Chamberlayne Edward

Angliae Notitia;

Or, the Present State of England the First and Second Part. Together with Divers Reflections Upon the Antient State Thereof. By Edward Chamberlayne. Fifth Edition

Chamberlayne Edward

Angliae Notitia;
Or, the Present State of England the First and Second Part. Together with Divers Reflections Upon the Antient State Thereof. By Edward Chamberlayne. Fifth Edition

ISBN/EAN: 9783337793364

Printed in Europe, USA, Canada, Australia, Japan

Cover: Foto ©Thomas Meinert / pixelio.de

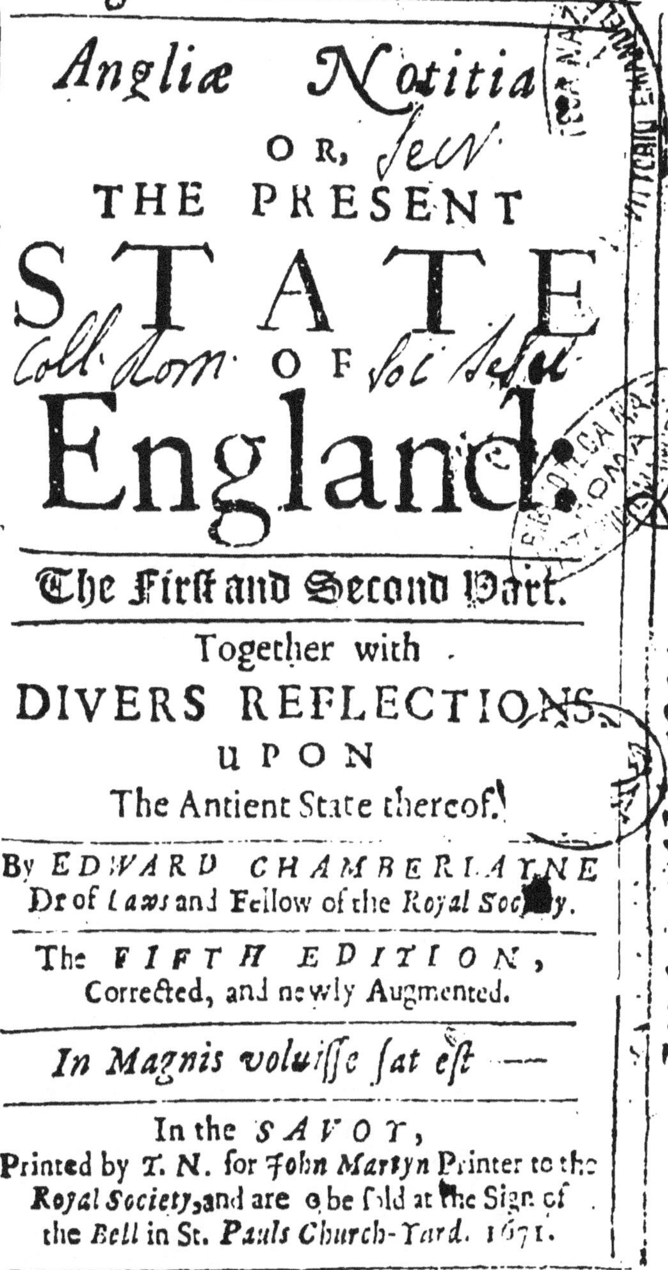

Angliæ Notitia
OR,
THE PRESENT STATE OF England.

The First and Second Part.

Together with

DIVERS REFLECTIONS UPON The Antient State thereof.

By EDWARD CHAMBERLAYNE Dr of *Laws* and Fellow of the *Royal Society*.

The *FIFTH EDITION*, Corrected, and newly Augmented.

In Magnis voluisse sat est ——

In the *SAVOY*,
Printed by *T. N.* for *John Martyn* Printer to the *Royal Society*, and are to be sold at the Sign of the *Bell* in St. *Pauls Church-Yard.* 1671.

To the Right Honorable

CHARLES

Earl of *Carlisle*, Vicount *Howard* of *Morpeth*, Baron *Dacre* of *Gilsland*, Lord Lieutenant in the Counties of *Cumberland* and *Westmerland*, One of the Lords of His Majesties Most Honorable Privy Council, heretofore Lord Ambassador Extraordinary to Three of the Northern Soveraign Princes, and late Ambassador Extraordinary to the High and Mighty Prince *CHARLES* the Eleventh of that Name, King of *Swedeland*.

My Lord,

S those very Honorable Employments abroad (whereof His Majesty hath judged your Excellency worthy, not onely for your most Noble Extraction and Eminent Degree, but also for your excellent Endowments, both Intellectual and Moral) have rendred you abundantly able to understand throughly the Present State *of divers Foreign Countreys; so that*

high Dignity wherewith the King hath been pleased to honor you at home (by placing you as one of His most faithful and vigilant Centinels in the Highest Watch-Tower of His cheif Kingdom, viz. *In that Noble, Honorable, and Reverend Assembly of Privy Counsellors) hath made you very capable of giving a large and judicious account of the* Present State *of this* Nation, *without any the least assistance from this Treatise; yet because your Excellency hath intimated some approbation of the Design, and lately owned the Designer for your Servant, he is encouraged to present the same to your Excellency; imploring your Patronage thereof, and the continuance of your Favor and assistance towards the like future endeavors of*

My Lord,
Your Excellencies
most humbly devoted Servant

Edw. Chamberlayne

To the

READER.

IN this small Treatise the *Reader* may not reasonably expect to have his *Fancy* much delighted.

(*Ornari res ipsa negat, contenta doceri.*)

but only to have his understanding informed; and therefore the Author hath industriously avoided all curious *Flowers of Rhetorick*, and made it his whole business to feed his Reader with abundant variety of Excellent Fruits.

Here are interspersed some observations, which though already known to many Engliſh men, yet may be unknown to moſt *Strangers* and *Foreigners*, for the information of whom this Book is *ſecondarily* intended ; and for that end is lately tranſlated into the *French Tongue*, and printed at *Amſterdam* ; whereby may be extinguiſht in ſome meaſure the Thirſt which Foreigners generally have to know the *Preſent State* of this *conſiderable Monarchy*.

Although the main aim is to inform all men of the *Preſent State* of this Kingdom, yet divers *Reflections* are made upon the *Paſt State* thereof; that ſo by comparing that with the preſent, ſome men may thereby not only be moved to endeavor the *Reſtauration* of what was heretofore better, and the *abolition* of what is now worſe; but alſo in ſome meaſure may *foreſee*

with-

without consulting our *Astrologers* and *Apocalyptick Men*, what will be the *Future State* of this Nation: according to that excellent Saying, *Qui respicit præterita & inspicit præsentia, prospicit etiam & futura. A good Historian by running back to Ages past, and by standing still and viewing the present times, and comparing the one with the other, may then run forward, and give a Verdict of the State almost Prophetick.*

In the many Reflections upon the Antient State of *England*, frequent use is made of divers grave Authors, as of *Glanvile*, *Bracton*, *Britton*, of *Horn* in his *Mirror of Justice*, *Fleta*, *Fortescue*, *Linwood*, *Stamford*, *Smith*, *Cosins*, *Camden*, *Cook*, *Spelman*, *Selden*, *&c.* And for the *Present State*, Consultation was had with several eminently learned

Perſonages yet living, to the end that the Reader might receive at leaſt ſome ſatisfaction in every particular, without the trouble and charges of a great *Library*. And as the Author doth ſometimes uſe both the *Words* of the *Living* and the *Writings* of the *Dead*, without quoting any, to avoid Oſtentation; ſo he hopes that this ingenuous Confeſſion being made at firſt, no man will be offended, though he give no notice when the Obſervation is theirs, and when it is his own; having taken ſpecial care that both in theirs and his own, there ſhould be nothing but the *Truth*: And although the Reader not perceiving every where by what Authority divers things are averred, may be apt to ſuſpect that ſome things are *gratis dicta*, yet if it ſhall pleaſe him to make

ſearch

ſearch, he will finde that generally they are *Vere & cum authoritate dicta.*

However in a Subject ſo Multiform as this, where ſo many marks are aimed at, no wonder if in ſome, the Author hath not hit the White; but whereſoever it hath appeared to him to have been miſled in the former Impreſſion, it is in this duly corrected.

Brevity, and a *Laconick Stile*, is aimed at all along, that ſo there might be *Magnum in Parvo*, that it might be *Mole minimus*, though *Re magnus*; that the whole State of *England* might be ſeen at once, Ὡς ἐν τύπῳ, or, as in a Map; that, as it will be a uſeful Book for all *Engliſhmen* at all times: So every one might without trouble, always carry it about with him as a Companion to conſult upon all occaſions.

For compleating this Structure, Materials were provided by the Author to give alſo a brief account of the particular Government of *England*, Eccleſiaſtical, Civil, and Military: Of all the Courts of Juſtice; of all cheif Offices belonging to theſe Courts; of the City of *London*; of the Two Univerſities; of the Inns of Court and *Chancery*; of the Colledge of Phyſitians; of the Royal Society, *&c.* All which is now publiſhed in a *Treatiſe* apart.

THE

THE TABLE.

A

B.

C.

D.

Deans

Queen

THE

OF ENGLAND in General.

CHAP. I.

Of its Name, Climate, Dimensions, Division, Air, Soil, Commodities, Moneys, Weights, Measures, and Buildings.

England, the better part of the best *Island* in the whole world, anciently with *Scotland* called *Britain*, and sometimes *Albion*; was about 800 years after the *Incarnation of Christ* (by special Edict of King *Egbert* descended from the the *Angles*, a people of the *Lower Saxony*, in whose possession the greatest part of this Countrey then was) named *Angle* or *Englelond*, thence by the *French* called *Angleterre*, by the Germans *Engeland*; and by the *Inhabitants England*. *Name.*

Climate. It is situated between the Degrees 17 and 42 of *Longitude*, equal with *Britany* and *Normandy* in *France*, and between 50 and 57 of Northern *Latitude*, equal with *Flanders*, *Zealand*, *Holland*, *Lower Saxony*, and *Denmark*.

The longest day in the most Northern part is 17 hours 30 minutes, and the shortest day in the most Southern parts is almost 8 hours long.

Dimensions. It is in *length* 386 miles, in *breadth* 279; in *compass* (by reason of the many *Bayes* and *Promontaries*) about 1300 miles; in *shape* triangular, contains by computation about 30 *Millions of Acres*, about the *thousandth* part of the *Globe*, and 333d part of the habitable earth, almost ten times as big as the *United Neatherlands*, five times as big as the *Spanish Neatherlands*; less than all *Italy* by almost one half, and in comparison of *France* is as 30 to 82.

Division. That part of *Britain*, now called *England*, was in the time of the Romans divided into *Britannia Prima*, *Britannia Secunda*, and *Maxima Cæsariensis*. The first of these contained the South part of *England*, the second all that Western part now called *Wales*, and the third the Nothern parts beyond *Trent*.

When the Britains had received the Christian Faith, they divided the same (for the better Government Ecclesiastical) into 3 Provinces or Archbishopricks; viz.

viz. the Archbishoprick of *London*, that contained *Britannia Prima*; the Archbishoprick of *York*, which contained that part called *Maxima Cæsariensis*; and the Archbishoprick of *Caerleon*, an antient great City of *South-Wales* upon the River *Uske*; under which was *Britannia Secunda*. Afterward the Heathen Saxons over-running this Country, and dividing it into Seven Kingdoms, the King of *Kent* being first converted to the Christian Faith by St. *Austin*, who lived and was buried at *Canterbury*, the Archiepiscopal See of *London* was there placed, and the other of *Caerleon* was translated to St. *Davids* in *Pembrook-shire*; and at last subjected to the See of *Canterbury*: the North part of *England* and all *Scotland* was put under the Archbishop of *York*, and all *England* divided into Dioceses, and in the year 630 it was for better Order and Government distinguisht into Parishes by the care and pains of *Honorius* Archbishop of *Canterbury*: almost 200 years before it was divided into Countries or Shires by King *Alfred*: by whom also those Shires (so called from the Saxon word *Scyre* a Partition or Division) were subdivided into Hundreds, which at first contained *ten Tythings*, and each Tything *ten Families*.

At present, *England* according to its Ecclesiastical Government, is divided first into 2 Provinces or Archbishopricks, *viz.* *Canterbury* and *York*, these 2 Provinces into 26 Dioceses, which are again divided into

60 Archdeaconr, and thoſe into Rural Deaneries, and thoſe again into Pariſhes.

According to the Temporal Government of *England* it is divided into 52 Countries or Shires, and thoſe into Hundreds, Laths, Rapes, or Wapentakes (as they are called in ſome Counties) and thoſe again into Tythings.

England without *Wales* is divided into 6 Circuits, allotted to the 12 Judges to hold Aſſizes twice a year (whereof more in a Treatiſe apart.) It is alſo divided by the kings Juſtices in *Eyre* of the Foreſt, and by the Kings at arms into North and South; that is, all Counties upon the North and South ſide of *Trent*.

There are in all *England* 25 Cities, 641 great Towns, called Market Towns, and 9725 Pariſhes; under ſome of which are contained ſeveral Hamlets or Villages as big as ordinary Pariſhes.

Aire. The *Aire* is far more mild and temperate (if not more healthy) than any part of the *Continent* under the ſame *Climate*.

By reaſon of the warm vapours of the Sea on every ſide, and the very often Winds from the huge Weſtern ſea, the *Cold* in *Winter* is leſs ſharp than in ſome parts of *France* and *Italy*, though more Southern.

By reaſon of the continual blaſts from Sea, the *Heat* in *Summer* is leſs ſcorching than in ſome parts of the *Continent*, that lies more Northward.

As

As in *Summer* the gentle *Winds* and frequent *Showres* qualifie all violent *Heats* aud *Droughts*, so in *Winter* the *Frosts* do only meliorate the cultivated Soyle, and the *Snow* keep warm the tender Plants. In a word, here is no need of Stoves in Winter, nor Grottes in Summer.

It is blessed with a very fertile wholesome *Soyle*, watered abundantly with *Springs* and *Streams*, and in divers parts with great *Navigable Rivers*; few barren *Mountains* or craggy *Rocks*, but generally gentle pleasant *Hills*, and fruitful *Valleys*, apt for *Grain*, *Grass*, or *Wood*. The Excellency of the English *Soyle* may be learnt (as *Varro* advised of *old*) from the *Complexion* of the *Inhabitants*, who therein excel all other Nations: or else from the high value put upon it by the *Romans* and the *Saxons*, who lookt upon it as such a precious spot of ground, that they thought it worthy to be *fenced* in like a *Garden-Plot* with a mighty *Wall* of fourscore miles in length, *viz.* from *Tinmouth* on the *German Sea*, to *Solwey Frith* on the *Irish* Sea (whereby the *Caledonian Bores* might be excluded) and with a monstrous *Dike* of fourscore and ten miles, *viz.* from the Mouth of the River *Wy* to that of the River *Dee* (whereby the *Cambro-Britan-Foxes* might be kept out.) Lastly, the Excellency of her *Soyle* may also be learnt from those transcendent *Elogies* bestowed on her by Antient and Modern Writers, calling *England* the *Grana-* *Soyle.*

ry of the *Western World*, the *Seat of Ceres*, *&c.* That her *Valleys* are like *Eden*, her *Hills* like *Lebanon*, her *Springs* as *Pisgah*, and her *Rivers* as *Jordan*. That she is a *Paradise* of *Pleasure*, and the *Garden* of *God*. *O fortunata & omnibus terris beatior Britannia, te omnibus cœli ac soli ditavit Natura, tibi nihil inest quod vitæ offendat, tibi nihil deest quod vita desideret, ita ut alter orbis extra orbem poni ad delicias humani generis videaris.* O happy and blessed *Britain*, above all other Countries in the World, *Nature* hath enricht thee with all the blessings of *Heaven* and *Earth*: Nothing in thee is hurtful to Mankind, nothing wanting in thee that is desirable, in so much that thou seemest another World placed besides, or without the great World, meerly for the delight and pleasure of Mankind.

Commodities. As it is divided from the rest of the World, so by reason of its great abundance of all things necessary for the life of Man, it may *without* the contribution of any other part of the World, more easily subsist than any of its neighbouring Countries.

Terra suis contenta bonis, non indiga mercis.

First, For wholesome *Food*; what plenty every where of *Sheep*, *Oxen*, *Swine*, *Fallow Deer*, *Coneys*, and *Hares*; It wants not *Red Deer*, *Goats*, nor *Roes*. What

What abundance of *Hens*, *Ducks*, *Geese*, *Turkeys*, *Pigeons*, and *Larks*? Of *Partridge*, *Phesants*, *Plovers*, *Teales*, *Thrushes*, *Merles*, *Field-Fares*, *Owsles*, or *Black birds*, *Wild ducks*, *Wild geese*, *Swans*, *Peacocks*, *Snipes*, *Quailes*, *Woodcocks*, *Lapwings*, It wants not *Sandlings*, *Knot*, *Curlew*, *bayning*, *Dotterel*, *Roe*, *Chur*, *Ruff*, *Maychit*, *Stint*, *Sea-Plover*, *Pewits*, *Redshanks*, *Rayles*, and *Wheat-ears*? *Herons*, *Cranes*, *Bitters*, *Bustards*, *Puffin Godwits*, *Heath-Coks*, *Mere-Poutes*, or *Grouse Thrushes*, and *Throstles*? What plenty of *Salmon*, *Trouts*, *Lampernes*, *Gudgeons*, *Carps*, *Tench*, *Lampreys*, *Pikes*, *Perches*, *Eeles*, *Bremes*, *Roch*, *Crefish*, *Flounders*, *Plaice*, *Shads*, *Mullets*? What great abundance of *Herrings*, *Whitings*, *Makerel*, *Soles*, *Smelts*, *Pilchards*, *Sprats*, *Oysters*, *Lobsters*, *Shrimps*, *Thornback*, &c. It wants not *Prawnes*, *Ruffes*, *Muscles*, *Cocles*, *Conger*, *Turbots*, *Cod*, *Scate*, *Mades*, *Escalops*, &c. What great plenty of *Apples*, *Pears*, *Plums*, and *Cherries*? How doth *England* abound with *Wheat*, *Barly*, *Rye*, *Pulse*, *Beans*, and *Oates*, with excellent *Butter* and *Cheese*; with most sorts of *Edible Roots* and *Herbs*, &c. It wants not *Apricocks*, *Peaches*, *Nectarins*, *Grapes*, *Figgs*, *Melons*, *Quinces*, &c. *Walnuts*, *Small Nuts*, *Filberts*, *Chesnuts*, *Medlers*, *Raspices*, *Strawberries*, *Currans*, *Gooseberries*, &c. Lastly, for *Drinks*, *England* abounds with *Beer*, *Ale*, *Sider*, *Perry*, and in some places with *Metheglin* or *Mede*.

Now of all these things there is such a constant continuance, by reason of the

Clemency of the *Climate*, that ſcarce the leaſt *Famine* which frequenteth other Countries, hath been felt in *England* theſe 400 years.

Then for *Rayment*; *England* produceth generally not onely very *Fine Wooll*, which makes our Cloth more *laſting* than other Countrey Cloth, and better *conditioned* againſt *Wind* and *Weather*; but alſo ſuch great *abundance* of Wooll, that not onely all ſorts from the higheſt to the loweſt are clothed therewith; but ſo much hath been heretofore tranſported beyond the Seas, that in honour of the *Engliſh Wooll*, that then brought ſuch plenty of Gold into the Territories of *Charles the puiſſant and bold Duke of Burgundy* (where the Staple for Engliſh Wooll was in thoſe days kept) he inſtituted that famous *Military Order* of the *Golden Fleece*, at this day in higheſt eſteem with the whole *Houſe* of *Auſtria*. This abundance and cheapeneſs of Wooll in *England*, proceeds not onely from the *goodneſs* of the *Soyle*, but alſo from the *freedom* from *Wolves* exceſſive *Heats* and *Colds*, which in other Countries create a charge of a conſtant guarding thier Sheep, and houſing them by night, and ſometimes by day. Alſo, for advancing the Manufacture of Cloth, that neceſſary Earth called *Fullers Earth*, is no where elſe produced in that abundance and excellency as in *England*.

Beſide, there is in *England* great plenty of excellent *Leather* for all ſorts of uſes

uses; nor wants it *Hemp* and *Flax*, at least, not ground fit to produce them.

For *Building*, it wants not *Timber* nor *Iron*, Stone, nor *Slate*, *Brick*, nor *Tiles*, *Marble* nor *Alabaster*, *Mortar* nor *Lime*, *Lead* nor *Glass*.

For *Firing*, either *Wood*, *Sea-Coal*, or *Pit Coal*, almost every where to be had at reasonable rates.

For *Shipping* no where better *Oak*, no where such *Knee-Timber*, as they call it; or *Iron* to make serviceable and durable *Guns*.

For *War*, for *Coach*, for *Highway*, and *Hunting*, no where such plenty of *Horses*; also for *Plough*, *Cart*, and *Carriages*: insomuch as *Mules* and *Asses* so generally made use of in *France*, *Italy*, and *Spain*, are utterly despised in *England*.

For *Dogs* of all sorts sizes and uses, as *Mastiffs*, *Greyhounds*, *Spaniels* for *Land* and *Water*, *Hounds* for *Stag*, *Buck*, *Fox*, *Hare*, or *Otter*, *Terriers*, *Tumblers*, *Lurchers*, *Setting-Dogs*, *Curs*, Little *Lap-Dogs*, &c.

Moreover, *England* produceth besides a mighty quantity of *Tinne*, *Lead*, and *Iron*, some *Brass* and *Copperas*, much *Alome*, *Salt*, *Hops*, *Saffron*, *Liquorix*, *Hony*, *Wax*, *Tallow*, *Cony-Furrs*, *Salt-peter*, *Woad*; and divers other beneficial Commodities; it wants not *Mines* of *Silver*, yielding more in their small quantities of *Ore*, and so, richer than those of *Potosi* in the *West-Indies*, whence the *King* of *Spain* hath most of his *Silver*; those yielding usually but one *Ounce* and a half of Silver in one hundred *Ounces* of *Ore*; whereas these in *Wales*, *Cornwal*, *Lancashire*, and the *Bishoprick* of *Durham*, yield ordinarily 6 or 8 *Ounces per Cent.* but these lying deep, are hard to come unto, and Workmen dear, which is otherwise in *Potosi*.

It wants not *Hot Baths*, and abounds in *Medicinal Springs*.

Vineyards have been heretofore common in most of the Southern and Middle parts of *England*, and *Silks* might be here produced, as it was once designed by King *James*; but a great part of the Natives prone to *Navigation*, supplying *England* at a very cheap rate, with all sorts of *Wines*, *Silks*, and all other Forreign Commodities (according to that of an antient Poet;

> *Quicquid amat luxus, quicquid desiderat usus,*
> *Ex te proveniet vel aliunde tibi.*)

it hath been found far better *Husbandry* to employ English ground rather for producing *Wooll*, *Corn*, and *Cattle*, for which it is most proper. In a word, though some Countries excel *England* in some things, yet in general, there is no one Country under Heaven whose *Aire* is better stored with *Birds* and *Fowls*, *Seas*, *Rivers*, and *Ponds* with *Fishes*; *Fields* with all sorts of *Corn*, the *Pastures* with *Cattle*, the *Forrests*, *Parks*, *Warrens*, and *Woods* with *Wild Beasts* onely for Recreation and Food; the *Mines* with *Metals*, *Coals*, and other *Minerals*; where are fewer *ravenous* and

and *hurtful Beasts*, fewer *venemous Serpents* or *noisome Flies*; fewer *Droughts*, *Inundations*, or *Dearths*; fewer *unwholsome Serenes*, *Pestilential Airs*, *Tempestuous Hurricanes*, or *Destructive Earthquakes*: Lastly, where there is a greater abundance of all things necessary for mans life, and more especially for all kind of Food; insomuch that it hath been judged that there is yearly as much *Flesh* and *Beer* consumed in *England* by overplentiful Tables, as would well serve three times the number of People. Add to all this, that being encompassed with the Sea and well furnisht with Ships and abundance of commodious and excellent Havens and Ports, it excels for *safety* and *security*, (which is no small praise) all the Neighbouring Countries, if not all the Countries in the World.

Moneys.

At first all Nations bartred and exchanged one Commodity for an other; but that being found troublesome; by a kind of Custom, good liking, or usage, amongst all Civilized Nations, *Silver* and *Gold*, as most *portable*, *pliable*, *beautiful*, and less subject to rust, hath been as early, as the days of *Abraham*, chosen to be the Instruments of *Exchange* and measure of all things, and were at first paid onely by *Weight*, till the Romans about 300 years before the Birth of Christ, invented *Coyning* or *Stamping* Gold and Silver.

When *Julius Cæsar* first entred this *Island*

Island, here were current instead of Money, certain *Iron Rings*, afterwards the Romans brought in the use of *Gold, Silver*, and *Brass Coyns.*

In the time of King *Richard* the First, Moneys coyned in the East parts of *Germany* being for its purity highly esteemed, some of those *Easterlings* were sent for over, and employed in our Mint, and thence our Money called *Esterling* or *Sterling* Money, as some think: (as the first Gold coyned in *England* was by King *Edward* the Third, and those Pieces called *Florences*, because Florentines were the first Coyners thereof) though others say of the *Saxon* word *Ster, Weighty.*

King *Edward* the First, since the *Norman* Conquest, established a certain *Standard* for *Coin* in this manner: Twenty four Grains made one *Penny Sterling*, 20 Penny weight one *Ounce*, and 12 Ounces made a *Pound Sterling*, consisting of 20 Shillings. Of these 12 Ounces, 11 Ounces two Penny weight *Sterling*, was to be of pure Silver, called *Leaf Silver*, and the weight of about 18 Penny *Sterling* in allay the *Minter* might add: So that anciently a *Pound Sterling* was a Pound of *Troy* weight, whereas now a *Pound Sterling* is but the *third* part of a *Pound Troy*, and little more than a 4 part of *Avoirdupois* weight.

The Money of *England* was abased and falsified for a long time, till Queen *Elisabeth* in the year 1605, to her great praise called in all such Money; since which time

no

no base Money hath been coyned in *England*, but onely of pure *Gold* and *Silver*, called *Sterling* Money; onely of latter times, in relation to the necessity of the *Poor*, and Exchange of great Money, a small piece of *Brass* called a *Farthing*, or Fourth part of a Penny, hath been permitted to be coined, but no man enforced to receive them in pay for Rent or Debt; which cannot be affirmed of any other State or Nation in the Christian World; in all which there are several sorts of *Copper* Money, as current with them for any payment as the purest *Gold* or *Silver*.

No Moneys in any Mint are made of pure *Silver*, because *Silver* in its purity is almost as *flexible* as *Lead*; and therefore not so useful, as when hardned with *Copper*.

Gold minted pure would also be too *flexible*, and therefore is in all Mints allayed with some *Copper*; and most Mints differ in more or less allay.

The Ordinary Silver Coyns at present in *England*, are according to weight, either the Ounce of *Troy*, the half Ounce, the 5th part, 10th part, 15 part, 20th part, 30th part, or 60th part; thus denominated, *The Crown*, *Half Crown*, *Shilling*, *Six Pence*, *Four Pence*, *Three Pence*, *Two Pence*, a *Peny*.

The Standard of *Sterling* Silver in *England* is *Eleven Ounces* and *Two Penny weight* of Fine Silver, and 18 Penny weight of *Allay* of *Copper* out of the Fire, and so proportionably; so that 12 Ounces of pure Silver, without any allay, is worth

worth 3 *l*. 4 *s*. 6 *d*. and an Ounce is worth 5 *s*. 4 *d*. 1 *ob*. but with allay is worth but 3 *l*. and the Ounce 5 *s*.

The Ordinary English Gold Coyns are now only the old *Carolus*, or 20 *s*. Piece, which by a late Proclamation is current at 21 *s*. 4 *d*. it weigheth 5 Penny weight 20 Grains. The *New Guinea* 20 *s*. weigheth 5 penny weight 10 Grains.

The Standard of the *English Carolus* piece, or Ordinary *Gold*, is in the pound weight *Troy* 22 *Carrats* of Fine Gold and 2 *Carrats* of Allay Silver or Copper; that is 11 Ounces of fine Gold and one Ounce of Allay Silver or Copper.

The *Spanish, French* and *Flemish* Gold is of equal fineness with the *English*.

The *English* Silver Money hath less Allay than the *French* or *Dutch*.

The *Moneyers* divide the Pound weight into 12 Ounces *Troy*.

The	*Ounce*	into	20 *Pen. w.*
	Pen. weight		24 *Grains,*
	Grain		20 *Mites.*
	Mite		24 *Droites.*
	Droite		20 *Perits.*
	Perit		24 *Blanks.*

The English Silver is coined at 3 *l*. 2 *s*. the pound of *Troy* weight, the 2 *s*. being allowed the Minters for Coinage.

The English Gold is coined at present at 44 *l*. 10 *s*. the pound *Troy* weight, whereof 15 *s*. is allowed the Minters for Coinage.

So

So that now the proportion of Gold to Silver in *England*. is as 1 to 14 and about $\frac{1}{3}$, that is to say, one Ounce of Gold is worth in Silver 14 Ounces and about $\frac{1}{3}$ or 3 *l*. 14 *s*. 2 *d*. of English Money.

That the English Coin may want neither the *purity* nor the *weight* required; it was most wisely and carefully provided, that once every year the *Chief Officers* of the *Mint* should appear before the *Lords of the Council* in the *Star Chamber* at *Westminster*, with some Pieces of all sorts of Moneys coined the foregoing year; taken at adventure out of the *Mint*, and kept under several Locks by several persons till that appearance, and then by a *Jury* of 24 able *Goldsmiths* in the presence of the said *Lords*, every Piece is most exactly assayed and weighed.

Since the happy restauration of His Majesty now raigning, the coining or stamping of Money by *Hammers* hath been laid aside, and all stampt by an Engine or Screw; whereby it is come to pass that our *Coins* for *neatness*, *gracefulness*, and *security* from *counterfeiting*, do surpass all the most excellent Coins, not only of the Romans, but of all the Modern Nations in the World.

Weights and Measures. For *Weights* and *Measures* at present used in *England*, there are very many excellent Statutes and Ordinances, and abundance of care taken by our Ancestors to prevent all cheating and deceit therein.

By the 27th Chapter of *Magna Charta* the

the *Weights* and *Measures* ought to be the same over all *England*, and those to be according to the *Kings Standards* of *Weights* and *Measures* kept in the Exchequer by a special *Officer* of His *House*, called the *Clerk* or *Comptroler* of the *Market*.

Of *Weights* there are two sorts used at present thorowout all *England*, *viz.* *Troy Weight* and *Avoirdupois*. In *Troy weight*, 24 Grains of Wheat make a *Peny weight Sterling*, 20 Penny weight make an *Ounce*, 12 Ounces make a *Pound*; so there are 480 Grains in the Ounce, and 5760 Grains in the Pound.

By this Weight are weighed *Pearls*, *Pretious Stones*, *Gold*, *Silver*, *Bread*, and all manner of *Corn* and *Grain*; and this Weight the *Apothecaries* do or ought to use, though by other Divisions and Denominations: their least measure is a *Grain*.

20 *Grains*	make	*a Scruple*,	markt	℈
3 *Scruples*	make	*a Drach*,	markt	ʒ
8 *Drachmes*	make	*an Ounce*,	markt	℥
12 *Ounces*	make	*a Pound*,	markt	℔

Avoir du pois hath 16 Ounces to the pound, but then the Ounce *Avoir du pois* is lighter then the Ounce *Troy* by 42 Grains in 480, that is near a 12th part; so that the *Avoir du pois* Ounce containeth but 438 Grains, and is as 73 to 80, that is 73 Ounces

73 Ounces *Troy* is as much as 80 Ounces *Avoir du pois*, and 60 pound *Avoir du pois*, is equal to 73 pounds *Troy*, and 14 Ounces *Troy* and an half, and the tenth part of a *Troy* Ounce make 16 Ounces *Avoirdupois*.

By this Weight are weighed in *England* all *Grocery Ware*, *Flesh*, *Butter*, *Cheese*, *Iron*, *Hemp*, Flax, *Tallow*, *Wax*, Lead, *Steel*, also all things whereof comes waste; and therefore 112 *l*. *Avoir du pois* is called a Hundred weight, and 56 *l*. Half a Hundred, and 28 *l*. a Quarter of a Hundred, or a Tod. Eight Pounds *Avoirdupois* amongst the Butchers is called a Stone.

Note, That when Wheat is at 5 *s*. the *Bushel*, then the *Penny Wheaten Loaf* is by Statue to weigh 11 Ounces *Troy*, and 3 *Half Penny Wheaten Loaves* to weigh as much, and the *Houshold Penny-Loaf* to weigh 14 *Troy* Ounces and Two third parts of an Ounce; and so more or less proportionably.

Note also, That here, as in other Countries, Silk-men use a Weight called *Venice* Ounce, which is 13 Penny weight and 12 Grains; so that 12 Ounces *Venice* is but 8 Ounces, 4 Penny *Troy*, and 9 Ounces *Avoirdupois*: but of this there is no Standard, nor doth the Magistrate allow of it.

Measures.

All *Measures* in *England* are either *Applicative* or *Receptive*.

The smallest *Mensura Applicationis* or

applicative

applicative measure is a *Barly Corn*, whereof 3 in length make a fingers breadth or *Inch*, 4 *Inches* make a *Handful*, 3 *Handful* a *Foot*, 1 *Foot* and a *half* makes a *Cubit*, 2 *Cubits* a *Yard*, 1 *Yard* and a *quarter* makes an *Ell*, 5 Foot make a *Geometrical Pace*, 6 Foot a *Fathom*, 16 Foot and a half make a *Perch*, *Pole*, or *Rod*, 40 *Perch* make a *Furlong*, 8 *Furlongs*, or 320 *Perch* make an *English Mile*; which according to the Statute of 11 *H*. 7. ought to be 1760 Yards, or 5280 Foot, that is 280 Foot more than the *Italian Mile*; 60 Miles, or more exactly 69 English Miles and a half, make a *Degree*, and 360 *Degrees*, or 25020 Miles compass the whole *Globe* of the *Earth*.

For measuring of Land in *England*, 40 Perch in length and 4 in breadth make an *Acre* of Land (so called from the *German* word *Acker*, and that from the Latine *Ager*) 30 Acres ordinarily make a *Yard-Land*, and one Hundred Acres are accounted a *Hide of Land*; but in this and also in some Weights and other Measures, the Custome of the place is otherwise, yet must be regarded.

In *France* about *Paris* 12 inches make a foot, 22 foot make a Perch, and 100 Perches make an Arpent.

Mensura receptionis, or the *Receptive* Measures, are twofold first of *Liquid* or *Moist* things, secondly of *Dry* things.

About a pound *Avoirdupois* makes the ordinary smallest *receptive* measure, called a *Pint*, 2 *Pints* make a *Quart*, 2 *Quarts*

Pottle, 2 *Pottles* a *Gallon*, 8 *Gallons* a *Firkin* of *Ale*: 2 such *Firkings* make a *Kilderkin*, and 2 *Kilderkins* or 32 *Gallons* make a barrel of *Ale*, 9 *Gallons* a *Firkin* of *Beer*, 2 such *Firkins* or 18 *Gallons* make a *Kilderkin*, 2 *Kilderkins* or 36 *Gallons* make a *Barrel of Beer*, 1 *Barrel* and a half, or 54 *Gallons*, make a *Hogshead*; 2 *Hogsheads* make a *Pipe* or *Butt*, and 2 *Pipes* a *Tun*, consisting of 1728 Pints or Pounds.

A Barrel of Butter or Soap is the same with a Barrel of Ale.

The English *Wine* Measures are smaller than those of *Ale* and *Beer*, and hold proportion as 4 to 5; so that 4 *Gallons* of *Beer* Measure are 5 Gallons of *Wine* Measure, and each Gallon of *Wine* is 8 pounds *Troy* weight. Of these Gallons, a *Rundlet* of Wine holds 18, Half a *Hogshead* 31 Gallons and a half, a *Tierce* of Wine holds 42 Gallons, a *Hogshead* 63 Gallons, a *Punchion* 84 Gallons, a *Pipe* or *Butt* holds 126, and a Tun 252 Gallons, or 2016 Pints.

To measure dry things, as *Corn* or *Grain* there is first the Gallon, which is bigger than the *Wine* Gallon, and less than the *Ale* or *Beer* Gallon, and is in proportion to them as 33 to 28 and 35, and is counted 8 pounds *Troy* weight. Two of these Gallons make a *Peck*, 4 *Pecks* a *Bushel*, 4 *Bushels* the *Comb* or *Curnock*, 2 *Curnocks* make a *Quarter*, and 10 *Quarters* a *Last* or *Weigh*, which contains 5120 Pints, and about so many Pounds; so that in a Garrison of 5000 men, allowing each but a pound

pound of bread *per diem*, they will consume near a *Last* or 80 Bushels every day, and 250 Men in a Ship of War will drink a *Tun* of *Beer* in 2 days, allowing each man but his *Pottle per diem*.

Buildings. *Churches* throughout all *England*, and all publick *Edifices*, are generally of *Solid Stone*, covered with *Lead*; *Cathedral* and *Collegiate Churches* every where ample and magnificent; and the Churches in Market-Towns and Opulent Villages spacious and solid enough, beautified either with very high Pyramids, or Steeples, or at least with stately high Towers. Houses in Cities, that were heretofore usually of *Wood*, are now built of good *Stone* or *Brick*, and covered with *Slate* or *Tile*; the Rooms within formerly *wainscotted*, are now *hung with Tapistry* or other convenient Stuffe; and all *Cieled* with *Plaister*, excellent against the rage of Fire, against the Cold, and to hinder the passage of all dust and noise.

The Modern Buildings have been far more slight and of less continuance than the Antient.

The houses of the Nobles and Rich, are abundantly furnisht with *Pewter*, *Brass*, *Fine Linnen*, and *Plate*. The mean Mechanicks and ordinary Husbandmen, want not *Silver Spoons*, or some *Silver plate* in their houses.

The *Windowes* every where *glased*, not made of *Paper* or *Wood*, as is usual in *Italy* and *Spain*.

Chimnies in most places; no *Stoves*, although the far more Southern parts of *Germany* can hardly subsist in the Winter without them.

CHAP.

CHAP. II.

Of the Inhabitants, and therein of their Law, Religion, Manners, and Punishments; of their Number, Language, Stature, Dyet, Attire, Recreations, Names, and Surnames; of their Computation and manner of Numbring.

ENgland hath been possest by *five* several Nations, and coveted by many more, and no wonder so *fair* and *rich* a *Lady* should have many *Lovers*, it being a Country (as was said of the tree in the midst of *Paradise*) *good for food, pleasant to the eyes, and to be desired*; whereas the *High-Lands* of *Scotland*, *Wales*, *Biscay*, *Switzerland*, and other like Countries, continue still in the possession of their *Aborigines*, of the first that laid claim unto them, none since judging it worth their pains to dispossess them. *Inhabitants.*

The first Inhabitants of *England* are believed to be the *Britains*, descended from the *Gauls*; whose language was once almost the same; subdued afterward by the *Romans*: who, by reason of their troubles nearer home, were constrained to abandon this Country about 400 years after *Christ*: whereupon the *Picts* Inhabitants of of *Scotland*, invading the *Britains*; they call to their aid the *Saxons*; who chasing away the *Picts*, soon made themselves Masters of the *Britains*: but these not able to endure the heavy yoke of the *Saxons*, after many Battels and Attempts to recover their lost Liberties and Country, retired, or were driven some of them into *Britain* in *France*, from whence some think they first came; but most of them into the two utmost *Western barren*, and *mountainous* parts of this Countrey, called afterwrrds by the *Saxons Walishland*, instead of *Gaulishland*, as the *Germans* still call *Italy Walishland*. because inhabited by the *Cisalpine Gauls*; and the *French* call our Countrey of *Britains*, *Le pais de Gales*.

The *Saxons* solely possest of all the best part of this *Isle*, were for a long time infested, and for some time almost subdued by the *Danes*, and afterwards wholly by the *Normans*, who drave not out the *Saxons*, but mixed with them; so that the *English bloud* at this day is a *mixture* chiefly of *Norman* and *Saxon*, not without a *tincture* of *Danish*, *Romish* and *British* Blood.

Their Laws. The English according to several Matters and Parts of the Kingdom; are governed by several Laws, *viz*. *Common Law*, *Statute Law*, *Civil Law*, *Canon Law*, *Forest Law*, and *Martial Law*; besides particular Customs and *By-Laws*: Of all which in brief (intending in a Trea-

tise

tise apart to speak more largely of them in the Particular Government of *England Ecclesiastique*, *Civil* and *Military*, together with all the Courts and Officers thereto belonging.

Common Law.

The *Common Law* of *England* is the Common Customs of the Kingdome, which have by length of time obtained the force of *Laws*: It is called *Lex non scripta* (not but that we have them written in the old *Norman Dialect*, which being no where vulgarly used, varies no more than the Latin, but) because it cannot be made by Charter or by Parliament; for those are always matters of *Record*; whereas Customs are onely matters of *Fact*, and are no where but in the *Memory of the People*; and of all Laws must be the best for the English: for the written Laws made in *England* by Kings or Privy-Councils, as *antiently*, or by Parliaments, as of *later times*; are imposed upon the Subject before any probation or trial, whether they are benificial to the Nation; or agreeable to the Nature of the People; but Customs bind not the People till they have been tryed and approved time out of mind; during which time no inconvenience arising to hinder, those Customs became Laws; and therefore when our Parliaments have altered any Fundamental points of our Common-Law, (as sometimes hath been done) those alterations have been by experience found so inconvenient, that the same Law by succee-

succeeding Parliaments hath soon been restored. This Common-Law is the Quintessence of the Customary Law of the *Mercians*, prevailing before the Conquest in the Middle Counties of *England*, called the Kingdom of *Mercia*, and of the *Saxons* amongst the West and South parts, and of the *Danes* amongst the *East-Angles*, all first reduced into one body by King *Edward* the *Elder*, about the year 900; which for some time almost lost, were revived by the good King *Edward* the Confessor, and by Posterity named his Laws. To these the Conquerour added some of the good Customs of *Normandy*, and then his Successor King *Edward* the First having in his younger years given himself satisfaction in the glory of Arms; bent himself (like another *Justinian*) to endow his Estate with divers notable Fundamental Laws, ever since practised in this Nation. The excellent conveniency and connaturalness of the Common Law of *England* to the temper of English Men, is such, that the serious consideration thereof induced King *James* in a Solemn Speech to prefer it as to this Nation, before the Law of *Moses*.

Statute-Law.

Where the *Common-Law* is silent; there we have excellent *Statute Laws*, made by the several Kings of *England*, by and with the Advice and Consent of all the Lords Spiritual and Temporal, and with the Consent of all the Commons of *England*, by their representatives in Parliament;

ment; whereunto the *English* easily submit, as made at their own earnest desire and request.

Where *Common* and *Statute-Law* take no Cognizance, use is made of that Law of Laws called the *Civil-Law*; wherein is to be had what all the wisest and Noblest Men of the most flourishing and puissant State that ever was in the World, could in the space of many hundred years by their own Wisdom or Reason devise, or from any other People learn: so that this Law may be lookt on as the Product of the Common Reason of all Mankind, and fitted for the Interest and Welfare not of one Nation onely; but contemplating and taking care for the general affairs of all People. Of this Law use is made in all Ecclesiastical Courts of Bishops, Arch-Deacons, Vicars-General, Chancellours, and Commissaries, when ever Cognizance is taken of Wills and Testaments, of Tythes, Oblations, Mortuaries, of Matrimony, Divorce, Adultery, Incest, Fornication, Chastity attempted; Of Sacred Orders, Institutions to *Church-Livings*, Celebration of Divine Offices, Reparation of Churches, Dilapidations, Procurations; of Heresie, Apostasy, Atheism, Schisme, Simony, Blasphemy, *&c.* So of this Law is made use in the Court of Admiralty, in all affairs immediately relating to the Royal Fleets, to all other Vessels of Trade, and to their Owners, to Mari-

Civil-Law.

ners, to Commanders at Sea; to Reprizals, to Pyracies, to Merchants Affairs, to all Contracts made at Sea or beyond Sea, in the way of Marine Trade or Commerce; to all matters touching Wrecks, *Flotsam*, *Jetsam*, *Lagam*, Marine Waifs, Deodands, *&c.* Moreover use is made of the Civil Law in the Court of the Earl Marshal, taking Cognizance of Crimes perpetrated out of *England*, of Contracts made in Foreign parts, of Affairs of War within and without *England*; of Controversies about Nobility and Gentry, or bearing of Coats of Arms; of Precedency, *&c.* Of this Law much use is made in Treaties with Foreign Potentates, where many points are to be determined and concluded, according to the direction of this most excellent and generally approved Law; and for this cause Forreign Princes take especial care to choose such persons for their Embassadors as are skilled in the Civil Law, and this Policy was heretofore duly observed by our English Princes with very good success, Lastly, the two Universities of *England* serve themselves of the Civil Law, for by their Priviledges no Student is to be sued at *Common-Law*, but in the Vicechancellours Court for Debts, Accounts, Injuries, *&c.*

Canon-Law. The Canons of many Antient General Councils of many National and Provincial English Synods, besides divers Decrees of the Bishops of *Rome* and Judgements

ents of Antient Fathers had been recei-
-d by the Church of *England*, and in-
-rporated into the Body of the Canon
aw: by which she did ever proceed in
ie exercise of her Jurisdidion, and doth
ill by vertue of the Statute 25 *Hen.* 8.
 far as the said Canons and Constitu-
-ons are not repugnant to the Holy Scrip-
ures, to the Kings Prerogative, or the
-aws, Statutes, and Customs of this
Realm; and those are called the Kings
Ecclesiastical Laws, which have several
proceedings and several ends from the
Temporal Laws; these inflicting punishment upon the Body, Lands, and Goods,
and to punish the outward man; but those
pro salute animæ, to reform the inward
man; both joyning in this, to have the
whole man outwardly and inwardly reformed.

The *Forest Laws* are peculiar Laws, *Forest Laws.*
different from the Common Law of *England*. *Forests* in *England* are exceeding
antient and before the making of *Charta
de Foresta*, Offences committed therein
were punisht at the pleasure of the King,
in so sharp and grievous a manner (as still
in *Germany*) that both Nobles and Commons did suffer many horrible inconveniences and oppressions, and even in that
Charter were some hard Articles, which
the Clemency of gracious Kings have since
by Statute thought fit to alter. *Per Assisas
Forestæ* in the time of *Edward* 3. *voluntas reputabitur pro facto*; so that if a man

be taken hunting a Deer, he may be arested as if he had taken a Deer. The Forrester may take and arest a man, if he be taken either at *Dog-draw*, *Stable-stand*, *Back-bear*, or *Bloody-hand*; for in these four a man is said to be taken with the manner, though three of them may be but presumptions.

Martial-Law. *Lex Castrensis Anglicanæ*, Is that Law that dependeth upon the Kings Will and Pleasure, or his Lieutenant in time of actual War; for although in time of Peace the King for the more equal temper of Laws towards all his Subjects, makes no Laws but by the consent of the Three Estates in Parliament: yet in times of War, by reason of great dangers arising suddenly and unexpectedly upon small occasions, he useth absolute Power, insomuch as his word goeth for a Law. Martial Law extends onely to Soldiers and Mariners, and is not to be put in practice in times of Peace, but onely in times of War, and then and there where the kings Army is on foot.

Peculiar and By-Laws. By the Kings Royal Charter granted to divers Cities of *England*, the Magistrates have a Power to make such Laws as may be beneficial for the Citizens, and not repugnant to the Laws of the Land; and these are binding only to the Inhabitants of the place, unless such Laws are for a general good, or against a general inconvenience; for then they bind Strangers.

Religio

Because Humane Laws can promote no other good, nor prevent any other evil, but what is open to publick cognizance, it is very necessary for the Socity of Mankind, and it is the great Wisdom of God so to ordain, That by Religion a Tribunal should be erected in every mans soul, to make him eschew evil and do good, when no Humane Law can take notice of either.

Of all Religions in the World, antiently only the Jews worshipt the true God in the true manner.

The Jews Religion in process of time by Traditions and Superstitions much corrupted, was partly abrogated, and the rest reformed, refined, and sublimated by our Saviour Christ, and since called the *Christian Religion*; which was planted in *England*, *Tempore ut scimus* (saith *Gildas*) *summo Tiberii Cæsaris*, which by computation will fall to be 5 years before *St. Peter* came to *Rome*, and about 5 years after the death of Christ.

It is also affirmed by antient and Modern Grave Authors expresly, that in the 12th year of the Emperour *Nero*, *St. Peter* preached here, baptized many, and ordained Bishops, Priests, and Deacons: That immediately after St. *Stephen*'s death and the Jews dispersion, *Joseph* of *Arimathea* with 12 others here preacht and died: That the first Fabrick of a Christian Church or Temple in all the World, was at *Glastenbury* in *Somerset-shire*, 31 years after Christs death, And that St.

Paul was permitted to preach here, before he was suffered so to do at *Rome*. Afterwards *Anno* 180 the Christian Faith was here first professed by publick Authority under King *Lucius* the first Christian King in the World; and with Christianity no doubt came in the Episcopal Government, as may be seen in the Catalogue of *British Bishops*, and it is certain that at the Council of *Arles Anno* 347. there were three British Archbishops, *viz*. of *London*, *York*, and *Caerleon*; whereof the first had for his Province under him the *South*, the second all the *North*, and the third all beyond *Severn*, or the *West* part of this Island as afore mentioned. Under these three Archbishops there were reckoned about that Age 28 Bishops, all which did observe the Customs and Orders of the Greek or Eastern Churches, and particularly that of *Easter* different from the Custom of the Latine or Western Churches: nor did they acknowledge *Rome* to be the Mother Church of the *Britannick* Church. *Britain* was then a Patriarchal Jurisdiction in substance, though perhaps not in name, and so continued until about the year 596. When *Austin* the Monk assisted by the fraud of 40 other Monks, and by the Power of the then Heathen *Anglo-Saxons* (who had long before driven the Britains into *Wales*) constraind the British Bishops to submit themselves to the Bishop of *Rome*; after which, by the Convenience or Concessions of the successive *Saxon* and *Norman* Kings, this Church was in some things sub-

subjected to the Bishop of *Rome* as its Patriarch or Primate; until *Henry* the Eight by His Royal Authority (as he and all other Kings might remove their Chancellours or other Officers, and dispose of their Offices to others) did remove the Primacy or Metropolitanship from the See of *Rome* to the See of *Canterbury*; as being far more agreeable to Civil Policy and Prudence; that such a high Power should be placed rather in a Subject of our own Nation than in a Soveraign Prince (for so is the Pope over several Territories in *Italy*) and he far remote beyond the Seas: Which ejection of the Popes Authority was not done, as in other Nations, by Popular Fury and Faction, but by the mature deliberate Counsel of Godly and Learned Divines assembled in Convocation, with the express Authority of the King, and ratified by the Three States in Parliament.

The minds of English Christians thus delivered from the Spiritual Tyranny of the Bishop of *Rome*, and the Dignity of English Kings from the Spiritual Slavery under him, the King and Clergy took this occasion to reform the many abuses and errours crept into the Church in length of time by the great negligence and corruption of Governours; wherein the Wisdom of the English Reformers is to be admired to all Posterity: which was briefly thus:

First, Care was taken lest that (as it oft

happens in indiscreet purges, and where ever the People only hath been the Reformer) the good should be taken away with the bad: It was therefore resolved not to separate farther from the Church of *Rome* in Doctrine or Discipline than that Church had separated from what she was in her purest Times. For Doctrine they embraced that excellent Counsel of the Prophet, *State super vias antiquas & videte quænam sit via recta & ambulate in ea*; they made a stand and took a view of the purest Primitive Christian Times, and thence saw which was the right way, and followed that. For the Discipline of this Reformed Church they considered what it was in the purest times of the first good Christian Emperours, for the Times of Persecution (before Temporal Princes embraced the Christian Faith) as they were most excellent Times for Doctrine and Manners; so very improper and unfit for a Pattern or Example of outward Government and Policy.

The Doctrine of the Church of *England* is contained in the 39 Articles of the Book of Homilies.

The Worship and Discipline is seen in the Liturgie and Book of Canons, by all which it will appear to impartial foreign eyes, that the Church of *England* may warrantably be said to be the most exact and perfect Patern of all the Reformed Churches in the World: and whosoever shall be so happy as to be a true Son of that Church, must confess that it is the

most

most incorrupt, humble, innocent, learned; the most Primative, most Decent; and Regular Church in *Christendome*; that her Doctrine is built upon the Prophets and Apostles, according to the explication of the Antient Fathers; the Government truly Apostolical, and in all essential parts thereof, of Divine Institution; the Liturgie an extract of the best Primitive Forms; the Ceremonies few but necessary, and such as tend only to Decency and increase of Piety: That she holds the whole truly Catholick Foundation according to the Scripture and the four first General Councils, that she adheres closely to Tradition truly Universal; that is, doth willingly receive *quod ab omnibus, quod ubique, quod semper receptum fuit*; which is the Old Rule of Catholicisme: so that none can say more truly with *Tertullian* than the English, *In ea regulas incedimus quam Ecclesia ab Apostolis Apostoli a Christo, Christus a Deo accepit.* search all the Religions in the World, none will be found more consonant to Gods Word for Doctrine, nor to the Primitive Example for Government. None will be found that ascribes more to God, or that constitutes more firm Charity amongst Men; none will be found so excellent not only in the Community as Christian, but also in the special Notion as Reformed, for it keepeth the middle way between the Pomp of Superstituous Tyranny, and the meanness of Fanatick Anarchy.

In two Points the Church of *England*

is truly Transcendent, First, It hath the Grand Mark of the true Church, which most *European* Churches seem to want, and that is Charity towards other Churches; for it doth not so engross Heaven to its own Professors, as to damn all others to Hell. Secondly, It is the great glory of the English Protestant Church; that it never resisted Authority; nor ingaged in Rebellion; a Praise that makes much to her advantage in the minds of all those who have read or heard of the dismal and devillish effects of the Holy League in *France*, by Papists, of the Holy Covenant in *Scotland* by Puritans, and of the late Solemn League and Covenant in *England* by Presbyterians

As for the Scandal begotten by the late Troubles and Murder of the late King, which some of the *Romish* endeavour to throw upon the English Religion; it is sufficiently known, that not one person that was a known Favourer and Practiser of that Religion by *Law* establisht in *England*, was either a beginner or active Prosecutor of that Rebellion, or any way an Abettor of that horrid Murther; for that our Religion neither gives such Rules, nor ever did set such Examples: nor indeed can that be truly said to be an Act either of the Parliament or People of *England*, but only of a few wretched Miscreants, Sons of *Belial*, that had no fear of God before their eyes.

About the year 1635 or 1636 the Church of *England*, as well as the State, seemed

to

to be in her full Stature of Glory; shining in Transcendent Empyreal Lustre and Purity of Evangelical Truth: Her Religious Performances, Her Holy Offices, ordered and regulated agreeably to the expedient of such Sacred Actions; Her Discipline-Model suitable to the Apostolick Form; the Set and Suit of Her Holy Tribe renowned for Piety and Learning; and these all in so Supereminent a Degree that no Church on this side the Apostolick can hardly or ever could compare with her in any one. And in this Felicity she might probably have continued, had she not been disturbed by a Generation of Hypocritical or at least blind Zealots; whose Predecessours in Queen *Elizabeth*'s time began to oppose that excellent begun Reformation, and then to contrive the Alteration of Government; beginning first very low at Caps and Hoods, Surplices, and Episcopal Habits; but these flew higher, proceeding at length to the height of all Impiety; subverted even Liturgie, Episcopacy, and Monarchy it self: all which our Most Gracious King upon his Restauration hath most wisely and piously restored, after the example of that good King *Hezekiah*, 2 *Chr.* 29. 2, 3: Since which we are able to render this joyful account of the Religion and Church of *England*, *viz.* That there is nothing wanting in order to Salvation: We have the Word of God, the Faith of the Apostles, the Creeds of the Primitive Church, the Articles of the Four First General

Coun-

Councils, a Holy Liturgie, Excellent Prayers, Due Administration of the Sacraments, the Ten Commandments, the Sermons of Christ, and all the Precepts and Councels of the Gospel. We teach Faith and Repentance, and the Necessity of Good Works, and strictly exact the severity of a Holy Life. We live in Obedience to God, ready to part with all for his Sake; We honour His Most Holy Name; We worship Him at the mention of His Name; we confess His Attributes; we have Places, Times, Persons, and Revenues, consecrated and set apart for the Service and Worship of our Great God Creatour of Heaven and Earth; we honour His Vicegerent the King, holding it damnable to use any other Weapons against him or his Army but Prayers and Tears: we hold a charitable respect toward all Christians: we confess our sins to God and to our Brethren, whom we have offended, and to Gods Ministers the Priests, in Cases of Scandal or of a troubled Conscience; and they duly absolve the Penitent Soul. We have an uninterrupted succession of Reverend, Learned, and Pious Bishops, who Ordain Priests and Deacons, Consecrate Churches, Confirm the Baptized at a due age, Bless the People, Intercede for them, Visit oft their respective Diocesses; taking care of all Churches, that they be served with as good and able Pastors as the small Maintenance can invite; they defend the Church Liberties, confer Institutions, in-

flict

flict Ecclesiastical Censures, dispence in certain Cases, keep Hospitality, as *St. Paul* admonisheth, and Preach as oft as necessity requireth. *Hodie enim neque Concionatorum paucitas uti olim, neque Infidelium multitudo hoc exigere videtur.* For now neither that scarcity of Preachers as was amongst the Primitive Christians nor multitude of Heathens as dwelt among them doth seem to require it.

Ever since the beginning of our Reformation, there are some few Families, in several parts of *England*, have persisted in the Romish Religion, and are usually called *Papists* from *Papa*, the old usual Name of the Bishop of *Rome*. Against these there are divers severe Laws still in force, but their number being not considerable, nor their Loyalty of later years questionable, those Laws are more rarely put in execution: besides the Clemency and gentle usage shewn them here, begets in *Romish* States and Potentates abroad the like gentle treatment of their Protestant Subjects, and of the English, living within their Dominions.

As for those other Perswasions whose Professors are commonly called *Presbyterians*, *Independents*, *Anabaptists*, *Quakers*, *Fifth-Monarchy-Men*, *Ranters*, *Adamites*, *Antinomians*, *Sabbatarians*, *Perfectionists*, *Family of Love*, and the rest of those Mushromes of *Christianity*; as most of them sprang up suddenly in the late unhappy night of Confusion, so it is to be presumed that they may in a short

time

time vanish in this blessed Day of Order; and therefore not worthy to be described here as Religions professed in *England*: for the State of *England* doth account them no other Members then the *Pudenda* of the Nation, and are ashamed of them, *Quippe ubi cætera Membra moventur ad arbitrium hominis, hæc sola tam turbida, inordinata ac effrænata sunt ut præter & contra voluntatem commoveri solent*; so neither doth the Church of *England* look upon those Professors as Sons but Bastards: or make account of any other interest in them then a man makes of those Vermin which breed out of his excrementitious sweat, or those *Ascarides* which come sometimes in his most uncleanly parts. Touching the *Jews* which by the late Usurper were admitted at *London*, and since continued by the bare permission of the King, and suffered to hire a Private House wherein to hold their *Synagogue*; they are not considerable either for Number, making not above 30 or 40 Familyes, nor for their Wealth or Abilities, being for the most part Poor and Ignorant.

Their Manners

As some years before the late Troubles, no people of any Kingdom in the World enjoyed more freedom from *Slavery* and *Taxes*, so generally none were freer from evil tempers and humors: none more *devoutly religius, willingly obedient to the Laws, truly Loyal to the King, lovingly hospitable to Neighbours, ambitiously*

tiously civil to Strangers, or more *liberally charitable to the Needy.*

No Kingdom could shew a more *valiant prudent Nobility*, a more *Learned Pious Clergy* or a more *contented loyal Commonalty.*

The *Men* were generally honest, the *Wives* and *Woemen* chaste and modest, *Parents loving, Children obedient, Husbands kind, Masters gentle*, and *Servants faithful.*

In a word, the *English* were then according to their *Native Tempers*, the best *Neighbours*, best *Friends*, best *Subjects*; and the best *Christians* in the World.

Amongst these excellent *Tempers*, amongst this goodly *Wheat*, whilst men slept, the Enemy came and sowed *Tares*, there sprang up of later years a sort of People *sowre, sullen, suspitious, querulous, peevish, envious, reserved, narrow-hearted, close-fisted; self-conceited, ignorant, stiff-necked, Children of Belial* (according to the genuine signification of the *word*) ever prone to *despise Dominion*, to *speak evil of Dignities*, to *gain-say Order, Rule*, and *Authority*; who have accounted it their honour to contend with *Kings* and *Governors*, and to *disquiet* the Peace of *Kingdoms*; whom no *deserts*, no *clemency* could ever oblige, neither *Oaths* or *Promises* bind, breathing nothing but *sedition* and *calumnies* against the establisht Government, *aspiring* without measure, *railing* without reason, and making their

own

own *wild fancies* the Square and Rule of their *Consciences*; hating, despising or disrespecting the *Nobility*, *Gentry* and *Superiour Clergy*, &c.

These lurking in all quarters of *England*, had at length with their pestilential breath infected some of the *worse natured* and *worse nurtured Gentry*, divers of the *inferiour Clergy*, most of the *Tradesmen*, and very many of the *Peasantry*, and prevailed so far, as not only to spoil the best governed State, and ruin the purest and most flourishing Church in *Christendome*, but also to corrupt the *minds*, the *humors*, and very *natures* of so many English; that notwithstanding the late happy Restauration of the *King* and *Bishops*, the incessant joynt endeavours and studies of all our Governours to reduce this people to their *pristine* happiness, yet no man now living can reasonably hope to see in his time the like blessed days again; without a transplantation of all those sons of *Belial* (as King *James* in his grave Testament to his Son did intimate) without an utter extirpation of those Tares, which yet the Clemency and meekness of the Protestant Religion seems to forbid.

The *Nobility* and chief *Gentry* of *England* have been even by Strangers compared to the *finest Flowre*, but the lower sort of common People to the *coursest bran*; the innate good nature, joyned with the liberal education and converse with Strangers in forreign Countries, ren-

der

der those exceeding civil; whereas the wealth, insolence, and pride of these, and the rare converse with Strangers, have rendred them so distasteful, not only to the few Strangers who frequent *England*, but even to their own Gentry, that they could sometimes wish that either the Country were less plentifull, or that the Impositions were heavier; for by reason of the great abundance of *Flesh* and *Fish*, *Corn*, *Leather*, *Wool*, *&c.* which the Soil of its own bounty with little labour doth produce, the *Yeomanry* at their ease and almost forgetting labour, grow rich, and thereby so proud, insolent, and careless, that they neither give that humble respect and awful Reverence which in other Kingdoms is usally given to *Nobility*, *Gentry*, and *Clergy*, nor are they so *industrious* or so *skilful* in *Manufactures* as some of our Neighbour Nations; so that in *England* it is no *Paradox* to affirm, that as too much *indigency* in the inferiour sort of people doth *depress* the spirits and dull the minds of them, so too *plentiful* and *wanton* a fortune, causeth in them a *laziness* and *less industry*, that State commonly enjoying most *peace* and *order* and *happiness*, where either the *moderate barrenness* of the Countrey, or *want of ground*, or *multitude* of *Imposts* (as in *Holland*) do necessitate the common people to be industrious in their Callings, and so to mind their own, as not to disturb the State and Church affairs.

Moreover, of the *English* especially it

hath

hath been formerly and unhapily observed, that then it is *happiest* with them, when they are somewhat *pressed*, and in a *complaining* condition; according to that old Riming Verse,

Anglica gens est optima flens & pessima ridens.

The *English* Common people anciently were, and at this day are very apt to hearken to *Prophesies*, and to create *Prodigies*; and then to interpret them according to their own extravagant conceits: to invent and then maintain any the most prodigious Opinions and Tenets in Divinity: some of the inferiour sort of late holding abominable opinions, unworthy even of men and such as in no Age were ever broacht before.

The *English national vices* were anciently *Gluttony* and the effects thereof *Lasciviousness*, (when they made four Meals in a day and most excessive *Feasting*, with great plenty of *French Wine*) when Women of *professed incontinency* were permitted to proffer their Bodyes to all Comers, in certain places called *Stews* or *Stoves*, or *Bathing places*; because men were wont to *bath* themselves there (as still in other Countreys) before they adrest themselves to *venerious acts*. Moreover *Pride* in *Apparel*, wherein they were anciently so extravagant and foolish, so superfluous and obscene, that divers *Statutes* before our *Reformation* in *Religion*, and *Homilies* since, have been made against

gainst that Excess, and an English Man was wont to be pictured naked with a pair of *Taylors Sheers* in his hand; and a piece of Cloth under his arme, with verses annext, intimating, that he knew not what fashion of Clothes to have.

Excess of drinking was antiently more rare in *England*, as appears by an old Poet.

Ecce Britannorum mos est laudabilis iste,
Ut bibat arbitrio pocula quisque suo.

The *Danes* in the time of King *Edgar* first brought it in, but it was afterward banisht hence, so that we find no ancient Statute since the Conquest against it; for though the Statutes heretofore made against Excess in *Apparel* and *Dyet* are ancient, yet those against *Drunkenness* are but of late date.

As the *English* returning from the Wars in the *Holy Land*, brought home the foul disease of *Leprosie*, now almost extinct here, though not yet in our Neighbouring Countries: so in our Fathers days the *English* returning from the service in the *Neatherlands*, brought with them the foul Vice of *Drunkenness*, as besides other Testimonies the Term of *Carous*, from *Gar auz*, *All out*, learnt of the *High Dutch* there in the same service; so *Quaffe*, &c. This Vice of late was more, though at present so much, that some persons, and those of quality may not safely be visited in an afternoon, without running the hazard of excessive drinking of *Healths* (whereby in a short time twice as much liquor is consumed as by the *Dutch*, who sip and prate) and in some places it is esteemed a piece of wit to make a man drunk; for which purpose some *swilling insipid Trencher-Buffoon* is always at hand.

However it may be truly affirmed that at present there is generally less Excess in *Drinking* (especially about *London*, since the use of *Coffee*) less excess in *Dyet*, but principally in *Apparel* than heretofore; insomuch that the poor Tradesmen is much pincht thereby; for as it is expedient for the benefit of the whole Common-wealth, that divers *unnecessary* and *superfluous* Commodities should be allowed; as *Tobacco*, *Coffee*, *Spices*, *Sugars*, *Raisins*, *Silks*, *Fine Linnen*, *&c.* so some less hurtful excesses (as in *Apparel*, *Diet*, *Building*, *Coaches*, *Lacqueys*, &c.) must either be connived at, or much of all the Money of the Nation must lie dead and unimployed (as it now doth in the *private*, *sullen*, *niggardly Non-Conformists* hand) and Tradesmen must either starve or be sustained by Almes.

The Sin of *Buggery* brought into *England* by the *Lombards*, as appears not onely by the word *Bugeria*, but also by *Rot. Parl.* 50. *Ed*, 3, *N.* 58. is now rarely practised amongst *English*, although sometimes discovered amongst *Aliens* in *England*, and then punisht by Death without any remission.

Im-

Impoysonments, so ordinary in *Italy*, are so abominable amongst *English*, as 21 *H.* 8, it was made High Treason, though since repealed; after which the punishment for it was to be put alive in a Caldron of Water, and there boyled to death: at present it is Felony without benefit of Clergy.

Stabbing in *England* is much more seldome than in *Italy*, the English being easie to be reconciled, to pardon and remit offences, not apt to seek revenge; the true well-bred English have more of inclination to goodness, which the Greeks called *Philantrophia*, than other Nations: the Nobility and well-bred Gentry delighting to be gracious and courteous to strangers, compassionate to the afflicted, and grateful to Benefactours, when their Purse or Estate not diverted by other extravagant expences, will give them leave to remember them.

The English according to the *Climate*, are of a *middle temper*. The *Northern Saturnine*, and the *Southern Mercurial temper* meeting in their Constitutions, render them *ingenious* and *active*, yet *solid* and *persevering*, which nourisht under a sutable liberty, inspires a courage *generous* and *lasting*.

Their *Ingenuity* will not allow them to be excellent at the *Cheat*, but subject in that point rather to take than give, and supposing others as open-hearted as themselves, are many times in Treaties overmatcht by them whom they overmatcht in

Arms and *true Valour*: which hath been very eminent in all ages, and almost in all Lands and Seas too of the whole world.

The *English* since the Reformation are so much given to Literature, that all sorts are generally the most knowing people in the World. They have been so much addicted to writing, and especially in their own Language, and with so much licenſe or connivence, that according to the obſervation of a Learned man, there have been during our late Troubles and Confusions *more good* and *more bad Books* printed and publiſhed in the Engliſh Tongue, than in all the vulgar Languages of *Europe*.

For ſolidity of Matter, for elegancy of Style and method in their *Sermons*, *Comedies*, *Romances*, as alſo in their Books of *Philoſophy*, *Phyſick*, *Hiſtory*, and all other ſolid Learning, no Nation hath ſurpaſſed the Engliſh, and few equalled them.

The Engliſh, eſpecially the *Gentry*, are ſo much given to *Prodigalitie* and *Slothfulneſs*, that Eſtates are oftner *ſpent* and *ſold* than in any other Countrey: They think it a piece of frugality beneath a Gentleman to *bargain* before-hand, or to *count* afterward, for what they eat in any place, though the rate be moſt *unreaſonable*; whereby it comes to paſs, that *Cooks*, *Vintners Innkeepers*, and ſuch mean fellows enrich themſelves, and begger and inſult over the Gentry. In a word, by *their prodigalitie* it comes to paſs, that not only thoſe, but *Taylours*, *Dancing-*

Maſters,

Masters, and such *Trifling Fellows*, arrive to that riches and pride as to ride in their *Coaches*, keep their Summer-Houses, to be served in Plate, *&c.* an insolence insupportable in other well-governed Nations.

Because the several *punishments* inflicted for several Crimes are different in most Countryes, and those of *England* much different from those of all other Countreys; a brief account of them may probably not be unaceptable to Forreigners especially. *Punishments of Criminals.*

All Crimes in *England* that touch the life of a Man, are either *High-Treason*, *Petit-Treason*, or *Felony*. Although some *High-Treasons* are much more heinous and odious than others; yet the punishment by Law is the same for all sorts (except for Coyning of Money) and that is that the Traitor laid upon a Hurdle or Sledge be drawn to the Gallows, there hanged by the Neck, presently cut down alive, his entrails to be suddenly pulled out of his Belly and burnt before the face of the Criminal, than his Head to be cut off, his Body to be divided into 4 parts, and lastly, that the Head and Body be hung up or impaled where the King shall command.

Besides all this, he shall forfeit all his Lands and Goods whatsoever, his Wife shall lose her Dower, his Children their Nobility, and all their Right of Inheriting him or any other Ancestor: Our Law thinking it most reasonable, that he who endeavoured to destroy the King, the Breath of of our Nostrils, and thereby to rend the Majesty of Government; his Body, Lands, Goods, and Posterity, should be rent torn and destroyed. For Coining of Money, though adjudged *High-Treason*, the Punishment having been onely drawing and hanging before the Statute of 25 *Ed.* 3 it remains so still.

Petit-Treason is either when a Servant killeth his Master or Mistriss, or a Wife killeth her Husband, or a Clergy-man his Prelate, to whom he oweth obedience; and for this Crime the Punishment is to be drawn (as before) and to be hanged by the Neck till he be dead. The punishment for a Woman convicted of *High-Treason* or *Petit-Treason*, is all one; and that is to be drawn and burnt alive.

Felonies are all other Capital Crimes; for which antiently there were several sorts of Punishments till *H.* 1. ordained that the Punishments for all Felonies should be to be hanged by the Neck till they are dead,

But if a Peer of the Realm commit *High-Treason*, *Petit-Treason*, or *Felony*, although his Judgement be the same with that of common persons; yet the King doth usually extend so much favour to such, as to cause them onely to be beheaded with an Axe upon a Block lying on the ground, and not as in all other Countreys by a Sword Kneeling or standing.

If a Criminal indicted of *Petit-Treason* or *Felony*, refuseth to answer, or to put himself upon a Legal Trial; then for such standing Mute, and Contumacy, he is presently to undergo that horrible punishment called *Paine forte & dure*; that is to be sent back to the Prison from whence he came, and there laid in some low dark Room upon the bare ground on his back, all naked besides his privy parts, his Arms and Legs drawn with Cords fastned to the several quarters of the room; then shall be laid upon his Body Iron and Stone, so much as he may bear or more: the next day he shall have three Morsels of Barly Bread without Drink; and the third day shall have Drink of the Water next to the Prison Door, except it be running Water, without Bread; and this shall be his Diet till he die. Which grievous kind of death some stout Fellows have sometimes chosen that so being not tried and convicted of their Crimes, their Estates may not be forfeited to the King, but descend to their Children; nor their Bloud stained.

But, in Case of *High-Treason*, though the Criminal stand mute, yet Judgment shall be given against him as if he had been convicted; and his Estate confiscated.

After Beheading or Hanging, the Criminals friends usually interr the Body decently where they please; onely if the Crime be very enormous, as for Murdering and Robbing any Person; than by Order, is the Criminal usually hanged by the neck till he be dead, and afterwards hanged in Chains till the Body rot; and in some Cases his Right Hand is first cut off and then hanged.

In all ſuch *Felonies* where the Benefit of *Clergy* is allowed (as it is in many) there the Criminal is to be markt with a hot Iron with a *T.* or an *M.* for *Thief* or *Manſlayer* on the Left Hand, and Wandring Rogues are to be burnt on the Shoulder with an *R.*

Antiently in the time of the Saxon Chriſtian Kings, and ſometime after the coming of the Norman Kings, men were rarely put to death for any Crime, but either paid grievous Fines, or for the more enormous Crimes, to looſe their Eyes or their Teſticles; and ſo remain living Monuments of their Impieties, as Puniſhments far worſe than death; which amongſt Chriſtians is believed to be but a paſſage from this life to a far better, and ſo more a Reward than a Puniſhment.

For *Petit Larceny* or *Smal Theft*, that is of the value of 12. *d* or under, the puniſhment antiently was ſometimes by loſs of an Ear, ſometimes by Cudgeling, but ſince *Edw.* 3. onely by Whipping; but if ſuch *Petit Thief* be found, by the Jury to have fled for the ſame, he forfeiteth all his Goods.

Perjury, by bearing falſe witneſs upon Oath, is puniſht with the Pillory called *Colliſtrigium*, burnt in the Fore-head with a *P.* his Trees growing upon his Ground to be rooted up, and his Goods confiſcated.

Forgery, *Cheating*, *Libelling*, *Falſe Weights* and *Meaſures*, *Fore-ſtalling the Market*, *Offences* in *Baking* and *Brewing*, are commonly puniſhed with ſtanding in the

the Pillory, and ſometimes to have one or both Ears nailed to the Pillory, and cut off, or there bored through the Tongue with a hot Iron.

The Puniſhment for *Miſpriſion* of *High-Treaſon*, that is for neglecting or concealing it, is forfeiture of the Profits of his Lands during life, and of all Goods, and alſo Impriſonment for life.

For *Striking in the Kings Court*, whereby Blood is drawn, the Puniſhment is, that the Criminal ſhall have his Right Hand ſtrucken off in a moſt ſad and ſolemn manner; as more at large may be ſeen in the Chapter of the Kings Court.

For ſtriking in *Weſtminſter-Hall* whilſt the Courts of Juſtice are ſitting, is Impriſonment during life, and forfeiture of all his Eſtate.

For one found in a *Præmunire*, is forfeiture of all his Eſtate, to be put out of the Kings Protection, and Impriſonment during the Kings Pleaſure.

The Puniſhment of *Petit Jurors* attainted of giving a Verdict contrary to Evidence wittingly is ſevere and terrible; they are condemned to loſe the Franchiſe or Freedom of the Law, that is, become infamous and of no credit, uncapable of being a Witneſs or of a Jury; their Houſes, Lands, and Goods ſhall be ſeiſed into the Kings hands, their Houſes pulled down, their Meadows ploughed up, their Trees rooted up, all their Lands layd waſte, and their Bodies impriſoned.

The like Puniſhment is alſo for thoſe

who shall conspire to indict an Innocent falsly and maliciously of *Felony*.

Any Man or Woman convicted, in the Bishops *Court* of *Heresie*, is to be delivered over to the Secular Power, and to be burnt alive.

Felo de se, that is one who wittingly killeth himself; is to be buried out of *Christian* Burial with a Stake driven thorow the Corps, and to forfeit his Goods.

Drunkards, Vagabonds, *&c.* are punished by setting their Legs in the Stocks for certain hours.

Scolding Women are to be placed in a *Trebuchet*, commonly called a *Cucking-stool*, placed over some deep water, into which they are let down and plunged under water thrice, to cool their choler and heat.

Other Misdemeanors are commonly punisht with Imprisonments or Fines, and sometimes with both.

As for breaking on the Wheel and other like Torturing Deaths, common in other Christian Countries, the English look upon them as too cruel for Christian Professors to use.

For putting any to the Rack, (unless perhaps in some Cases of *High-Treason*) it is by the English believed to savour of too much slavishness; besides they contemning and despising death, and yet not enduring Torture, will sooner acknowledge themselves guilty of any the foulest Crime whatsoever, then be put to the Rack; and the People not acustomed to such cruelty, would

would be apt to pity the party tortured, and abominate the Sovereign and his Judges, for introducing such a Custom; and the Jury would easily quit the Prisoner of whatever Confession should be thus extorted.

England contains 9725 Parishes, now allowing to each Parish one with another 80 Families, there will be 778000 Families, and to each Family 7 persons, there will be found in all Five Millions four hundred forty six thousand souls, and amongst them about one Million of Fighting Men. *Number of Inhabitants.*

The *English Tongue* being at present much refined, exceedingly *copious*, *expressive*, and *significant* (by reason of a liberty taken by the Natives of borrowing out of all other Languages, what ever might conduce thereunto) is (as their blood) a *mixture* chiefly of the Old *Saxon* (a *Dialect* of the *Teutonick*) and the Old *Norman* (a *Dialect* of the *French*) not without some savour of the *Brittains*, *Romans* and *Danes* *Langages*. *Their Language.*

The *Romans* possessing *England*, caused their Tongue, the *Latine* once, to be generally used in this Countrey.

The *Saxons* succeeding, introduced their *Language* wheresoever they seated themselves.

The *Normans* afterwards getting possession of *England*, caused the *Norman* or *French* Tongue to be learnt at School by the *Saxons*, and for a long time had all

Laws, *Pleadings*, *Sermons*, &c. in *French*.

The *Latine* Tongue at present is made use of in *Court Rolls*, *Records*. *Processes* of *Courts*, in *Charters*, *Commissions*, *Patens*, *Writs*, *Bonds*, & some statuts are still Kept in that language.

The Names of all *Shires*, *Cities*, *Towns*, and *Villages*, *Places*, and *Men*, in *England*, are generally *Saxon*, and so are most *Nouns Appellative*, and a great part of the *Verbs*.

In *French*, or rather *Norman*, are still written the *Common Laws*, and learnt by young Students thereof. Also some *Pleadings*, and all *Moots* and *Law Exercises*, are wholly *French*. Declarations upon original writs, & all Reports are written in French, some old statutes are still in that tongue. In Parliaments, the assent or dissent to Bills made by the King lords or Commons is in French. Almost all our Termes in *Hunting*, in *Hawking*, *Dicing*, *Dancing*, *Singing*, &c. are still *French*.

Stature. The *Natives* of *England* (by reason of the *Temperate Climate*, *Milde Air*, not rendred unequal by high *Mountains*, and unhealthy by many *Marshes*, plenty of wholsome food, and the use of Beer rather then Wine) *Pour la belle taille & le beau teinct au visage*, as the French say, For a just hansome large *proportion* of body, for clear *complexions* and pleasing *features*, do surpass all the Nations of the World.

Dyet. The English are generally great *Flesh-eaters*, although by the nearness of the *Sea*

and

and abundance of *Rivers* and *Fish-ponds*; there is no want of Fish. In former times their Table was in many places covered four times a day; they had *Break-fasts*, *Dinners*, *Beverages*, and *Suppers*, and every where *set Dinners* and *Suppers* untill the time of the late troubles: wherein many eminent Families were much impoverisht; a Custom was taken up by some of the Nobility and Gentry, of eating a more plentiful *Dinner*, but little or no *Supper*; as on the contrary the *Romans* and *Jews* anciently, and the hotter *Climats* at this day have little or no *Dinners*, but *Set Suppers*.

The English are not now so much addicted to *Gluttony* and *Drunkenness* as of late years, but unto *Tobacco* more.

Feasting also is not now so common and profuse as antiently; for although the *Feasts* at *Coronations*, at the *Installation* of *Knights* of the *Garter*, *Consecration of Bishops*, *Entertainments* of *Ambassadors*, the Feasts of the *Lord Mayor* of *London*, of the *Sergeants at Law*, and *Readers Feasts* in the *Innes of Court*, are all very sumptuous and magnificent in these times; yet compared to the Feasts of our *Ancestors*, seem to be but niggardly and sparing: for *Richard Earl of Cornwall*, Brother to *Henry* 3, had at his Marriage Feast, as is recorded; Thirty thousand Dishes of Meat; and King *Richard* the Second at a *Christmas* spent daily 26 Oxen, 300 Sheep, besides Fowl and all other Provision proportionably: So antiently at a *Call* of *Sergeants* at law, each *Sergeant* (saith *Fortescue*) spent sixteen hundred Crowns in feasting which in those dayes was more than 1600 *l.* now.

The English that feed not over liberally (whereto the great plenty and variety of Viands entice them) nor drink much *Wine*, but content them selues with Small *Ale* or *Sider*, (but especially the later) are observed to be much more *healthy* and far *longer lived* than any of our Neighbourg Nations,

Since the late Rebellion, *England* hath abounded in variety of Drinks (as it did before in variety of Religions) above any Nation in *Europe*. Besides all sorts of the best *Wines* from *Spain*, *France*, *Italy*. *Germany*, *Grecia*; and there are sold in *London* above 20 sorts of other *Drinks*, as *Coffee*, *Chocolate*, *Tee*, *Aromatick*, *Mum*, *Sider*, *Perry*, *Beer*, *Ale*; many sorts of *Ales* very different, as *Cock*, *Stepony*, *Stich-Back*, *Hull*, *North-Down*, *Sambidge*, &c. a piece of Wantonness whereof none of our Ancestours were ever guilty.

Attire. For *Apparrel* or *Clothing*, the *French Mode* hath been generally used in *England* of late years: In the time of Queen *Elizabeth* sometimes the *High Dutch*, sometimes the *Spanish*, and sometimes the *Turkish* and *Morisco Habits*, were by the *English* worn in *England* when the Women wore *Doublets* with *Pendant Codpieces* on the Breast, full of *Tags* and *Cuts*; moreover *Gallygascons*, *Fardingales*, and *Stockings* of *divers Colours*: but since the Restauration of the King now raigning, *England* never saw, for matter of wearing

Apparel,

Apparel, less prodigality, and more modesty in Clothes, more plainness and comeliness than amongst her Nobility, Gentry, and Superiour Clergy; onely the Citizens, the Countrey people, and the Servants, appear clothed for the most part above and beyond their Qualities, Estates, or Conditions. Since our last breach with *France*, the English Men (though not the Women) have quitted the French Mode, and taken a grave Wear, much according with the Oriental Nations.

Recreations. For Variety of *Divertisements*, *Sports* and *Recreations*, no Nation doth Excel the English.

The King hath abroad his *Forests*, *Chases*, and *Parks*, full of variety of Game; for Hunting *Red* and *Fallow Deer*, *Foxes*, *Otters*; *Hawking*, his *Paddock Courses*, *Horse Races*, &c. and at home, *Tennis*, *Baloon*, *Billiards*, *Enterludes*, *Balls*, *Ballets*, *Masks*, &c. The Nobility and Chief Gentry have their *Parks*, *Warrens*, Decoys, *Paddock Courses*, *Horse-Races*, *Hunting*, *Coursing*, *Fishing*, *Fowling*, *Hawking*, *Setting-dogs*, *Tumblers*, *Lurchers*, *Duck-hunting*, *Cockfighting*, *Guns for Birding*, *Low-Bells*, *Bat-fowling*; *Angling*, *Nets*, *Tennis*, *Bowling*, *Billiards*, *Tables*, *Chesse*, *Draughts*; *Cards*, *Dice*, *Catches*, *Questions*; *Purposes*, *Stage-Plays*, *Masks*, *Balls*, *Dancing*, *Singing*, all sorts of *Musical Instruments*, &c. The Citizens and Peasants have *Hand-Ball*, *Foot Ball*, *Skittles*, or *Nine-Pins*, *Shovel-boards*,

Stow-Ball, *Goffe*, *Trol-Madam*, *Cudgels*; *Bear-Baiting*; *Bull-baiting*, *Bow* and *Arrow*, *Throwing at Cocks*, *Shuttlecock*, *Bowling*, *Quaits*, *Leaping*, *Wrest-ling*, *Pitching the Bar* and *Ringing of Bells*, a Recreation used in no other Countrey of the World.

Amongst these *Cock-Fighting* seems to all Forreigners too *childish* and *unsuitable* for the *Gentry*, and for the Common People, *Bull-baiting*, and *Bear-baiting* seem too *cruel*, and for the Citizens, *Foot-Ball*, and throwing at *Cocks*, very *uncivil*, *rude* and *barbarous*, within the City.

English Names. *Nomina quasi Notamina*, Names were first imposed upon Men for distinction sake by the *Jews* at their *Circumcision*, by the *Romans* at the ninth day after *Birth*, and by the *Christians* at the *Baptisme*; of such signification for the most part that might denote the future good hope or good wishes of Parents toward their Children.

The English Names of *Baptisme* are generally either *Saxon*, as *Robert*, *Richard*, *Henry*, *William*, *Edward*, *Edmund*, *Edwin*, *Gilbert*, *Walter*, *Leonard*, &c. Which are all very significative; or else out of the *Old* and *New Testament*, as *Abraham*, *Isaack*, *Jacob*, *John*, *Thomas*, *James*, &c. Or sometimes the Mothers Surname, and rarely two Christian Names, which yet is usual in other Countreys, especially in *Germany*.

Surnames Names super-added to the Christian Names the French call *Surnoms* (*i. e.*) *supernomina*. The

The *Hebrews*, *Greeks*, and most other ancient Nations; had no *Surnames* fixt to their Families as in these days, but counted thus, for example among the *Hebrews*, *Melchi Ben Addi*, *Addi Ben Casam*, &c. So the *Britains*, *Hugh ap Owen*, *Owen ap Rhese*, so the *Irish Neal mac Con*, *Con mac Dermoti*, &c.

As Christian Names were first given for distinction of Persons, so Surnames for distinction of Families.

About *Anno* 1000 the *French* Nation began to take Surnames with *de* prefixt of a place, and *le* prefixt for some other qualification; as at this day is their usual manner. The English also took to themselves Surnames, but not generally by the Common People, till the Raign of *Edw.* I.

Great Offices of Honour have brought divers Surnames, as *Edward Fitz-Theobald* being long ago made Butler of *Ireland*, the Duke of *Ormond* and his Ancestors descended from him, took the Surname of *Butler*; so *John* Count *Tanquirvile* of *Normandy* being made Chamberlain to the King of *England* above 400 years ago, his Descendants of *Sherborn* Castle in *Oxford-shire*, and of *Prestbury* in *Glocester shire*, bear still the same Coat of Arms by the Name of *Chamberlyne*.

At first, for Surnames the English Gentry took the Name of their Birth-place or Habitation, as *Thomas* of *Aston* or *East Town*, *John* of *Sutton* or *South-Town*; and as they altered their Habitation, so they altered their Surname, After, when they became Lords of places, they called themselves *Thomas Aston* of *Aston*, *John Sutton* of *Sutton*.

The Saxon Common People for Surnames added their Fathers Name with *Son* at the end thereof, as *Thomas Johnson*, *Robert Richardson*. They also oft took their Fathers Nick-name or Abbreviation, with addition of s as *Gibs* the Nick name or Abbreviation, of *Gilbert*; *Hobs* of *Robert*, *Nicks* of *Nicholas*, *Bates* of *Bartholomew*, *Sams* of *Samuel*, *Hodges* of *Roger*; and thence also *Gibson*, *Hobson*, *Nickson*, *Batson*, *Samson*, *Hodson*, and *Hutchinson*; &c. Many also were surnamed from their *Trade*, as *Smith*, *Joyner*, *Weaver*, *Walker*, that is *Fuller* in Old English; and *Goff*, that is *Smith* in Welsh, *&c.* Or from their *Offices*, as *Porter*, *Steward*, *Shepheard*; *Carter*, *Spencer*, that is *Steward*, *Cook*, *Butler*; *Kemp*, that is in Old English *Soldier*: Or from their *place of Abode*, as *Underwood*, *Underhil*, also *Atwood*, *Atwell*, *Athill*; which three last are shrunk into *Wood*, *Wells*, *Hill*, Or from their Colour or Complexion, as *Fairfaix*, that is *Fair locks*; *Pigot*, that is *Speckled*; *Blunt* or *Blund*, that is *Flaxen Hair*; so from *Birds*, as *Arundel*, that is *Swallow*; *Corbet*, that is *Raven*: *Wren*, *Finch*, *Woodcook*, &c. so from *Beasts*, as *Lamb*, *Fox*, *Moyle*, that is *Mule*.

The Normans at their first coming into *England* brought Surnames for many of their Gentry with *de* prefixt, as the French Gentry doth generally at this day, and their

their Christian names were generally German; they being originally descended from *Norway* inhabited by *Germans*. And some for about 200 years after the Conquest, took for Surnames their Fathers Christian Name, with *Fitz* or *Fils* prefixt as *Robert Fitz-William*, *Henry Fitz Gerard*, &c.

The *Britains* or *Welsh* more lately refined did not take Surnames till of late years, and that for the most part onely, by leaving out *a* in *ap*, and annexing the *p* to their Fathers Christian Name; as instead of *Evan ap Rice*, now *Evan Price*; so instead of *ap Howel*, *Powel*; *ap Hughe*, *Pughe*, *ap Rogers*, *progers* &c.

The most ancient Families and of best account for Surnames in *England*, are either those that are taken from Places in *Normandy* and thereabouts in *France*, and from some other Transmarine Countreys, or else from Places in *England* and *Scotland*; as *Evreux*, *Chaworth*, *Seymour*, *Nevile*, *Montague*, *Mohun*, *Biron*, *Bruges*, *Clifford*, *Berkley*, *Arcy*, *Stourton*, *Morley*, *Courtney*, *Grandison*, *Hastings*, &c. which antiently had all *de* prefixt, but of later times generally neglected or made one word as *Devereux*, *Darcy* &c.

English Computation.

In *England* at the beginning of Christianity they counted as all other Christians, according to the then Roman Account by *Olympiads* or space of five years. Afterwards (in the Raign of *Constantine* the first Christian Emperour) by *Indictions* or Fifteen years; at length in the Raign

Raign of the Emperour *Justinian*, 532 years after *Christs* Incarnation (and not before, all Christians generally began to count *ab Anno Christi Incarnati*; at which time one *Dionysius Exiguus* or *Abbas*, a worthy Roman, had finisht a *Cycle* for the Observation of *Easter*, which was then generally received, and is still observed by the Church of *England*, the ground whereof is this. The *Vernal Equinox* at that time was accounted to be the 21 of *March*, and by consequence must be the earliest *Full Moon*, and then *March* the 8 must be the earliest *New Moon*; and *April* the 18 the latest *Full Moon*; which happening on a *Sunday* (as it will when the *Dominical* Letter is *C*. and the *Golden Number* 8) then *Easter* that year will be *April* 25. So when the New Moon shall be on *March* 2. (as it will when the Dominical Letter is *D*: and the Golden Number 16) then *Easter* will be on the 22 *March*, as was in the year 1668.

But the Romish Church inventing new Rules for finding of *Easter*, it happens sometimes that their *Easter* is full 5 weeks before ours, and sometimes with ours, but never after ours; for Pope *Gregory* the 13 in the year 1582, having observed that upon exact account the year contained above 365 days, not ful 6 hours (as had been from the time of *Julius Cæsar* hitherto reckoned) but only 5 hours 49 minutes and 16 seconds, and that this difference of almost 11 minutes in the

space

ſpace of about 134 years, maketh one whole day, which not conſidered ſince the Regulation of *Eaſter*, had brought back the year at leaſt 10 days; inſomuch that the *Vernal Equinox* which was at firſt on the 21 of *March*, was now on the 11th of *March*; by reaſon whereof ſometimes 2 Full Moons paſt between the *Equinox* and *Eaſter*, contrary to the Primitive Inſtitution thereof, which was, that *Eaſter* ſhould always be obſerved on the Sunday following the firſt Full Moon after the *Vernal Equinox*, Pope *Gregory* then having obſerved theſe inconveniences, reſolved at once to take away 10 days, and that out of the Moneth of *October*, by calling the 5th day thereof the 15th and that for that year thoſe Feſtivals which fell in thoſe ten days, which by reaſon of the Vintage time were but few, ſhould be celebrated upon the 15, 16, and 17th days of that Moneth. And that the *Equinox* might never *retrocede* for the future, it was then provided that every 400 years 3 *Biſſextile years* ſhould be left out, that is, in the years 1700, 1800, and 1900, and ſo again in 2100, 2200, and 2300, leaving the year 2000 to have its *Biſſextile*, and ſo every 400th year.

The Engliſh Nation, as all other States that withdrew themſelves from under the Biſhop of *Rome's* uſurped Authority, before the ſaid year 1582, except *Holland* and *Zealand*, obſerve ſtill the antient Accouut made by *Julius Cæſar* 43 years before

before the Birth of Christ; and is therefore called the *Old* Style or *Julian Account*: the other observed by those still under the *Romish* Yoke, is called the *New* Style or *Gregorian Account*; and is (by reason of the aforesaid 10 days taken away) 10 days before ours for the begining of Moneths, and for all fixt Festivals; but various for all Moveable Festivals.

Easter and the other *Moveable Feasts* in *England*, are most certainly thus found. *Shrove-Tuesday* is always the first *Tuesday* after the first *New Moon* after *January*, and the Sunday following is *Quadragessima*, and the Sixth Sunday after is *Easter Day*, and the Fifth Sunday after *Easter* is *Rogation Sunday*, and the Thursday following, being 40 days after the Resurrection, is *Ascention day*; 10 days after which, or 50 days after *Easter* is *Pentecost* or *Whitsunday*, and the Sunday following is *Trinity Sunday*: which Computation of the Church of *England* agrees with all the Eastern Christian Churches, for they and we find *Eas*[illegible] Rules which were generally receiv[illegible] all *Christendom*, *Anno* 532; and ever since, till 1582, it was altered by the Pope, as aforesaid, yet cannot it be denied but that this old Computation is become erroneous; for by our Rules, two *Eastens* will be observed in one year, as in the year 1667, and not one *Easter* in another year as in 1668, as this Author observed formerly in his Proposals to the Parliament.

Advent

Advent Sunday hath a peculiar Rule, d is always the Fourth *Sunday* before *ristmas Day*, or the nearest Sunday to . *Andrews* day, whether before or after.

The year in *England* according to the *ycles* of the *Sun* and *Moon*, and according to *Almanacks*, begins on the First f *January*; but the English Church and tate begins the year from the day of *hrists Incarnation*; *viz.* on the 25th of *March*, which also is observed in *Spain*; yet the *Portugues* (as in divers Countreys in *Africa*) begin their year on the 29th of *August*, the *Venetians* on the first of *March* according to the *Epact*, the *Græcians* on the longest day, as the old *Romans* did on the shortest day; which two last seem to have most reason, as beginning just at the *Periodical* day of the Suns return.

The *Natural* day consisting of 24 hours is begun in *England* at *Midnight*, and counted by 12 hours to *Midday*, and again by 12 hours to next *Midnight*; whereas in *Italy*, *Bohemia*, *Poland*, and some other Countreys, their account is from Sun-setting by 24 of the clock to the next Sun setting, and at *Noremberg* and *Wirtemberg* in *Germany*, according to the old *Babylonian* Account they begin at the first hour after Sun-rising, to count one of the Clock, and so again at the first hour after Sun-set.

English Numbring.

There was a time when those Names of Number now in use amongst all civilized Nations

Nations were unknown, and probably men applied their Fingers of one or both Hands to things they desired to keep account of, and thence it may be that the Numeral words are but *Ten* in any Nation, and in some Nations but *Five*; and then they begin again, as after *decem*, *undecim*, *duodecim*, &c.

The *Hebrews* and the *Greeks* instead of Numeral Words used the Letters of their *Alphabets*, beginning again after the tenth Letter.

The *Latines* made use onely of 7 of their *Capital Alphabet*, viz.

MDCLXVI, all comprehended in this Figure, and all made use of in the same order, in the fatall year 1666, which never did happen before, nor ever will happen again.

The *English* (as all the Western Christian World till about 400 years ago) used only *Numeral Words* in all Writings; but since use the *Figures* 1, 2, 3, &c. which the Christians learnt first of the *Maures* or *Arabs*, and they of the *Indians*.

CHAP.

CHAP. III.

Of the Government of ENGLAND *in general.*

OF Governments there can be but three Kinds, for either One, or More, or All, must have the Soveraign Power of a Nation. If One, then it is a *Monarchy*; If More (that is; an Assembly of Choice Persons) then it is an *Aristocracy*; If All (that is, the General Assembly of the People) then it is a *Democracy*.

Of all Governments the Monarchical, as most resembling the *Divinity*, and nearest approaching to *perfection* (Unity being the perfection of all things) hath ever been esteemed the most excellent.

Οὐκ ἀγαθὸν πολυκοιρανίη : εἷς κοίρανος ἔστω.
Εἷς βασιλεὺς——

For the transgressions of a Land, many are the Princes or Rulers thereof, Prov. 28. 2.

Of Monarchies some are *Despotical*, where the Subjects like Servants are at the Arbitrary Power and Will of their Soveraign, as the *Turks* and *Barbarians*: Others *Political* or *Paternal*, where the Subjects like Children under a Father, are

are governed by equal and just Laws consented and sworn unto by the King; as is done by all Christian Princes at their Coronations.

Of *Paternal* Monarchies, some are *Heriditary*, where the Crown descends either only to Heirs Male, as in *France*, hath been long practised; or next of Blood, as in *Spain, England*, &c. Others *Elective*, where upon the death of every Prince, without respect had to the Heirs or next of Bloud, an other by Solemn Election is appointed to succeed, as in *Poland* and *Hungary*, and till of late in *Denmark* and *Bohemia*.

Of Heriditary *Paternall* Monarchies, some are *dependent* and holden of Earthly Potentates, and are obliged to do homage for the same; as the Kingdoms of *Scotland* (though this be stifly denied by Scotch Writers) and of *Man*, that held in *Capite* of the Crown of *England*, and the Kingdom of *Naples*, holden of the Pope; others *independent*, holden only of God, acknowledging no other Superiour upon Earth.

England is an *Heriditary Paternal Monarchy*, governed by one *Supreme, Independent*, and *Undeposable Head*, according to the known Laws and Customs of the Kingdom.

It is a *Free* Monarchy, challenging above many other *European* Kingdoms, a freedom from all subjection to the Emperour or Laws of the Empire; for that the *Roman Emperours* obtaining antiently ly the Dominion of this Land by force of Arms; and afterwards abandoning the same, the Right by the Law of Nations returned to the former Owners *pro direlicto*, as *Civilians* speak.

It is a Monarchy free from all manner of Subjection to the *Bishop* of *Rome*, and thereby from divers inconveniencies and burdens, under which the neighbouring Kingdoms groan: as *Appeals to Rome* in sundry *Ecclesiastical Suits*, *Provisions*, and *Dispensations*, in several cases to be procured from thence; many *Tributes* and *Taxes* paid to that Bishop, &c.

It is a *Monarchy* free from all *Interregnum*, and with it from many mischiefs whereunto Elective Kingdoms are subject.

England is such a Monarchy, as that, by the necessary subordinate Concurrence of the Lords and Commons in the making and repealing all Statutes or Acts of Parliament, it hath the main advantages of an *Aristocracy* and of a *Democracy*, and yet free from the disadvantages and evils of either.

It is such a Monarchy, as by a most admirable temperament affords very much to the *Industry*, *Liberty*, and *Happiness* of the *Subject*, and reserves enough for the *Majesty* and *Prerogative* of any King that will own his People as Subjects, not as Slaves.

It is a Kingdom that of all the Kingdoms of the World is most like the Kingdom of *Jesus Christ*; whose yoke is easy, whose burden is light. It

It is a Monarchy that without interruption hath been continued almost 1000 years, (and till of late) without any attempts of change of that Government: so that to this sort of Government the English seem to be naturally inclined, and therefore during the late *Bouleversations* or over-turnings, when all the Art that the Devil or man could imagine, was industriously made use of to change this Monarchy into a *Democracy*, this Kingdom into a Common-wealth, the most and the best of English men, the general Spirit and Genius of the Nation (not so much the Presbyterian or Royalist) by mighty, though invisible, influence, concurred at once to restore their exiled Soveraign, and re-establish that antient Government.

CHAP.

CHAP. IV.

Of the KING *of* ENGLAND, *and therein of his Name, Title, Arms, Dominions, Patrimony, Revenue, and Strength: Of his Person, Office, Power, Prerogative, Supremacy, Soveraignty, Divinity, and Respect.*

THe *King* is so called from the *Saxon* word *Koning*, intimating *Power* and *Knowledge*, wherewith every Soveraign should especally be invested. *Names.*

The *Title* antiently of the *Saxon* King *Edgar* was *Anglorum Basileus & Dominus quatuor Marium*, viz. the *British*, *German*, *Irish*, and *Deucaledonian Seas*; and sometimes *Anglorum Basileus omniumque Regum, Insularum, Oceanique Britanniam circumjacentis. cunctarumque Nationum quæ infra eam includuntur, Imperator & Dominus.* *Title.*

The Modern Title more modest ; is, *Dei Gratia of England, Scotland, France and Ireland King, Defender of the Faith.*

The King onely is *Dei Gratia* simply (*i. e.*) from the favour of none but God; and the Archbishops and Bishops, to whom that Title is given, must understand, *Dei gratia & Regis*, or *Dei gratia & voluntate Regis.*

Defen-

Defender of the Faith, was antiently used by the Kings of *England*, as appears by several Charters granted to the University of *Oxford*, but in the year 1521 more affixt by a *Bull* from Pope *Leo* the Tenth for a Book written by *Henry* the Eighth against *Luther*, in defence of some points of the Romish Religion; but since continued by Act of Parliament for defence of the *Antient Catholick* and *Apostolick Faith*.

Primogenitus Ecclesiæ belongs to the Kings of *England*, because their Predecessor *Lucius* was the first King that embraced Christianity.

Christianissimus was by the *Lateran Council* under Pope *Julius* the 2d, conferred on the Kings of *England* in the 5th year of *Henry* the 8th though before used by *Henry* the 7th and since only by the French King.

The Title of *Grace* was first given to the King about the time of *H.* 4. to *H.* 6. *Excellent Grace*, to *Ed.* 4. *High and Mighty Prince*, to *Hen.* 8. first *Highness* then *Majesty*, and now *Sacred Majesty*, after the Custom of the Eastern Emperours, that used Ἁγία Βασιλεία.

The King of *England* in his Publick Instruments and Letters, stiles himself *Nos*, *We*, in the Plural Number; before King *John*'s time the Kings used the Singular Number, which Custom is still seen in the end of Writs, *Teste me ipso apud Westm.*

In speaking to the King is used often (be-

(besides *Your Majesty*) *Syr* from *Cyr*, in the *Greek* Κυρ an Abbreviation of Κύριος and Κῦρος, *Dominus*, much used to the *Greek* Emperours; but *Syr* or *Domine* is now in *England* become the ordinary word to all of better rank, even from the King to the Gentleman. It was antiently in *England* given to *Lords*, afterwards to *Knights*, and to *Clergimen*, prefixt before their Christian Names; now in that manner only to *Baronets* and *Knights of the Bath*, and *Knights Batchelours*: yet in *France Syr* or *Syre* is reserved only for their King.

About the time that our Saviour lived on Earth, there was a Jewish Sect, whose Ring-leader was one *Judas* of *Galilee*, mentioned *Acts* 5. 37. that would not give this Title of *Sir* or *Dominus* to any man; affirming that it was proper only to God, and stood (not unlike our new Fanaticks, called *Quakers*) so perversely for such Nominal Liberty (being in other points meer *Pharisees*) that no penalties could force them to give this honorary Title to any man, no not to the Emperour; *uti videre est apud Josephum & alios. Sed hoc obiter.*

Arms are Ensigns of Honour born in a Shield for distinction of Families, and descendable as heriditary to Posterity; but were not fixed generally in *England* nor *France* till after the Wars in the *Holy-Land*, about 400 years ago, unless it were in the Kings of *Europe*. *Arms.*

The *Saxon* Kings before the Conquest bare *Azure* a *Crosse Formy* between four *Martlets Or*.

Afterward the *Danish* Kings raigning in *England* bare *Or Semi de Harts Gules*, 3 *Lyons Passant Gardant Azure*.

After the Conquest the Kings of *England* bare two *Leopards*, born first by the Conquerour as Duke of *Normandy*, till the time of *Hen.* 2. who in right of his Mother annext her Paternal Coat, the *Lyon* of *Aquitaine*, which being of the same *Field*, *Metal*, and *Form* with the *Leopards*, from thenceforward they were joyntly marshalled in one *Shield*, and *Blazoned* 3 *Lyons*, as at present.

King *Edward the Third* in right of his Mother claiming the Crown of *France*, with the Arms of *England* quartered the Arms of *France*, which then were *Azure*, *Semy Flower-deluces Or*: afterwards changed to 3 *Flower deluces*: whereupon *H*. 5. of *England* caused the *English* Arms to be changed likewise: King *James* upon the Union of *England* and *Scotland*, caused the Arms of *France* and *England* to be quartered with *Scotland* and *Ireland*, and are thus blazoned:

The King of *England* beareth for his Soveraign *Ensigns Armorial* as followeth:

In the first place *Azure*, 3 *Flower-deluces Or*; for the *Regal* Arms of *France* quartered with the *Imperial* Ensigns of *England*, which are *Gules three Lyons Passant Gardant in Pale Or*. In the second place,

place, within a double *Tressure counter-flowered de lys Or*, *a Lyon rampant Gules* for the *Royal* Armes of *Scotland*. In the third place, *Azure* an *Irish Harp Or*, *stringed Argent*, for the *Royal* Ensigns of *Ireland*. In the fourth place as in the first, All within the *Garter*, the chief Ensign of that most Honourable Order, above the same an *Helmet* answerable to His Majesties Soveraign Jurisdiction; upon the same a rich *Mantle* of Cloth of Gold *doubled Ermine*, adorned with an *Imperial* Crown, and surmounted for a Crest by a *Lyon Passant Gardant Crowned* with the like; supported by a *Lyon Rampant Gardant Or*, *Crowned* as the former, and an *Unicorn Argent Gorged*, with a Crown; thereto a *Chain* affixt, passing between his fore-legs and reflext over his back *Or*; both standing upon a Compartment placed underneath, and in the Table of the Compartment His Majesties Royal *Motto*, *Dieu & mon Droit*.

The Supporters used before the Union of *England* and *Scotland* were the *Dragon* and *Lyon*.

The Arms of *France* placed first, for that *France* is the greater Kingdom, and because from the first bearing, those *Flowers* have been always *Ensigns* of a *Kingdom*; whereas the Arms of *England* were originally of *Dukedoms* as aforesaid, and probably because thereby the French might be the more easily induced to acknowledge the *English Title*.

The Motto upon the Garter, *Honi soit*

qui mal y pense; that is, *Shame be to him that evil thereof thinketh*, was first given by *Edward* 3. the Founder of that Order, who at first made a solemn Invitation to the most Illustrious Martial Persons of *Europe* to be of this new Order, and that none might believe his design therein was any other than just and honourable, he caused those words to be wrought in every Garter that he bestowed; whereof more in the Chapter of Knights of the Garter.

The Motto *Dieu & mon Droit*, that is, *God and my Right*, was first given by *Richard the First*, to intimate, that the King of *England* holdeth his Empire not in Vassallage of any mortal man, but of God only; and afterward taken up by *Edward* 3, when he first claimed the Kingdom of *France*. The device of the *Portcullis* of a Castle yet to be seen in many places was the Badge or Cognizance of the *Beauforts* Sons of *John* of *Gaunt* Duke of *Lancaster*, because they were born at his Castle of *Beaufort* in *France*.

Dominions. The Antient *Dominions* of the Kings of *England*, were first *England* and all the *Seas* round about *Great Britain* and *Ireland*, and all the *Isles adjacent*, even to the *Shores* of all the Neighbour-Nations; and our Law saith the *Sea* is of the *Ligeance* of the King, as well as the *Land*: and as a mark thereof, all ships of *Foreigners* have antiently demanded leave to fish and pass in these Seas, and do at this

this day *Lower* their *Top-sailes* to all the Kings Ships of War; and therefore children born upon those Seas (as it sometimes hath happened) are accounted natural born Subjects of the King of *England*, and need no Naturilazation, as others born out of his Dominions.

To *England*, *Henry* 1. annext *Normandy*, and *Henry* 2 *Ireland*, being stiled only Lord of *Ireland* till 33 *H.* 8. although they had all Kingly Jurisdiction before.

Henry 2. also annext the Dukedomes of *Guien* and *Anjou*, the Counties of *Poictou*, *Turein*, and *Mayn*. *Edward the first* all *Wales*, and *Edward the Third* the Right, though not the possession of all *France*.

King *James* added *Scotland*, and since that time there have been super added sundry considerable Plantations in *America*.

The Dominions of the King of *England* are at this day in Possession (besides his just Right and Title to the Kingdom of *France*) all *England*, *Scotland*, and *Ireland*, Three Kingdoms of large extent, with all the Isles, above 40 in number small and great; whereof some very considerable: and all the Seas adjacent. Moreover the Islands of *Jersey*, *Garnsey*, *Alderny*, and *Sark*, which are Parcel of the Dutchy of *Normandy*; besides those profitable Plantations of *New-England*, *Virginia*, *Barbados*, *Jamaica*, *Florida*, *Bermudos*, *New-Neatherlands*, with

with several other Isles and Places in those Quarters, and some in the *East-Indies* and upon the Coast of *Africa*; also upon the North parts of *America*, by right of first discovery to *Estoitland*, *Terra Corterialis*, *New-found-Land*, and to *Guiana*, in the South, the King of *England* hath a Legal Right, though not Possession.

Patrimony. King *William* the Conquerour getting by right of Conquest all the Lands of *England* (except Lands belonging to the Church, to Monasteries, and Religious Houses) into his own hands in *Demesne*, as Lawyers speak, soon bestowed amongst his Subjects a great part thereof, reserving some retribution of Rents and Services, or both to him and his Heirs Kings of *England*; which reservation, is now, as it was before the Conquest, called the Tenure of Lands; the rest he reserved to himself in *Demesne*, called *Corona Regis Dominica*, *Domaines*, and *Sacra Patrimonia*, *Prædium Domini Regis*, *Directum Dominium*, *cujus nullus est Author nisi Deus*: all other Lands in *England* being held now of some Superiour, and depend mediately or immediately on the Crown; but the Lands possest by the Crown, being held of none, can *escheat* to none; being *sacred*, cannot become *prophane*, are or should be permanent and inalienable. And yet they have been (by Time, the Gift and Bounty of our Kings, and some Necessities for the preservation of the Weal Publick) much alienated

The

The certain *Revenues* of the Kings of *England* were antiently greater than of any King in *Europe*, they enjoying in Domains and Fee-Farm Rents, almoſt enough to diſcharge all the Ordinary expences of the Crown, without any Tax or Impoſt upon the Subject. *Revenues.*

Upon the happy Reſtauration of our preſent King, the Lords and Commons aſſemblede in Parliament finding the Crown Revenus much alienated, and the Crown Charges exceedingly encreaſed by reaſon of the late vaſt augmentation of the Revenues and Strength by Sea and Land of our two next Neighbour Nations abroad, and of the many factious, mutinous and rebellious ſpirits at home, did unanimouſly conclude that for the Peace and Security, for the Wealth and Honour of the King and Kingdom, it would be neceſſary to ſettle upon His Majeſty an early Revenue of Twelve hundred thouſand Pounds ? and accordingly with the Kings Conſent, at the humble Requeſt of the Lords and Commons, there was eſtabliſht by Impoſts upon Imported and Exported Goods, upon Liquors drank in *England*, and upon Fire-Hearths, ſo much as was judged would bring up the former impaired Crown Revenues to the ſaid ſumm. Notwithſtanding which, the whole yearly Revenues of the King of *England* are not above the Twelfth part of the Revenues of His Kingdom; whereas the King of *France* hath yearly above One hundred and fifty Millions of Livers that is about Eleven millions of Pounds *Sterling*, and above a Fifth part of the whole Reveunes of *France*.

If this Revenue of our King be truly paid to the King, and brought into the Kings Exchequer (that great Sea, wherein-to so many Rivers & Rivolets empty themselves, and from whence are exhaled by the Sun those kind vapors, wherewith it watereth this whole Land, and whereby all His Majesties Land and Sea Forces (by whose vigilancy we sleep quietly in our Beds) are maintained; and whereby do subsist the several Courts of the King and Royal Family (by which the Honour and Splendor of this Nation is preserved) the several Ambassadors abroad, Great Officers of the Crown, and Judges at home, &c.) If this Revenue be truly paid and brought into the Exchequer, it is sure that in all *Europe* there is no one Treasury, that with less deceit, or less charge of Officers proportionably doth re-imburse the same.

It was complained by *Hen.* 4. of *France*, *Que les despens que faisoyent les Officiers de l' Espargne montoyent a plus que la Taille*; That the Charges of the Exchequer Officers exceeded the Income; and that there were then Thirty thousand Officers to collect and wait on the Revenues: whereas there cannot be any other just complaint in *England*, but only that the necessary Charges of the Crown are of late so great, that the Kings setled Revenue

venue cannot defray them; and yet too many of his Subjects grudge to have those Revenues augmented, looking upon every little payment through a Magnifying Glass, whereby it appears a great Grievance, and never making use of those Prospective Glasses (Moral and Civil Science) whereby they might see afar off the calamity that is coming on like an armed man, and cannot without such payments be prevented.

The King of *England*'s Revenues were never raised by any of those sordid base ways used in other Countries, as by sale of Honours, sale of Magistracies, sale of Offices of Justice and Law, by Merchandising, by a General Impost upon all manner of Victuals and Clothes, by *Puertos secos*, or Impost upon all Goods at the entrance into any Inland County, or Inland City; by Pensions from Confederates, upon pretence of Protection, *&c.*

But the Revenues of the King of *England* consist either in Demesnes, (as afore) or in Fee-Farm Rents, in Lands belonging to the Principallity of *Wales*, Dutchy of *Cornwall*, and Dutchy of *Lancaster*, in Tenths and First-Fruits, in Reliefs, Fines, Amercements, and Confiscations; but more especially of late in those few Imposts afore mentioned.

The mighty power of the King of *England* before the Conjunction of *Scotland*, and total subjection of *Ireland*, which were usally at enmity with him, was notoriously *Strength* toriously known to the World, and sufficiently felt by our Neighbour-Nations: What his Strength hath been since, was never fully tried by King *James* or King *Charles the First*, their Parliaments and People having upon all occasions been refractory, and thwarting those good Kings dèsigns; but now, that the Parliaments of all the Three Kingdoms seem to vie which shall more readily comply with their Sovereign's Desires and Designs, it is not easie to comprehend what mighty things His Majesty now raigning might attempt and effect. But let him be considered abstractly, as King only of *England*, which is like a huge Fortress or Garrisoned Town, fenced not only with strong Works, her Port-Towns, with a wide and deep Ditch the Sea, but guarded also with excellent Out-Works, the strongest and best built Ships of War in the World; then so abundantly furnisht within with Men and Horse, with Victuals and Ammunition, with Clothes and Money, that if all the Potentates of *Europe* should conspire (which God forbid) they could hardly distress it. *Her home-bred Wares are sufficient to maintain her, and nothing but her home-bred Wars enough to destroy her.*

This for the Defensive strength of the King of *England*, now for his Offensive Puissance; how formidable must he be to the World, when they shall understand that the King of *England* is well able, when ever he is willing, to raise of Eng-

lish

lish men Two hundred thousand, and of English Horse Fifty thousand (for so many during the late Rebellion, were computed to be in Arms on both sides) yet (which is admirable) scarce any miss of them in any City, Town or Village; and when they shall consider that the valiant and martial Spirit of the English, their natural agility of Body, their patience, hardiness, and stedfastness is such, and their fear of death so little, that no Neighbour-Nation upon *equal Number and Terms* scarce durst ever abide Battle with them either at Sea or at Land: when they shall consider, that for transporting of an Army, the King of *England* hath at command 100 excellent Ships of War, and can hire 200 stout English Merchant Ships, little inferiour to ships of War; that he can soon man the same with the best Sea-soldiers (if not the best Mariners) in the whole World. And that for maintaining such a mighty Fleet sufficient money for a *competent time* may be raised only by a Land Taxe, and for a *long time* by a moderate Excise upon such Commodities only as naturally occasion Excess or Luxury, Wantonness, Idleness, Pride, or corruption of Manners.

In a word, when they shall consider, that by the most commodious and advantageous Scituation of *England*, the King thereof must be Master of the Sea, and that as on Land, whosoever is Master of the Field, is said to be also Master of every Town when it shall please him; so he that is is Master of the Sea, may be said in some sort to be Master of every Country, at least bordering upon the Sea, for he is at libety to begin or end a War, where, when, and upon what Terms he pleaseth, and to extend his Conquests even to the *Antipodes*.

Person. *Rex Angliæ est persona mixta cum Sacerdote*, say our Lawyers. He is a Priest as well as a King.

He is anointed with *Oyle*, as the Priests were at first, and afterward the Kings of *Israel*, to intimate that his Person is *Sacred* and *Spiritual*: and therefore at the Coronation hath put upon him a *Sacerdotal Garment* called the *Dalmatica*, or *Colobium*, and other Priestly Vests; and before the Reformation of *England*, when the Cup in the Lords Supper was denied to the Laity, the King as a Spiritual Person received in both Kinds: He is capable of *Spiritual Jurisdiction*, of holding of *Tythes*; all *Extra-Parochial Tythes*, some Proxies, and other Spiritual Profits belong to the King, of which Lay-men both by Common and Canon Law are pronounced uncapable.

He is an *External Bishop* of the Church, as *Constantine* the Emperour said of himself, Ἐγὼ δὲ τῶν ἐκ ὁ ὑπὸ Θεοῦ καθεςαμένος. Ἐπίσκοπος ἂν εἶμι; *But I am constituted Bishop for external things of the Church.*

Rex idem hominum Phœbique Sacerdos.

He is, as the Romam Emperors, Christian as well as Heathen, stiled themselves,

Pontifex

Pontifex Max. He is the Supreme *Pastor* of *England*, and hath not only Right of Ecclesiastical Government, but also of exercising some Ecclesiastical Function, so far as *Solomon* did, 1 *Kings* 8. when he blessed the People, consecrated the Temple, and pronounced that Prayer which is the Pattern now for Consecration of all Churches and Chappels; but all the Ministerial Offices are left to the *Bishops* and *Priests*, as the Administration of Sacraments, Preaching, and other Church Offices and Duties.

Of this *Sacred Person* of the King, of the *life* and *safety* thereof, the Laws and Customs of *England* are so *tender*, that they have made it *High-Treason*, onely to imagine or *intend* the *death* of the *King*. And because by imagining or conspiring the death of the Kings *Counsellors* or *Great Officers* of his *Houshold*, the destruction of the King hath thereby sometimes ensued, and is usually aimed at (saith *Stat.* 3. *H.*) that also was made *Felony*, to be punisht with death, although in all other Cases Capital the Rule is *Voluntas non reputabitur pro facto*, and an English Man may not in other Cases be punisht with death, unless the Act follow the Intent.

The Law of *England* hath so high esteem the Kings *Person*, that to offend against those *Persons* and those *things* that represent his *Sacred Person*, as to Kill some of the *Crown Officers*, or the *Kings Judges* executing their Office, or to counterfeit the *Kings Seals*, or his *Moneys*, is made

made *High-Treason* ; because by all these the Kings *Person* is represented : and High-Treason is in the Eye of the Law so horrid, that besides loss of Life and Honour, Real and Personal Estate to the Criminal, *his Heirs* also are to lose the same for ever, and to be ranked amongst the *Peasantry* and *Ignoble*, till the King shall please to restore them. *Est enim tam grave crimen* (saith *Bracton*) *ut vix permittatur hæredibus quod vivant.* High Treason is so grievous a Crime, that the Law not content with the Life and Estate and Honour of the Criminal, can hardly endure to see his heirs survive him.

And rather than Treason against the Kings *Person* shall go unpunisht, the Innocent in some Cases shall be punished; for if an Idiot or Lunatick (who cannot be said to have any will, and so cannot offend) during his Idiocy or Lunacy, shall Kill, or go about to Kill the King, he shall be punisht as a Traytor; and yet being *Non compos mentis*, the Law holds that he cannot commit Felony or Petit-Teason, nor other sorts of High-Treason.

Moreover, for the precious regard of the *Person* of the *King*, by an Antient Record it is declared, that no *Physick* ought to be administred to him, without good *Warrant*, this Warrant to be signed by the Advice of his *Council*; no other Physick but what is mentioned in the Warrant to administer to him; the *Physitians* to prepare all things with their own hands, and not by the hands of any *Apothecary*; and to use

th

the assistance only of such *Chirurgeons* as are prescribed in the Warrant.

And so precious is the *Person* and *Life* of the King, that every Subject is obliged and bound by his Allegeance to defend his Person in his *Natural* as well as *Politick* Capacity, with his own *Life* and *Limbs*; wherefore the Law saith, that the *Life* and *Member* of every *Subject* is at the Service of the *Sovereign*. He is *Pater Patriæ &* *Dulce erit pro Patre Patriæ mori*, to lose Life or Limb in defending him from Conspiracies, Rebellions, or Invasions, or assisting him in the Execution of his Laws, should seem a pleasant thing to every Loyal hearted Subject.

The *Office* of the *King* of *England* in the Laws of King *Edward* the *Confessour* is thus described, *Rex quia Vicarius summi Regis est, ad hoc constituitur ut Regnum terrenum & populum Domini & super omnia Sanctam Ecclesiam ejus veneretur, regat & ab injuriosis defendat*; and (according to the Learned *Fortescue*) is, *Pugnare bella populi sui & eos rectissime judicare*. To fight the Battles of his People, and to see Right and Justice done unto them. *Office*.

Or (according to another) it is to protect and govern his People, so that they may (if possible) lead quiet and peaceable lives in all Godliness and Honesty under him.

Or more particular (as is promised at the Coronation) to preserve the *Rights* and

and *Priviledges* of the *Church* and *Clergy*, the *Royal Prerogatives* belonging to the Crown, the *Laws* and *Customes* of the Realm, to do Justice, shew Mercy, keep Peace and Unity, &c.

Power and Prerogative. The *King* for the better performance of this great and weighty *Office*, hath certain *Jura Majestatis*, extraordinary Powers, Preeminences, and Priviledges, inherent in the Crown, called antiently by Lawyers *Sacra Sacrorum*, and *Flowers of the Crown*, but commonly *Royal Prerogatives*; whereof some the King holds by the *Law* of *Nations*, others by *Common Law*, (excellent above all Laws in upholding a free Monarchy, and exalting the Kings Prerogative) and some by *Statute-Law*.

The King only, and the King alone, by His Royal Prerogative, hath Power without Act of Parliament to *declare War*, *make Peace*, *send and receive Ambassadours*, *make Leagues* and *Treaties* with any Foreign States, give *Commissions* for *levying Men* and *Arms* by Sea and Land, or for pressing Men if need require; dispose of all *Magazines*, *Ammunition*, *Castles*, *Fortresses*, *Ports*, *Havens*, *Ships* of *War*, and *Publick Moneys*; appoint the *Metal*, *Weight*, *Purity*, and *Value* thereof, and by his *Proclamation* make any *Forreign Coyn* to be lawful Money of *England*.

By His *Royal Prerogative* may of his meer Will and Pleasure *Convoke*, *Adjourn*, *Prorogue*, *Remove* and *Dissolve* Parliaments;

ments; may to any *Bill* passed by both *Houses* of *Parliament*, refuse to give (without rendring any reason) His *Royal Assent*, without which a *Bill* is as a Body without a Soul. May at pleasure encrease the Number of the Members of both Houses, by creating more *Barons*, and bestowing *Priviledges* upon any other Towns to send *Burgesses* to *Parliament*. May call to *Parliament* by Writ whom he in His Princely Wisdome thinketh fit, and may refuse to send His Writ to some others that have sate in former *Parliaments*. Hath alone the choice and nomination of all *Commanders* and other Officers at Land and Sea; the choice and nomination of all *Magistrates*, *Counsellours*, and *Officers of State*, of all *Bishops*, and other *High Dignities* in the *Church*, the bestowing of all Honours both of higher and of lower Nobility of *England*; the Power of determining *Rewards* and *Punishments*.

By his *Letters Patent* may erect new *Counties*, *Universities*, *Cities*, *Burroughs*, *Colledges*, *Hospitals*, *Schools*, *Fairs*, *Markets*, *Courts of Justice*, *Forests*, *Chases*, *Free-Warrens*, &c.

The King by His Prerogative hath power to *enfranchise* an *Alien* and make him a *Denison*, whereby he is enabled to purchase Leases of Houses and Lands, and to bear some Offices. Hath power to grant Letters of *Mart* or *Reprisal*.

The King by His Prerogative hath had at all times the Right of *Purveyance* or *Pre-*

Pre-emption of all ſorts of Victuals near the Court, and to take *Horſes*, *Carts*, *Boats*, *Ships*, for His Carriages at reaſonable Rates; alſo by Proclamation to ſet reaſonable Rates and Prices upon *Fleſh*, *Fiſh*, *Fowl*, *Oats*, *Hay*, *&c.* which His Majeſty now Raigning was pleaſed to releaſe, and in lieu thereof, to accept of ſome other recompence.

Debts due to the King, are in the firſt place to be ſatisfied, in caſe of *Excecutorſhip* and *Adminiſtratorſhip*; and until the Kings Debt be ſatisfied, he may *protect* the *Debtor* from the *Arreſt* of other *Creditors*.

May diſtrain for the *whole Rent* upon *one* Tenant that holdeth not the whole Land; may require the *Anceſtors* Debt of the *Heir*, though not eſpecially bound, is not obliged to *demand* his Rent as others are. May ſue in what Court he pleaſe, and diſtrain where he liſt.

No Proclamation can be made but by the King.

No Protection for a Defendant to be kept off from a Suit, but by him, and that becauſe he is actually in his Service.

He only can give *Patents*, in caſe of loſſes by Fire or otherwiſe, to receive the *Charitable Benevolences* of the People; without which no man may ask it publickly.

No Foreſt, Chaſe, or Park to be made, nor Caſtle to be built, without the Kings Authority.

The

The sale of his *Goods* in an open Market will not take away his property therein.

Where the King hath granted a Fair with Toll to be paid, yet his Goods there shall be exempted from all Toll.

No Occupancy shall be good against the King, nor shall Entry before him prejudice him.

His *Servants* in ordinary are priviledged from serving in any Offices that require their attendance, as *Sheriff*, *Constable*, *Churchwarden*, &c.

All *Receivers* of Moneys for the King, or *Accomptants* to him for any of his *Revenues*, their *Persons*, *Lands*, *Goods*, *Heirs*, *Executors*, *Administratours*, are chargeable for the same at all times, for, *Nullum tempus occurrit Regi.*

His *Debtor* hath a kind of Prerogative remedy by a *Quo minus* in the Exchequer against all other Debtors, or against whom they have any cause of Personal Action; supposing that he is thereby disabled to pay the King: and in this Suit the Kings Debtor being Plaintiff, hath some Priviledges above others.

In *Doubtful Cases*, *Semper præsumitur pro Rege.*

No Statute restraineth the King, except he be *especially named* therein. The quality of his Person alters the descent of *Gavelkind*, the Rules of *Joynt Tenancy*; no *Estoppel* can bind him, nor *Judgement final* in a *Writ of Right.*

Judge-

Judgments entred against the Kings Title, are entred with a *Salvo Jure Domini Regis*, That if at any time the Kings Council at Law can make out his Title better; that Judgment shall not prejudice him, which is not permitted to the Subject.

The King by His Prerogative might have demanded reasonable *Aid-Money* of His Subjects to Knight His eldest Son at the age of Fifteen, and to marry His eldest Daughter at the age of Seven years: Which reasonable Aid is Twenty shillings for every Knights Fee, and as much for every Twenty pound a year in *Soccage*. Moreover, if the King be taken Prisoner, Aid-Money is to be paid by the Subjects to set Him at liberty.

The King upon reasonable causes, Him thereunto moving, may *protect* any Man against Suits at Law, *&c.*

In all Cases where the King is *party*, His Officers with an *Arrest* by force of a *Process* at Law, may *enter* (and if entrance be denied) may *break open* the House of any Man, although every Mans House is said to be his Castle, and hath a priviledge to protect him against all other Arrests.

A Benefice or Spiritual Living is not *full* against the King by *Institution* onely, without *Induction*, although it be so against a Subject.

None but the King can hold plea of false Judgements in the Court of his Tenants.

The King of *England* by His Prerogative is *Summus Regni Custos*, and hath the custody of the Persons and Estates of such

as

for want of understanding, *cannot govern* *mselves* or serve the King ; so the Persons l Estates of *Ideots* and *Lunaticks* are in custody of the King, that of *Ideots* to own use, and that of *Lunaticks* to the of the next Heir. So the Custody or rdships of all such Infants whose An-:ors held their Lands by Tenure in *Capite* Knight-service, were ever since the Con-:st in the Kings of *England*, to the great ıor and benefit of the King and King-n; though some abuses made some of the ıple out of love with their good, and the htof that part of His just Prerogative.

The King by His Prerogative is *Ultimus* *res Regni*, and is (as the *Great Ocean* of all Rivers) the *Receptacle* of all ates when no Heir appears ; for this ıse all Estates for want of Heirs, or by :feiture, Revert or Escheat to the King. l Spiritual Benefices for want of Presen-ion by the Bishop, are lapsed at last to King: All *Treasure-Trove* (that is, *ney*, *Gold*, *Silver*, *Plate*, or *Bullion*, ınd (and the owners unknown) belongs the King; so all *Wayfs*, *Strays*, *Wrecks*, : granted away by Him, or any former ıgs; all *Waste Ground* or *Land* recovered m the *Sea*; all *Lands* of *Aliens* dying ore *Naturalization* or *Denization*, and things whereof the property is not own. All *Gold* and *Silver Mines*, in ose Ground soever they are found. *Roy-* *Fishes*, as *Whales*, *Sturgeons*, *Dolphins*, c. *Royal Fowl*, as *Swans*, not markt and imming at liberty on the River, belong the King.

In

In the *Church*, the Kings Prerogative and Power is extraordinary great. He onely hath the *Patronage* of all *Bishopricks*, none can be chosen but by His *Conge d'Eslire*, whom He hath first *nominated*; none can be *consecrated* Bishop, or take possession of the Revenues of the Bishoprick, without the Kings special Writ or Assent. He is the *Guardian* or *Nursing Father* of the *Church*, which our Kings of *England* did so reckon amongst their principal cares, as in the Three and twentieth year of King *Edward* the First, it was alledged in a pleading and allowed. The King hath power to call a *National* or *Provincial Synod*, and with the advice and consent thereof, to make *Canons*, *Orders*, *Ordinances*, and *Constitutions*, to introduce into the Church what *Ceremonies* He shall think fit; *reform* and *correct* all *Heresies*, *Schisms*, punish *Contempts*, &c. and therein, and thereby to declare what *Doctrines* in the *Church*, are fit to be *published* or *professed*, What *Translation of the Bible to be allowed*; what *Books* of the *Bible* are *Canonical*, and what *Apocryphal*, &c.

The King hath a Power, not onely to unite, consolidate, separate, enlarge, or contract the limits of any old *Bishoprick*, or other *Ecclesiastical Benefice*; but also by His Letters Patents, may erect new *Bishopricks*, as *Henry* the Eighth did six at one time; and the late King *Charles* the Martyr intended to do at S. *Albans*, for the honor of the *First Martyr* of *England*, and for Contracting the too large extent of

the

the *Bishoprick* of *Lincoln*, may also erect new *Archbishopricks*, *Patriarchats*, *&c.*

In the Twenty eighth of *Elizabeth*, when the House of Commons would have passed Bills touching Bishops granting *Faculties*, conferring *Holy Orders*, *Ecclesiastical Censures*, the Oath *Ex Officio*, *Non Residency*, *&c.* The Queen much incensed, forbad them to meddle in any *Ecclesiastical Affairs*, for that it belonged to Her Prerogative, &c.

The King hath power to pardon the violation of *Ecclesiastical Laws*, or to abrogate such as are unfitting or useless; to dispence with the rigor of *Ecclesiastical Laws*, and with any thing that is onely *Prohibitum* or *malum per accidens*, *&* *non malum in se*. As for a *Bastard* to be a *Priest*, for a *Priest* to hold *Two Benefices*, or to succeed his *Father* in a *Benefice*, or to be *Non-Resident*, *&c.* For a *Bishop* to hold a vacant *Bishoprick*, or other *Ecclesiastical Benefice* in *Commendam* or *Trust*.

Hath power to dispence with some *Acts* of *Parliament*, *Penal Statutes*, by *Non Obstantes*, where himself is onely concerned, to moderate the rigor of the *Laws* according to *Equity* and *Conscience*; to alter or suspend any particular *Law*, that He judgeth hurtful to the *Commonwealth*; to grant special *Priviledges* and *Charters* to any Subject, to pardon a Man, by *Law* condemned; to interpret by His *Judges Statutes*, and in Cases not defined by *Law*, to determine and pass *Sentence*.

And

And this is that *Royal Prerogative*, which in the Hand of a King, is a *Scepter of Gold*; but in the Hands of Subjects, is a *Rod of Iron*.

This is that *Jus Coronæ*, a *Law* that is parcel of the *Law* of the *Land*; part of the *Common Law*, and contained in it; and hath the precedence of all *Laws* and *Customs* of *England*; and therefore void in *Law*, is every *Custom*, *Quæ exaltat se in Prerogativam Regis*.

Some of these *Prerogatives*, especially those that relate to *Justice* and *Peace*, are so essential to *Royalty*, that they are for ever inherent in the *Crown*, and make the *Crown*: They are like the *Sun* [illegible] the *Sun*, and as inseparable from [illegible]eams [illegible] and therefore it is held by great *Lawyers*, [illegible] at *Prerogative in Point of Government*, cannot be restrained or bound by *Act of Parliament*, but is as unalterable as the *Laws* of the *Medes* and *Persians*: Wherefore the *Lords* and *Commons* (*Rot. Parl.* 42 *Edw.* 3. *Numb.* 7.) declared, That they could not assent in *Parliament* to any thing, that tended to the *disherison* of the King and the Crown, whereunto they were sworn; no, though the King should desire it. And every King of *England*, as he is *Debitor Justitiæ* to His People, so is He in Conscience, obliged to defend and maintain all the Rights of the *Crown* in possession, and to endeavor the recovery of those, whereof the *Crown* hath been dispossest; and when any King hath not religiously observed His duty in this point, it hath proved of very dreadful consequence; as the first fatal blow to the Church of *England*, was given when *Henry* the Eighth, waving His own Royal Prerogative, referred the Redress of the Church to the *House of Commons* (as the Lord *Herbert* observes, *Hist. Hen.* 8.) So the greatest blow that ever was given to Church and State, was, when the late King parting with His absolute Power of *Dissolving Parliaments*, gave it (though onely *Pro illa vice*) to the *Two Houses of Parliament*. And indeed, it greatly concerns all Subjects (though it seem a *Paradox*) to be far more sollicitous, That the King should maintain and defend His own *Prerogative* and *Preeminence*, then their *Rights* and *Liberties*; the truth whereof will appear to any Man that sadly considers the mischeifs and inconveniencies that necessarily follow the diminution of the *Kings Prerogative*, above all that can be occasioned by some particular infringements of the Peoples Liberties. As on the other side, it much concerns every King of *England*, to be very careful of the Subjects just Liberties, according to that Golden Rule of the best of Kings, *Charles* the First, *That the Kings Prerogative is to defend the Peoples Liberties, and the Peoples Liberties strengthen the Kings Prerogative.*

Supremacy and Soveraignty.

Whatsoever things are proper to *Supream Magistrates*, as *Crowns*, *Scepters*, *Purple Robe*, *Golden Globe*, and *Holy Unction*, have as long appertained to the King of *England*,

England, as to any other Prince in *Europe*. He holdeth not His Kingdom in *Vassallage*, nor receiveth His *Investiture* or *Installment* from another. Acknowledgeth no *Superiority* to any, but *God* onely. Not to the *Emperor*; for, *Omnem potestatem habet Rex Angliæ in Regno suo quam Imperator vendicat in Imperio*; and therefore the Crown of *England*, hath been declared in *Parliaments* long ago to be an *Imperial Crown*, and the King to be Emperor of *England* and *Ireland*, and might wear an *Imperial Crown*, although he chuseth rather to wear a *Triumphant Crown*: Such as was anciently worn by the Emperors of *Rome*, and that, because His Predecessors have triumphed; not onely over Five Kings of *Ireland*, but also over the *Welsh*, *Scotch*, and *French* Kings.

He acknowledgeth onely Precedence to the Emperor, *Eo quod Antiquitate Imperium omnia Regna superare creditur*.

As the King is 'Αὐτοκράτωρ in the *State*, so He is 'Αρχιεπίσκοπος in the *Church*. He acknowledgeth no *Superiority* to the Bishop of *Rome*, whose long arrogated *Authority* in *England*, was, One thousand five hundred thirty five, in a full *Parliament* of all the *Lords Spiritual* as well as *Temporal*, declared null; and the King of *England* declared to be by *Antient Right*, in all Causes, over all Persons, as well Ecclesiastical as Civil, *Supream Governor*.

The King is *Summus totius Ecclesiæ Anglicanæ Ordinarius*, Supream Ordinary in all the Diocesses of *England*: 'Επίσκοπος

τῶν

τῶν Ἐπισκόπων, and for His Superintendency over the whole Church, hath the *Tenths* and *First-Fruits* of all Ecclesiastical Benefices.

The King hath the Supream Right of Patronage through all *England*, called *Patronage Paramount*, over all the Ecclesiastical Benefices in *England*; so that, if the mean Patron as aforesaid, present not in due time; nor the Ordinary, nor Metropolitan, the Right of Presentation comes to the King, beyond whom it cannot go. The King is *Lord Paramount, Supream Landlord*, of all the Lands of *England*; and all Landed Men are mediately, or immediately His Tenants, by some Tenure or other: For no Man in *England*, but the King, hath *Allodium & Directum Dominium*, the sole and independent Property or Domain in any Land. He that hath the Fee, the *Jus perpetuum*, and *Utile Dominium*, is obliged to a duty to His Soveraign for it: So it is not simply his own, he must swear Fealty to some Superior.

The King is *summus totius Regni Anglicani Justiciarius*, *Supream Judge*, or *Lord Cheif Justice* of all *England*. He is the Fountain from whence all Justice is derived, no Subject having here as in *France*, *Haute moyenne & basse Justice*. He alone hath the Soveraign Power in the Administration of Justice, and in the Execution of the Law; and whatsoever power is by Him committed to others, the *dernier resort* is still remaining in Himself; so that He may sit in any Court, and take Cogniſance of any Cauſe (as anciently Kings ſate in the Court, now called *The Kings Bench*, *Henry* the Third in His *Court of Exchequer*, and *Henry* the Seventh; and King *James* ſometimes in the *Star-Chamber*) except in Felonies, Treaſons, &c. wherein the King being Plaintiff, and ſo Party, He ſits not perſonally in Judgment, but doth perform it by Delegates.

From the King of *England*, there lies no Appeal in Eccleſiaſtical Affairs to the Biſhop of *Rome*, as it doth in other Principal Kingdoms of *Europe*; nor in Civil Affairs to the Emperor, as in ſome of the *Spaniſh*, and other Dominions of *Chriſtendom*; nor in either to the People of *England* (as ſome of late have dreamed) who in themſelves, or by their *Repreſentatives* in the *Houſe of Commons* in *Parliament*, were ever *Subordinate*, and never *Superior*, nor ſo much as co-ordinate to the King of *England*.

The King being the onely *Soveraign* and *Supream Head*, is furniſhed with Plenary Power, Prerogative, and Juriſdiction to render Juſtice to every Member within His Dominions; whereas ſome Neighbor Kings do want a full power to do Juſtice in all Cauſes, to all their Subjects, or to puniſh all Crimes committed within their own Dominions, eſpecially in *Cauſes Eccleſiaſtical*.

In a word, *Rex Angliæ neminem habet in ſuis Dominiis Superiorem nec Parem; ſed omnes ſub illo, ille ſub nullo niſi tantum ſub Deo, a quo ſecundus, poſt quem primus, ante*

ante omnes & super omnes (in suis ditionibus) Deos & Homines.

The title of *Dii*, or *Gods*, plurally is often in *Holy Writ*, by *God Himself*, attributed to *Great Princes*; because as *Gods Vicars* or *Vice Dii* upon Earth, they represent the Majesty and Power of the *God of Heaven and Earth*: And to the end, that the people might have so much the higher esteem, and more reverend awfulness of them; for if that fails, all *Order* fails; and thence all *Impiety* and *Calamity* follows. *Divinity.*

The substance of the Titles of *God* was also used by the Ancient Christian Emperors, as *Divinitas nostra & Æternitas nostra, &c.* As imperfectly and analogically in them, though essentially and perfectly onely in God; and the good Christians of those times, out of their excess of respect, were wont to swear by the Majesty of the Emperor (as *Joseph* was wont by the life of *Pharaoh*) and *Vegetius*, a Learned Writer of that Age, seems to justifie it: *Nam Imperatori* (saith he) *tanquam præsenti & corporali Deo fidelis est præstanda Devotio & pervigil impendendus famulatus; Deo enim servimus cum fideliter diligimus eum, qui Deo regnat Autore.* For a faithful devotion to the Emperor, as to a corporal god upon Earth, ought to be performed, and a very diligent service to be paid: For then we truly serve *God*, when with a loyal affection we love Him, whom *God* hath placed to raign over us.

So the Laws of *England* looking upon the King, as a *God upon Earth*, do attribute unto Him divers excellencies that belong properly to *God* alone, as Justice in the Abstract; *Rex Angliæ non potest cuiquam injuriam facere*. So also Infallibility, *Rex Angliæ non potest errare*. And as *God* is perfect, so the Law will have no imperfection found in the King.

No Negligence or Laches, no Folly, no Infamy, no Stain or Corruption of Blood; for by taking of the Crown, all former, though just Attainders (and such Attainder made by *Act of Parliament*) is *ipso facto* purged. No Nonage or Minority; for His Grant of Lands, though held in His Natural, not Politick Capacity, cannot be avoided by Nonage: Higher then this the Law attributeth a kinde of immortality to the King, *Rex Angliæ non moritur*; His death is in Law termed the *Demise* of the King, because thereby the Kingdom is demised to another. He is said not subject to Death, because He is a Corporation in Himself, that liveth for ever, all *Interregna*, being in *England* unknown, the same moment that one King dies, the next Heir is King fully and absolutely without any Coronation, Ceremony, or Act to be done *Ex post facto*.

Moreover, the Law seemeth to attribute to the King a certain *Omniprescency*, That the King is in a manner every where, in all His *Courts of Justice*; and therefore cannot be non-suited (as Lawyers speak) in all His *Palaces*, and therefore all Subjects stand bare in the *Presence Chamber*, wheresoever the *Chair of State* is placed, though the King be many miles distant from thence. And His Majesties good Subjects usually bow toward the said *Chair*, when they enter into the *Presence Chamber*, or into the *House of Lords* in *Parliament*.

He hath a kinde of *Universal Influence* over all his Dominions, every Soul within His Territories, may be said to feel at all times His *Power* and His *Goodness*, *Omnium Domos Regis Vigilia defendit, Omnium Otium illius Labor, Omnium Delicias illius Industria, Omnium vacationem illius Occupatio, &c.*

So a kinde of *Omnipotency*, that the King can, as it were, raise Men from Death to Life, by pardoning whom the Law hath condemned; can *create* to the highest Dignity, as *Lord Chancellor*, *Lord Treasurer*, *&c.* and annihilate the same at pleasure.

Divers other semblances of the *Eternal Deity* belong to the King. He in His own Dominions (as *God*) saith, *Vindicta est mihi*; for all punishments do proceed from Him, in some of His Courts of Justice, and it is not lawful for any Subject to revenge himself.

So He onely can be Judge in His own Cause, though He deliver His Judgment by the Mouth of His Judges.

And yet there are some things that the King of *England* cannot do. *Rex Angliæ nihil injuste potest*, and the King cannot divest Himself, or His Successors, of any part of His *Regal Power*, *Prerogative*, and *Authority*, inherent and annext to the Crown: Not that there is any defect in the *Kings Power* (as there is none in *Gods Power*, though He cannot lie, nor do any thing that implies Contradiction:) Not but that the King of *England* hath as absolute a Power over all His Subjects, as any *Christian Prince* rightfully and lawfully hath, or ever had: Not but that He still hath a kinde of *Omnipotency* not to be disputed, but adored by His Subjects: *Nemo quidem de factis ejus præsumat disputare* (saith *Bracton*) *multo minus contra factum ejus ire, nam de Chartis & Factis ejus non debent nec possunt Justiciarii, multo minus privatæ personæ, disputare.* Not but that the King may do what He please, without either *opposition* or *resistance*, and without being questioned by His Subjects; for the King cannot be impleaded for any Crime; no *Action* lieth against His Person, because the Writ goeth forth in His own Name, and He cannot Arrest Himself. If the King should seise the Lands (which *God* forbid) or should take away the Goods of any particular Subject, having no Title by Law so to do; there is no remedy. Onely this, *Locus erit* (saith the same *Bracton*) *supplicationi quod factum suum corrigat & emendet, quod quidem si non fecerit, sufficit ei ad pœnam quod Dominum Deum expectet Ultorem.* There may be Petitions and Supplications made, that His Majesty will be

pleased

pleased to rule according to Law, which if He shall refuse to do, it is sufficient that He must expect, that the *King of Kings* will be the *Avenger* of oppressed *Loyal Subjects*.

His *Counsellors* may also disswade Him, His Officers may decline His unlawful Commands, the persecuted may flie, all may use *Prayers* and *Tears*, the onely Weapons of the *Primitive* and *Best Christians*, and (rather then resist by *force* and *arms*) meekly to suffer *Martyrdom*, the Crown whereof is utterly taken away by all resistence.

But there are also divers things which the King cannot do, *Salvo Jure*, *Salvo Juramento*, & *Salva Conscientia sua*; because by Oath at His Coronation, and indeed without any Oath, by the Law of *Nature*, *Nations*, and of *Christianity*, He holds Himself bound (as do all other Christian Kings) to protect and defend His People, to do Justice, and shew Mercy, to preserve Peace and Quietness amongst them, to allow them their just Rights and Liberties, to consent to the Repealing of bad Laws, and to the enacting of good Laws. Two things especially the King of *England* doth not usually do without the consent of His Subjects, *viz. Make new Laws*, and *raise new Taxes*, there being something of *odium* in both of them; the one seeming to diminish the Subjects Liberty; and the other to infringe His Property: Therefore, that all occasion of disaffection towards the King (the

Breath of our Nostrils, and the Light of our Eyes, as He is stiled in *Holy Scripture)* might be avoided; it was most wisely contrived by our *Ancestors*, that for both these, should *Petitions* and *Supplications* be first made by the Subject.

These, and divers other *Prerogatives*, rightfully belong, and are enjoyed by the King of *England*.

Nevertheless, the Kings of *England* usually govern this Kingdom, by the ordinary known *Laws* and *Customs* of the Land (as the *Great God* doth the World by the *Laws of Nature*) yet in some cases, for the benefit, not damage of this Realm, they make use of their *Prerogatives*, as the *King of Kings* doth of his extraordinary power of working of *Miracles*.

Lastly, To the Kings of *England*, *Quatenus* Kings, doth appertain one *Prerogative* that may be stiled *Super-excellent*, if not *Miraculous*, which was first enjoyed by that pious and good King *Edward* the Confessor; that is to remove and to cure the *Struma* or *Scrofula*, that stubborn disease, commonly called *The Kings Evil*.

Which manifest Cure, is ascribed by some malignant *Non-Conformists*, to the power of Fancy, and exalted Imagination; but what can that contribute to small Infants, whereof great numbers are cured every year. The manner of the Cure is briefly thus:

There is an appointed short Form of *Divine Service*, wherein are read (besides some

some short Prayers pertinent to the occasion) two portions of Scripture taken out of the *Gospel*, and at these words, [*They shall lay their hands on the sick, and they shall recover*] the King gently draws both His Hands over the sore of the sick person; and those words are repeated at the touch of every one.

Again, at these words [*That light was the true light, which lighteth every man that cometh into the world*] pertinently used, If it be considered that that light did never shine more comfortably, if not more visibly, than in the healing of so many leprous and sick persons. At those words, the King putteth about the neck of each sick person a Piece of Gold, called (from the Impression) an *Angel*, being in value about two Thirds of a French Pistol.

In consideration of these and other transcendent Excellencies, no King in Christendom, nor other Potentate receives from his Subjects more *Reverence*, *Honor*, and *Respect*, than the King of *England*. All His People at their first addresses *kneel* to Him, He is at all times served upon the *Knee*, all Persons (not the Prince, or other Heir Apparent excepted) stand bare in the presence of the King, and in the Presence Chamber; though in the Kings absence, all men are not onely bare, but also do or ought to do reverence to the Chair of State. Onely it was once indulged by Queen *Mary*, for some emi- *Respect.*

nent

nent services performed by *Henry Ratcliff*, Earl of *Sussex*, that (by Patent) he might at any time be covered in Her Presence; but perhaps, in imitation of the like liberty, allowed by King *Philip* Her Husband, and other Kings of *Spain* at this day, to some of the principal Nobility there called *Grandees* of *Spain*.

Any thing or act done in the Kings Presence, is presumed to be void of all deceit and evil meaning; and therefore a *Fine* levied in the Kings Court, where the King is presumed to be present; doth bind a *Feme Covert*, a married Woman, and others, whom ordinarily the Law doth disable to transact.

The Kings onely Testimony of any thing done in His Presence, is of as high a nature and credit as any *Record*; and in all *Writs* sent forth for dispatch of *Justice*, He useth no other witness but Himself, *viz.* *Teste me ipso*.

CHAP. V.

Of Succession to the Crown of England, *and of the Kings Minority, Incapacity, and Absence.*

THe King of *England* hath right to the Crown by *Inheritance*, and the *Laws* and *Customs* of *England*.

Upon the death of the King, the next of Kinred, though born out of the Dominions of *England*, or born of Parents, not Subjects of *England*, as by the *Law* and many examples in the *English Histories* it doth manifestly appear, is, and is immediately King before any *Proclamation*, *Coronation*, *Publication*, or consent of *Peers* or *People*.

The Crown of *England* descends from *Father* to *Son*, and His Heirs; for want of *Sons*, to the eldest *Daughter*, and Her Heirs; for want of *Daughters*, to the *Brother* and His Heirs; and for want of *Brother*, to the *Sister* and Her Heirs. The *Salique Law*, or rather Custom of *France*, hath here no more force then it had anciently among the *Jews*, or now in *Spain*, and other Christian Hereditary Kingdoms. Among *Turks* and *Barbarians*, that *French* Custom is still and ever was in use.

In case of descent of the Crown (contrary to the Custom of the descent of Estates among Subjects) the *Half Blood* shall

shall inherit; so from King *Edward the Sixth* the Crown and Crown Lands descended to Queen *Mary* of the half blood, and again to Queen *Elizabeth* of the half blood to the last Possessor.

At the death of every King, die not only the Offices of the Court, but all Commissions granted to the Judges *durante bene placito*, and of all Justices of Peace.

Minority If the King be likely to leave his Crown to an Infant, he doth usually by *Testament* appoint the person or persons that shall have the tuition of him; and sometimes for want of such appointment, a fit person of the Nobility or Bishops is made choice of by the Three States assembled in the name of the Infant King, who by Nature or Alliance hath most Interest in the preservation of the Life and Authority of the Infant, and to whom least benefit can accrue by his Death or Diminution; as the *Uncle* by the *Mothers* side, if the Crown come by the *Father*, and so *vice versa*, is made *Protector*; so during the minority of *Edward 6* his Uncle by the Mothers side, the *Duke of Somerset* had the tuition of him, and was called Protector; and when this Rule hath not been observed (as in the minority of *Edward* the Fifth) it hath proved of ill consequence.

Incapacity. If the King of *England* be *Non compos mentis*, or by reason of an incurable disease, weakness, or old age, become uncapable

capable of governing, then is made a *Regent, Protector*, or *Guardian*, to govern.

King *Edward* the Third being at last aged, sick, and weak, and by grief for the death of the *Black Prince*, sore broken in body and mind, did of his own will create his Fourth Son, *John* Duke of *Lancaster*, Guardian, or Regent of *England*.

If the King be absent upon any Forreign Expedition, or otherwise, (which anciently was very usual) the Custom was to constitute a *Vicegerent* by Commission under the *Great Seal*, giving him several Titles and Powers according as the necessity of affairs have required; sometimes he hath been called *Lord Warden*, or *Lord Keeper* of the Kingdom, and therewith hath had the general power of a King, as was practised during the *Absence* of *Edward* the First, Second and Third, and of *Henry* the Fifth, but *Henry* the Sixth to the Title of Warden or Guardian added the Stile of *Protector* of the *Kingdom* and of the *Church* of *England*; and gave him so great power in his *absence*, that he was *tantum non Rex* swaying the *Scepter* but not wearing the *Crown*; executing Laws, Summoning Parliaments under his own *Teste* as King, and giving his assent to Bills in Parliament, whereby they became as binding as any other Acts.

Absence

Sometimes during the Kings *absence* the Kingdom hath been committed to the care

of

of several *Noblemen*, and sometimes of *Bishops*, as less dangerous for attempting any usurpation of the Crown; sometimes to one Bishop, as *Hubert* Archbishop of *Canterbury* was Viceroy of *England* for many years; and when *Edward* the Third was in *Flanders* (though his Son then but nine years old, had the Name of *Protector*) *John Stratford* Arch-bishop of *Canterbury* was Governour both of the Kings Son and of the Realm, so King *Henry* the First during his absence (which was sometimes three or four years together) usually constituted *Roger* that famous Bishop of *Salisbury* sole Governour of the Realm a Man excellently qualifyed for Government.

Lastly, Sometimes to the Queen, as two several times during the absence of *Henry* the Eigth in *France*.

CHAP. VI.

Of the QUEEN *of* ENGLAND.

Name. THe *Queen*, so called from the *Saxon Koningin*, whereof the last syllable is pronounced by Forreigners as *gheen* in English, it being not unusual to cut off the first Syllables, as an *Almes-house* is sometimes called a *Spital* from *Hospital* and *Sanders* from *Alexander*.

She hath as high Prerogatives, Dignity, and State, during the life of the King, as any Queen of *Europe*.

From the *Saxon* times the Queen *Consort* of *England*, though she be an *Alien* born, and though during the life of the King she be *femme covert* (as our Law speaks) yet without any Act of Parliament for *Naturalization* or Letters Patents for *Denization*, she may purchase Lands in *Fee-simple*, make Leases and Grants in her own Name without the King, hath power to give, to sue, to contract, as a *femme sole* may receive by gift from her Husband, which no other *femma covert* may do.

Prerogatives.

She may present by herself to a Spiritual Benefice, and in a *Quare Impedit* brought by Her, plenarty by the presentation of another is no more a Bar against Her, then it is against the King.

She shall not be amerced if she be Nonsuited in any Action, &c.

Had anciently a Revenue of *Queen Gold* or *Aurum Reginæ*, as the Records call it, which was the tenth part of so much as by the name of *Oblata* upon Pardons, Gifts and Grants, &c. came to the King.

Of later times hath had as large a Dower as any Queen in Christendome, hath her Royal Court apart, her Courts and Officers, &c.

The Queen may not be *impleaded* till first petitioned, if she be *Plaintiff* the Summons in the Process need not have the solemnity of 15 dayes, &c.

Is

Dignity. Is reputed the Second Person in the Kingdom.

The Law setteth so high a value upon her, as to make it High-Treason to conspire her death, or to violate her Chastity.

Her Officers, as *Atturney* and *Sollicitor*, for the Queens sake have respect above others, and place within the *Barr* with the Kings Council.

The like honour, the like reverence and respect that is due to the King, is exhibited to the Queen both by Subjects and Foreigners, and also to the Queen *Dowager* or Widow Queen, who also above other Subjects looseth not her Dignity, though she should marry a private Gentleman; so Queen *Katharina*, Widow to King *Henry* the Fifth, being married to *Owen ap Theodore* Esquire, did maintain her Action as Queen of *England*; much less doth a Queen by inheritance, or a Queen *Soveraign* of *England*, follow her Husbands condition, nor is subject as other Queens; but Soveraign to her own Husband, as Queen *Mary* was to King *Philip*.

CHAP.

CHAP. VII.

Of the Sons *and* Daughters *of* ENGLAND.

THE Children of the King of *England* are called the *Sons and Daughters of England*; because all the Subjects of *England* have a special interest in them, though the whole power of Education, Marriage, and disposing of them, is only in the King.

The Eldest Son of the King is born Duke of *Cornwall*, and as to that Dutchy, and all the Lands, Honours, Rents, and great Revenues belonging thereunto, he is upon his Birth-day presumed, and by Law taken to be of full age, so that he may that day sue for the *Livery* of the said Dukedom, and ought of right to obtain the same, as if he had been full 21 years of age. Afterwards he is created *Prince of Wales*, whose *Investiture* is performed by the Imposition of a *Cap of Estate* and *Coronet* on his Head, as a Token of Principality, and putting into his Hand a *Verge* of *Gold*, the Emblem of Government, and a *Ring* of Gold on his Finger, to intimate, that he must be a Husband to his Countrey, and Father to her Children. Also to him is given and granted Letters Patent to hold the said Principality *Eldest Son.*

ty.

ty to him and his Heirs Kings of *England*, by which words the seperation of this Principality is prohibited. His Mantle which he wears in Parliament is once more doubled, or hath one Guard more then a Dukes, and his Coronet of *Crosses* and *Flowers de luce* and his Cap of State indented.

Since our present Kings happy Restauration it was solemnly ordered, that the Son and Heir apparent of the Crown of *England*, shall use and bear his Coronet of *Crosses* and *Flower deluces* with one Arch, and in the midst a *Ball* and *Cross*, as hath the Royal *Diadem*. That the Duke of *York* and all the immediate Sons and *Brothers* of the Kings of *England*, shall use and bear their Coronets composed of *Crosses* and *Flower de luces* only, but all their sons respectively having the Title of Dukes shall bear and use their Coronets composed of *Crosses* and *Flower de luces* such as are used in the Composure of the Coronets of Dukes, not being of the Royal Family.

Title. From the day of his Birth he is commonly stiled the *Prince*, a Title in *England* given to no other Subject. The Title of Prince of *Wales* is antient, and was first given by King *Edward* the First to his Eldest Son; for the *Welsh* Nation till that time unwilling to submit to the yoke of strangers, that King so ordered, that his Queen was delivered of her first Child in *Caernarvan Castle* in *Wales*, and then deman-

demanded of the Welsh, as some affirm, *If they would be content to subject themselves to one of their own Nation, that could not speak one word of* English, *and against whose life they could take no just exception.* Whereunto they readily consenting, the King nominated this his new-born Son, and afterwards created him Prince of *Wales*, and bestowed on him all the Lands, Honours and Revenues belonging to the said Principality.

The Prince hath ever since been stiled Prince of *Wales*, Duke of *Aquitaine* and *Cornwall*, and Earl of *Chester* and *Flint*, which Earldoms are always conferred upon him by Letters Patent. Since the Union of *England* and *Scotland*: his Title hath been *Magnæ Britaniæ Princeps*, but more ordinarily the Prince of *Wales*. As Eldest Son to the King of *Scotland* he is Duke of *Rothsay* and Seneschal of *Scotland* from his Birth.

The King of *Englands* Eldest Son (so long as *Normandy* remained in their hands) was alwayes stiled *Duke of Normandy*.

Antiently the Princes Arms of *Wales* whilest they were Soveraigns, bare *quarterly Gules*, and *Or 4 Lyons passant gardant counterchanged*.

The Armes of the Prince of *Wales* differ from those of the King only by addition of a *Label* of three Points charged with nine *Tortcaux*, and the *Device* of the Prince is a *Coronet* beautified with three *Ostrich* Feathers, inscribed with *Ich*

dien,

dien which in the German, or old Saxon Tongue is *I serve*, alluding perhaps to that in the *Gospel*, *The Heir, whilest his Father liveth differeth not from a Servant.* This *Device* was born at the Battel of *Cressy* by *John* King of *Bohemia*, as serving there under the King of the French, and there slain by *Edward, the Black Prince*, and since worn by the Princes of *Wales*, and by the *Vulgar* called the *Princes Armes.*

Dignity. The Prince by our Law is reputed as the same Person with the King, and so declared by a Statute of *Henry* the Eight, *Coruscat enim Princeps* (say our Lawers) *radiis Regis Patris sui & censetur una persona cum ipso.* And the Civilians say, the Kings Eldest Son may be stiled a King.

Priviledges. He hath certain Priviledges above other persons.

To *imagine* the death of the Prince, to *violate* the Wife of the Prince, is made High-Treason.

Hath heretofore had priviledge of having a *Purveyour*, and taking *Purveyance* as the King.

To retain and qualifie as many *Chaplains* as he shall please.

To the Prince at the Age of 15 was a certain *Aid* of Money from all the Kings Tenants and all that held of him in *Capite*, by *Knights-Service*, and *Free-Socage*, to make him a Knight.

Yet as the Prince in nature is a distinct Person from the King, so in Law also in some

some cases, he is a Subject, holdeth his Principallities and Seignories of the King, giveth the same respect to the King as other Subjects do.

The Revenues belonging to the Prince, since much of the Lands and Demesnes of that Dutchy have been aliened; are especially out of the *Tinn Mines* in *Cornwall*, which with all other profits of that Dutchy amount yearly to the summ of *Revenues.*

The Revenues of the Principality of *Wales* surveyed 200 years ago was above 4680 *l.* yearly, a rich Estate according to the value of Money in those days.

At present his whole Revenues may amount to

Till the Prince come to be 14 years old, all things belonging to the Principality of *Wales*, were wont to be disposed of by Commissioners consisting of some principal Persons of the Clergy and Nobility. *Cadets.*

The *Cadets* or younger Sons of *England*, are *created*, not *born*, Dukes or Earls of what Places or Titles the King pleaseth.

They have no certain *Appanages* as in *France*, but onely what the good pleasure of the King bestows upon them.

All the Kings Sons are *Consiliarii nati*, by Birth-right Counsellors of *State*, that so they may grow up in the weighty affairs of the Kingdom.

The

The Daughters of *England* are stiled Princesses, the eldest of which had an *Aid* or certain rate of Money paid by every Tenant *in Capite*, *Knights Service*, and *Soccage*, towards her Dowry or Marriage Portion; and to violate her unmarried is High-Treason at this day.

To all the Kings Children belong the Title of *Royal Highness*; All Subjects are to be uncovered in their presence, to kneel when they are admitted to *kiss* their hands, and at Table they are *(out of the Kings Presence)* served on the *Knee*.

The Children, the Brothers and Sisters of the King, if *Plaintiffs*, the Summons in the Process need not have the solemnity of 15 dayes, as in case of other Subjects.

All the Kings, Sons, Grandsons, Brothers, Unkles, and Nephews of the King, are by *Stat.* 31 *Henry* 8. to precede others in *England*; It is true the word *Granson* is not there *in terminis*, but is understood as Sir *Edward Coke* holds by *Nephew*, which in Latin being *Nepos*, signifies also, and chiefly a *Grandson*.

The *Natural*, or illegitimate Sons and Daughters of the King, after they are acknowledged by the King, have had here as in *France*, precedence of all the Nobles under those of the Blood Royal.

They bear what Surname the King pleaseth to give them, and for Arms the Arms of *England*, with a Baston or a Border Gobionne, or some other mark of illegitimation. Some Kings of *England* have

have acknowledged many, and had more illegitimate Sons and Daughters.

King *Henry the First* had no fewer than sixteen illegitimate Children.

Henry the Eighth amongst others had one by *Elizabeth Blount*, named *Henry Fitzroy*, created by him Duke of *Somerset* and *Richmond*, Earl of *Nottingham*, and Lord High *Admiral* of *England*, *Ireland*, and *Aquitain*.

CHAP. VIII.

Of the present KING *of* ENGLAND *and therein of His Name, Surname, Genealogie, Birth, Baptisme, Court, Education, Restauration, Marriage,* &c.

Name. THe *KING* now raigning is *CHARLES* the Second of that Name. His Name of Baptisme *Charles* in the German Tongue signifies one of a Masculine strength or vertue.

Surname The Royal, and also the most Princely and Antient Families of *Europe*, at this day have properly no *Surnames*, for neither is *Burbon* the Surname, but the Title of the Royal Family of *France*, nor *Austria* of *Spain*, nor *Stuart* of *England*, since the coming in of King *James*, nor *Theodore* or *Tudor* for his 5 immediate Ancestors in *England*, nor *Plantagenet* for

for 11 Generations before, as some vainly think; for althongh *Geffery* Duke of *Anjou* was surnamed *Plantagenet* from a *Broom Stalke* commonly worn in his Bonnet, yet his Son *Hen.* 2. King of *England*, was surnamed *Fitz-Empress*, and his Son *Richard Cœur de Lyon*: So *Owen* Grandfather to King *Henry* 7. was *ap Meridith*, and he *ap Theodore*, pronounced *Tyder*, Surnames being then but little in use amongst the *Cambrobritains*; So *Walter* Father to *Robert* King of *Scotland*, from whom our present King is descended, was only by Office *Grand Seneschal* or *High Steward* or *Stewart* of *Scotland*, though of later times by a long vulgar errour it hath so prevailed, that they are accounted Surnames of many Families descended from him.

Steward is a Contraction from the *Saxon* word *Stedeward*, that is in Latine *Locum-tenens*, in French *Lieu-Tenant*, because the Lord High Steward was *Regis locum tenens*, a Name not unfit for any King, who is *Dei locum tenens*, Gods Stuart or Lieutenant or Vicegerent upon Earth.

Genealogies. The King now Raigning is Son to King *Charles* the Martyr and the Princess *Henrietta Maria*, Daughter of King *Henry* the *Great* of *France*; from which two Royal Stocks he hath in his Veins all the Royal Blood of *Europe* concentred.

Is descended lineally and lawfully from the *British*, *Saxon*, *Danish*, *Norman*, and *Scottish Kings* and Princes of this Island.

From

From the first *British* Kings the 139th Monarch, from the *Scotish* in a continued succession for almost 2000 years the 109th, from the *Saxon* the 46th, and from the first of the *Norman* Line the 26th King. So that for Royal Extraction and long Line of just descent, His Majesty now raigning excels all the Monarchs of all the Christian, if not of the whole World.

Is the first Prince of *Great Britain* so born, and hath in possession *larger* Dominions than any of his Ancestors.

He was born the 29th of May, 1630. *at the Royal Palace of St. James*, over which House the same day at Noon was by thousands seen a star, and soon after the Sun suffered an Eclipse, a sad presage as some then divined, that this Prince's Power should for some time be eclipsed, as it hath been; and some subject signified by a star, should have extraordinary splendor. *Birth.*

Was *Christened* the 27th of *June* following by the then Bishop of *London* Doctor *Laud*. *Baptisme.*

Had for Godfathers his two Uncles *Lewis* the 13th King of *France*, and *Frederick* Prince *Palatine* of the *Rhine*, then called King of *Bohemia*, represented by the Duke of *Richmond* and Marquis *Hamilton*; his Godmother being his Grandmother then Queenmother of *France*, represented by the Dutchess of *Richmond*.

Had for Governess *Mary* Countess of *Dorset*, Wife to *Edward* Earl of *Dorset*. In *May* 1638. he was first knighted, and immediately after he was made Knight of the Garter, and installed at *Windsor*.

Court. About this time by Order, not Creation, he was first called Prince of *Wales*, and had all the profits of that Principallity, and divers other Lands annexed, and *Earldom* of *Chester* granted unto him; and held his Court apart from the King.

Education. At the Age of Eight he had for *Governour* the Earl afterwards Marquis and now Duke of *Newcastle*, and after him the late Earl of *Berkshire*: and for Tutor or *Preceptor*, Doctor *Duppa* then Dean of *Christchurch*, after Bishop of *Salisbury*, and lately of *Winchester*.

At the Age of 12 was with the King his Father at the Battle of *Edgehill*, and soon after at *Oxford* was committed to the care of the Marquis of *Hertford*.

About 14 years old was in the Head of an Army in the West of *England*.

At the Age of 15 a Marriage was proposed between him and the Eldest Daughter of the King of *Portugal*, the *Infanta Joanna* since deceased.

Two years after was from *Cornwal* transported to the Isle of *Scilly*, and after to *Jersey*, and thence to his Royal Mother to St. *Germains* near *Paris*.

In 1648 was at *Sea* with some Naval Forces

Forces, endeavouring to rescue the King his Father, then in the Isle of *Wight*, out of the wicked hands of his rebellious Subjects. Not many moneths after, upon the sad news of the horrid *Murther* of his Royal Father, he was in *Holland* first saluted *King*, and soon after proclaimed in *Scotland*, being not yet 19 years of age.

At the age of 20 from *Holland* he landed in *Scotland*, *June* 1650, and in *January* following was crowned at *Scoon*.

The 3d of *September* 1651 fought the Battle of *Worcester*, whence after the unfortunate loss of his whole Army, wandring in disguise about *England* for *Six Weeks*, and most wonderfully preserved, he was at length transported from a Creek near *Shoram* in *Sussex* to *Feccam* near *Havre de Grace* in *France*; in which Kingdom, with his Royal Brothers and divers English Nobility, Clergy, and Gentry, he was for some years received and treated as King of *England*, and by his mediations and interest with the Prince of *Conde*, and Duke of *Lorrain*, then in the Head of two great and mighty Armies against the *French* King, quenched the then newly kindled fires of a great and universal rebellion against him, much resembling that of *England*; and was a means of recalling the then fled and banished Cardinal *Mazarine*: After which in *Germany*, *Flanders*, *Spain*, &c. he passed the residue of his time in the Studies and Exercises most befitting a Prince, in sollliciting the Aid of Christian Princes, and in advi-

advising and vigorously promoting the several attempts of his Friends in *England*, until the year 1660, at which time being at *Brussels* within the Spanish Territories, and perceiving a general inclination and disposition of all *England* to receive him, he providently removed himself to *Breda*, within the Dominions of the *United Neatherlands*, in the moneth of *April*, thence in *May* to the *Hague*; from whence, after a magnificent Entertainment and an humble Invitation by English Commissioners sent from the then Convention at *Westminster*, he embarkt at *Scheveling* the 23 of *May* 1660. and with a gallant English Fleet a gentle gale of Wind, landed the 25th at *Dover*, and on the 29th following, being his Birth-day, and then just 30 years of age, he entred into *London*, was there received with the greatest and most universal Joy, Acclamations, and Magnificence that could possibly be expressed on so short a warning.

On the first of *June* following, His Majesty sate in *Parliament*, and on the 22 of *April* 1661. rode in triumph from the *Tower* to *Westminster*, on the next day, being St. *Georges*, was Crowned with great Ceremony.

On the 28th of *May* following, declared to his Parliament to marry the *Infanta* of *Portugal*, who accordingly in *May* 1662, being landed at *Portsmouth*, was there espoused to the King by then bishop of *London*, now Archbishop of *Canterbury*.

His

His Majesties life hath been full of wonders, but three passages especially seem miraculous. First, at his Birth a Bright Star seen over him at Noon-day by many thousands, Secondly, His escape in and after the Battel of *Worcester*, when being in the very heart of *England*, forsaken by all, a sum of Money by Publick Act promised to those that should discover him, and penealty of High Treason to any one that should conceal him; when he was seen and known to many persons of all sorts and conditions; whereof divers were very indigent, and so very subject to be tempted with the proposed reward, and divers of the female sex, and so most unapt to retain a secret, when he was necessitated to wait so many weeks, and appear in so many places and companies, before a fit opportunity of transportation could be found. Thirdly, His Majesty's Restauration (*quippe impossibile fuit Filium tot Precationum, tot Lacrymarum, & tot Miraculorum periisse*) that after so many years dispossession, his most inveterate, potent, subtil enemies in full aud quiet possession, on a sudden the desire of him should like Lightning, or a mighty Torrent, run over all *England* in such a manner, that he should be solemnly invited, magnificently conducted, triumphantly received, without Blood, Blows, Bargain, or any Obligation to any Foreign Prince or Potentatee.

This was the Lords doing, and must for ever be marvellous in our eyes.

CHAP. IX.

Of the present QUEEN of ENGLAND.

DONNA CATHERINA, *Infanta of Portugal*, being Queen Consort of *England*, and the Second Person in the Kingdom, was Daughter of Don *Juan* the Fourth of that name, King of *Portugal*, descended from our English *John* of *Gaunt*, Duke of *Lancaster*, and King of *Castile*; and *Leon*, Fourth Son of *Edward* the Third, King of *England*; and of *Donna Lucia*, Daughter of Don *Guzmam el buono*, a Spaniard; Duke of *Medina Sidonia*, who was lineally descended from *Ferdinando de la Cerde*, and his Consort *Blanche*, to whom S. *Lewis*, King of *France* Her Father, relinquished His Right and Title to *Spain*, descended to Him by His Mother *Blanche*, Eldest Daughter and Heir of *Alphonso*, the Spanish King.

She was born the Fourteenth of *November* 1638. at *Villa Vicosa* in *Portugal*, She was Baptized *Catherina*, signifying in Greek *Pure*; Her Father being then Duke of *Braganza* (though right Heir of the Crown of *Portugal*) the most potent Subject in *Europe*; for a Third Part of *Portugal* was then holden of him in Vassal-

lage;

lage; and is onely Sister at present of Don *Alphonso* the Sixth of that name, and the Three and twentieth King of *Portugal*, 1643.

Hath one Brother more called Don *Pedro*, born 1648. now called Prince of *Portugal*.

Had another Brother called Don *Theodosio*, the eldest Son of that King, who was the most gallant and hopeful Prince of all *Europe*, but died 1653, aged but 18 years, yet his life thought worthy to be written by divers grave Authors of *Portugal*.

Having been most carefully and piously educated by her Mother, and at the age of 22 desired in Marriage by King *CHARLES* the Second, and the Marriage not long after concluded by the Negotiation of Don *Francesco de Melo Conde de Ponte Marquis de Sande*, then Extraordinary Ambassadour of the King of *Portugal*, and solemnised at *Lisbon*. She embarkt for *England* upon the 23d of *April* 1662. being the Festival of *St. George*, *Patron* as well of *Portugal* as *England*, and was safely by the Earl of *Sandwich* conducted by a Squadron of Ships to *Portsmouth*; where the King first met her, and was re-married.

On the 23d of *August* 1662 her Majesty comming by water from *Hampton Court*, was with great Pomp and Magnificence first received by the Lord Mayor and Aldermen of *London* at *Chelsey*, and thence conducted by water to *Whitehall*.

The Portion she brought with her was Eight hundred Millions of *Reas* or two Millions of *Crusado's*, being about Three hundred thousand pounds *Sterling*; together with that important place of *Tangier* upon the Coast of *Africk*, and the Isle of *Bombaim* near *Goa* in the *East-Indies*, with a Priviledge that any Subjects of the King of *England* may Trade freely in the *East* and *West-Indie*-Plantations belonging to the Portugueses.

Her Majesties *Joynture* by the Articles of Marriage is Thirty thousand pounds *Sterling per annum*, and the King out of his great affection toward her, hath as an addition setled upon her 10000 *l. per annum* more.

The Queens Arms as Daughter of *Portugal*, is *Argent 5 Scutcheons Azure crossewise, each Scutcheon* charged with 5 *Plates Argient Saltier-wise*, with a Point Sable. The Border *Gules*, charged with 7 *Castles Or*. This Coat was first worn by the Kings of *Portugal*, in memory of a Signal Battel obtained by the first Kings of *Portugal Don Alphonso* against 5 King of the *Moors*, before which Battel appeared *Christ crucified* in the Air, and a voice heard, as once to *Constantine the Great*, *In hoc signo vinces*: before which time the *Portugal* Armes were *Argent* a *Cross Azure*.

Queen *CATHERINE* is a personage of such rare perfections of Mind and Body, of such eminent Piety, Modesty, and other Vertues, that the English Nation

tion may yet promise all the happiness they are capable of from a Succession of Princes to govern them to the end of the World.

CHAP. X.

Of the Queen Mother.

THe Third Person in the Kingdom was the *Queen-Mother*, or *Dowager*, *Henrietta Maria de Bourbon*, *Daughter* to the *Great* King *Henry* the Fourth, *Sister* to the *Just* King *Lewis* the 13th, *Wife* to the glorious *Martyr* King *Charles* the First, Mother to our *Gracious* Soveraign King *Charles* the Second, and Aunt to the present *Puissant* King *Lewis* the 14th.

She was born the 16 of *November*, married first at *Nostre Dame* in *Paris* by Proxy 1625, and shortly after in the moneth of *June* arriving at *Dover*, was at *Canterbury* espoused to King *Charles* the First. In the year 1629 was delivered of her First born, a Son that died shortly after; in 1630 of her Second, our present Soveraign whom God long preserve; in 1631 of her Third, *Mary*, the late Princess of *Orange*, a Lady of Admirable Vertues, who had the happiness to see the King her Brother restored 6 or 7 Moneths before her death. In 1633 of her Fourth, *James*, now *Duke of York*. In 1635 of her Fifth,

named

named *Elizabeth*, who being a Princess of incomperable Abilities and Vertues, died for grief soon after the murther of her Father. In 1636 of her Sixth, named *Anna*, who died young. In the year 1640 of her Seventh Child *Henry* of *Oatland*, designed Duke of *Glocester*, who living till above 20, being most excellently accomplished in all Princely Endowments died four moneths after the Restauration of the King. In the year 1644 of her Eighth, the Lady *Henrietta*, late Dutchess of *Orleans*.

In the year 1641, Her Majesty foreseeing the ensuing storm of *Rebellion*, and seeing the groundless *Odium* raised already against her self, timely withdrew her self with her eldest Daughter (then newly married to Prince *William*, onely Son to *Henry* Prince of *Orange*) into *Holland*, whence in 1643, after a most furious storm and barbarous fierce pursuit of the English Rebels at Sea, she landed at *Burlington Bay* with Men, Money, and Ammunition, and soon after with a considerable Army met the King at *Edge-hill*, and thence was conducted to *Oxford*.

In *April* 1644, marching with competent forces from *Oxford* towards *Exeter*, at *Abington* took her last farewel of the King, whom she never saw again.

In *July* following embarkt at *Pendennis* Castle, she sailed into *France*, where entertained at the charges of her Nephew the present King of *France*, she passed a solitary retired life until the moneth of

October

October 1660 when upon the Restauration of her Son to the Crown of *England*, she came to *London*, and having setled her Revenues here, she went again with her youngest Daughter the Lady *Henrietta* into *France*, to see her espoused to the then Duke of *Anjou*, now of *Orleans*; and in the moneth *July* 1662. being returned into *England*, she setled her Court at *Somerset-House*, where she continued till *May* 1665, then crossed the Seas again, and hath ever since continued in *France* her Native Countrey till her death.

She needeth no other Character then what is found in the Seventh Chapter of that inimitable Book compiled by him that knew her best.

CHAP. XI.

Of the present Princes *and* Princesses *of the Blood*

THe first Prince of the Blood (in *France* called *Monsieur sans queue*) is the Most Illustrious Prince *James* Duke of *York*, Second Son to King *Charles* the *Martyr*, and only Brother to the present King our Soveraign.

He was born *October* 14. 1633. and forthwith proclaimed at the Court Gates, Duke of *York*, the 24th of the same month was baptized, and afterward committed

mitted to the Government of the then *Countess* of *Dorset*.

The 27 of *July* 1643, at *Oxford* was *created* by *Letters Patent* Duke of *York* (though called so by special command from his Birth) without those Solemnities (the iniquity of the times not admitting thereof) that were used to the King his Father 1605, when being Second Son to King *James*, and so Duke of *Albany* in *Scotland*, was created Duke of *York* with the preceding Solemn Creation of divers young Noblemen to be Knights of the *Bath*, and the *Robes of State* put upon him, the *Cap of State* on his Head, and the *Golden Rod* into his Hand, the Prime Nobility and the Heralds assisting at that Ceremony.

After the Surrender of *Oxford*, his Royal Highness was in 1646, conveyed to *London* by the then prevailing disloyal part of the two Houses of Parliament, and committed with his Brother *Glocester* and Sister *Elizabeth* to the care of the Earl of *Northumberland*.

In 1648 aged about 15, was by Colonel *Bampfield* conveyed in a disguise or habit of a Girle beyond Sea, first to his Sister the Princess Royal of *Orange* in *Holland*, and afterward to the Queen his Mother, then at *Paris*, where he was carefully educated in the *Religion* of the Church of *England*, and in all Exercises meet for such a Prince.

About the Age of 20. in *France* he went into the *Campagne*, and served with much

Gallantry under that great Commander the then Proteſtant *Mareſchal de Turenne* for the *French* King againſt the *Spaniſh* forces in *Flanders*.

Notwithſtanding which, upon a Treaty between the *French* King and *Cromwel* in 1655, being obliged with all his retinue to leave the French Dominions, and invited into *Flanders* by Don *Juan* of *Auſtria*, he there ſerved under him againſt the *French* King, then leagued with the *Engliſh* Rebels againſt *Spain*: where his *Magnanimity and Dexerity in Martial affairs*, (though unſuccesful) were very eminent.

In the year 1660 came over with the King into *England*, and being Lord *High Admiral*, in the year 1665, in the War againſt the *United States of the Neatherlands*, commanded in perſon the whole *Royal Navy* on the Seas between *England* and *Holland*, where with incomperable valour and extraordinary hazard of his own Royal Perſon, after a moſt ſharp diſpute he obtained a *Signal Victory* over the whole *Dutch* Fleet commanded by Admiral *Opdam*, who periſht with his own and many more Dutch Ships in that Fight.

He married *Anne* the Eldeſt Daughter of *Edward Earl of Clarrendon*, late Lord High Chancellour of *England*, by whom he hath had a numerous iſſue, whereof are *living* firſt the Lady *Mary*, born 30 *April* 1662, whoſe Godfather was *Prince Rupert*, and Godmothers the Dutcheſſes of *Buckingham* and *Ormond*. Secondly, the Lady *Anne*, born in *Febr.* 1664. whoſe

Godfa-

Godfather was *Gilbert Lord Archbishop of Canterbury*, her Godmothers were the young Lady *Mary* her Sister and the Dutchess of *Monmouth*. She was lately for her health transported into *France*. Thirdly, 15 *Sept.* 1667, was born *Edgar*, lately created Duke of *Cambridge* by *Letters Patent* under the Great Seal of *England*, whose Godfathers were the Duke of *Albemarle* and the Marquis of *Worcester*, his Godmother the Countess of *Suffolk*.

The Titles of his Royal Highness, are *Duke* of York *and* Albany, *Earl of* Ulster, *Lord High Admiral of* England Ireland, *and all Forreign Plantations, Constable of* Dover-Castle, *Lord Warden of the* Cinque Ports, *Governout of* Portsmouth, &c.

Of the Prince of Orange.

Next to the Duke of *York* and his Issue, is *William* of *Naussau* Prince of *Orange*, onely Issue of the lately deceased Princess Royal *Mary*, eldest Daughter to King *Charles* the First, and wedded 1641, to *William* of *Nassau*, the onely Son to *Henry* Prince of *Orange*, Commander in Chief of all the Forces of the States General both by Land and Sea.

His Highness the present Prince was born 9 dayes after his Fathers death on the 14th *Novemb.* 1650, had for Godfa-

thers

thers the Lords *States General* of *Holland* and *Zealand*, and the Cities of *Delft*, *Leyden*, and *Amsterdam*.

His Governess was the English Lady *Stanhop*, then Wife to the Heer *Van Hemvliet*.

At Eight years of age was sent to the *University* of *Leyden*.

His yearly Revenue is about 60000 *l.* *Sterling*, besides Military advantages enjoyed by his Father and Ancestors, which amounted yearly to about 30000 *l.* *Sterling* more.

He is a Prince in whom the high and Princely quallities of his Ancestors already appear.

Of the Princess Henrietta.

The next Heir (after the forenamed) to the English Crown, was the *Princess Henrietta* youngest Sister to the present King of *England*.

She was born the 16th day of *June* 1644 at *Exeter* during the heat of the late Rebellion, after the surrender of *Exeter*, conveyed to *Oxford*, and thence 1646, to *London*, whence with her Governess the Lady *Dalkeith*, she escaped into *France*, was there educated as became her high Birth and Quality, but being left wholly to the care and maintainance of the *Queen* her *Mother* at *Paris*, embraced the *Romish Religion*.

At

At the age of 16 years came with the Queen Mother into *England*, and six months after returning into *France*, was Married to the only Brother of the French King the Illustrious Prince *Philip* then *Duke* of *Anjou*, till the death of his Uncle, and now *Duke* of *Orleans*, whose *Revenue* is 1100000 *Livers Tournois*, besides his *Appanage*, nor yet setled.

Her portion was 40000 *l. Sterling*, her Joynture was to be the same with the present Dutchess *Dowager* of *Orleans*.

This Princess left issue two Daughter. She was usually stiled *Madame* only, as being the first Lady in *France*; She died suddenly in *June* 1670.

The Elder called *Madamoiselle* only, or *sans queve* κατ' ἐξοχὴν because she is the first Gentlewoman of *France*.

The younger Sister is called *Madamoiselle de Valois*; if she had had a Son, the French King was to allow him 50000 *Crowns* yearly, and the *Appanage* after the death of the present Duke *reverts* to the Crown.

Of

Of the Prince Elector Palatine.

There being left alive no more of the Off-spring of King *Charles* the First, the next Heirs of the Crown of *England*, are the Issue and Descendants of *Elizabeth*, late Queen of *Bohemia*, onely Sister to the said King, who was married to *Frederick*, Prince *Palatine* of the *Rhine*, afterwards stiled King of *Bohemia*, whose eldest Son living, is *Charles Lodowick*, Prince Elector *Palatine* of the *Rhine*, commonly called the *Palsgrave*, from the High Dutch *Pfaltzgraff*, *Palatii Comes*, was born the Two and twentieth of *December*, 1617, at *Heidelbergh*; and afterwards at the Age of Three or four years, conveyed thence into the Countreys of *Wittenberg* and *Brandenburgh*, then into *Holland*, and at the *Hague*, and the University of *Leyden*, was educated in a Princely manner. At the age of Sixteen, was made Knight of the Garter, and at the age of Eighteen years came into *England*; about Two years after, fought a Battel at *Ulota* in *Westphalia*. In the year 1639. passing *incognito* thorow *France*, to take possession of *Brisach* upon the *Rhine*, which the Duke of *Saxon Weymar* intended to deliver up unto him, together with the command of his Army, he was by that quick-sighted Cardinal *Richlieu* discovered at *Moulins*, and thence

thence sent back prisoner to the *Bois de Vincennes*, whence after Twenty three weeks imprisonment, he was by the mediation of the King of *England* set at liberty.

In the year 1643, he came again into *England*, and with the Kings *secret consent* (because the King could not continue unto him the wonted Pension, whil'st the Rebels possest the greatest part of His Majesties Revenues) made his Addresses to, and abode with the disloyal part of the Lords and Commons at *Westminster*, until the Murder of the said King, and the Restauration of the *Lower Palatinat*, according to the famous *Treaty* at *Munster* 1648, for which he was constrained to quit all his Right to the *Upper Palatinat*, and accept of an *Eighth Electorship*, at a juncture of time when the King of *England* (had he not been engaged at home by an impious Rebellion) had been the most considerable of all other at that Treaty, and this Prince his *Nephew* would have had the greatest advantages there.

In 1650, he espoused the Lady *Charlotte*, at *Cassel*, Daughter to *William* 5th *Landgrave* of *Hesse*, and of *Elizabeth Emilia* of *Hanaw*, by whom he hath one Son named *Charles*, born 31 of *March* 1651, and one Daughter named *Lovise*, born in *May* 1652.

Of

Of Prince Rupert.

Next to the issue of the Prince *Elector Palatine*, is Prince *Rupert*, born at *Prague* 17 *Decem.* 1619, not long before that very unfortunate Battle there fought, whereby not only all *Bohemia* was lost, but the *Palatine Family* was for almost 30 years dispossest of all their Possessions in *Germany*.

At 13 years of age he marcht with the then Prince of *Orange* to the *Siege of Rhineberg*.

And at the age of 18 he commanded a *Regiment* of *Horse* in the German Wars, aud in the Battle of *Lemgou* 1638, being taken by the Imperialists under the Command of Count *Hatzfield*, he continued a Prisoner above three years.

In 1642, returning into *England*. in *April* this Prince at a Chapter held at *York* was elected Knight of the *Garter*, and soon after made General, of the Horse to the King, fights and defeats Colonel *Sands* near *Worcester*, routed the Rebels Horse at *Edge Hill*, took *Cirencester* raised the Siege of *Newark*, recovered *Lichfield* and *Bristol*, raised the long siege before *Latham House*, fought the great Battle at *Marston Moor*, was created *Earl* of *Holderness*, and Duke of *Cumberland*

Cumberland, after the extinction of the Male Line of the *Cliffords* 1643. Finally the Kings forces at land being totally defeated, he transported himself into *France*, and was afterward made *Admiral* of such Ships of War as submitted to King *Charles* the Second, to whom after divers disasters at Sea, and wonderful preservations, he returned to *Paris* 1652, where, and in *Germany*, sometimes at the *Emperours Court*, and sometimes at *Heydelberg*, he passed his time in Princely Studies and exercises, till the Restauration of His Majesty now raigning; after which, returning into *England*, was made a *Privy Counsellour* in 1662, and in 1666, being joyned *Admiral* with the Duke of *Albermarle*, first attackt the whole *Dutch Fleet* with his *Squadron*, in such a bold resolute way, that he put the Enemy soon to flight.

He enjoys a *Pension* from His Majesty of 4000 *l. per Annum*, and the Government of the Castle of *Windsor*.

High Steward. After Prince *Rupert*, the next Heirs to the Crown of *England* are 3 *French Ladies*, daughters of Prince *Edward* lately deceased, who was a younger Son of the Queen of *Bohemia*, whose Widow the Princess *Dowager*, Mother to the said three Ladies, is Sister to the late Queen of *Poland*, Daughter and *Coheir* to the last Duke of *Nevers* in *France*. amongst which three Daughters there is a Revenue of about 12000 *l*, *Sterling* a year.

The

The Eldest of these is married to the Duke *d'Enghien* Eldest Son to the Prince of *Conde*. The Second is married to *John Frederick* Duke of *Brunswick* and *Lunenburg* at *Hanover*.

After these is the Princess *Elizabeth*, Eldest Sister living to the Prinee *Elector Palatin*, born 26 *Decemb.* 1618. unmarried and living in *Germany*, is Abbesse of *Hervorden*, but of the Protestant Religion.

The next is another Sister, called the Princess *Louisa*, bred up at the *Hague* with the Queen her Mother in the *Religion* of the Church of *England*, at length embracing the *Romish Religion*, is now Lady *Abbess* of *Maubuisson* at *Ponthoise*, not far from *Paris*.

Last of all is the Princess *Sophia*, youngest Daughter to the Queen of *Bohemia*, born at the *Hague*, 13 *Octob.* 1630. and in 1658. wedded to *Ernest Auguste* Duke of *Brunswick* and *Lunenburg*, Bishop of *Osnaburg*, by whom she hath had divers Children.

Of these three Princesses it is said, that the first is the most *learned*, the second the greatest *Artist*, and the last one of the most accomplisht Ladies in *Europe*.

CHAP.

CHAP. XII.

Of the Great Officers *of the* Crown.

NExt to the King and Princess of the Blood are reckoned the *Great Officers* of the *Crown*; whereof there are Nine, *viz.* the Lord *High Steward* of *England*, the Lord *High Chancellour*, the Lord *High Treasurer*, Lord *President* of the *Kings Council*, the Lord *Privy Seal*, the Lord *Great Chamberlain*, the Lord *High Constable*, the *Earl Marshal*, and the Lord High *Admiral*.

High-Steward. The first *Great Officer* of the Crown, according to the account of our Ancestors, was the Lord *High Steward* of *England*, or *Viceroy*; for so the word *Steward* imports in the *Saxon* Tongue, from *Stede* and *ward Locum tenens*, in French *Lieutenant*, and was the same Officer with the *Reichs Drotzet*, that is, *Regni vice* Rex in *Sweden*, and the *Stadtholder* in *Denmark*, who is also called *Viceroy* or *Lieutenant du Roy*. Our Common Lawyers stile him *Magnus Angliæ Seneschallus*, of *Sen* in Saxon *Justice*, and *Schals* a *Governour* or *Officer*.

He was antiently the Highest Officer under the King, and his power so exorbitant, that it was thought fit not longer to to trust it in the hands of any Subject, for his Office was *Supervidere & regulare sub Rege & immediate post Regem* (as an antient Record speaks) *totum Regnum Angliæ & omnes ministros Legum infra idem regnum temporibus pacis & guerrarum.*

The last that had a State of inheritance in this High Office, was *Henry* of *Bullingbrook* (Son and Heir to the great Duke of *Lancaster, John* of *Gaunt*, afterwards King of *England*) since which time they have been mede only *pro hac vice*, to officiate either at a Coronation, by vertue of which Office he sitteth judicially and keepeth his Court in the Kings Palace at *Westminster*, and there receiveth the Bills and Petitions of all such Noblemen and others, who by reason of their Tenure, or otherwise, claim to do Services at the New Kings Coronation, and to receive the Fees and Allowances due and accustomed; as lately at the *Coronation* of King *Charles* the Second, the *Duke of Ormond* was made for that occasion Lord *High Steward* of *England*, and (marching immediately before the King, above all other Officers of the Crown) bore in his hands St. *Edwards Crown*: Or else for the Arraignment of some Peer of the Realm, their Wives or Widows, for Treason or Felony, or some other great Crime, to judge and give sentence, as the antient High Stewards were wont to do; which ended, his Commission expireth: During such Trial he sitteth under a Cloth of Estate, and they that speak to him say, *May it please your Grace my Lord High Steward of England.* His Commission is to proceed *Secundum Legem & consuetudinem Angliæ.* He is sole Judge, yet doth call all the Twelve Judges of the Land to assist him. Is *not sworn*, nor the Lords who are the Triers of the Peer arraigned.

During his Stewardship he bears a *White Staffe* in his Hand, and the Trial being over, openly breaks it, and so his Office takes an end.

Lord Chancellour. Jeffreys 86

Next, The Lord *High Chancellour*, *Summus Cancellarius*, so called, because all *Patents*, *Commissions*, *Warrants*, coming from the King, and perused by him, are *signed*, if well, or *cancelled*, if amiss; or else because antiently he sate *intra cancellos*, that is, such a partition as usually now seperates the Church from the Chancel.

Dignity. He is after the King and Princes of the Blood in *Civil Affairs* (there being now no Lord *High Steward*) the *highest* Person in the Kingdom, as the *Arch-bishop* of *Canterbury* is in *Ecclesiastical affairs*.

Office. His Office is to keep the Kings *Great Seal*, to judg, not according to the *Common Law*, as other Civil Courts do, but to moderate the rigor of the Law, and to judge according to *Equity*, *Conscience*, or *Reason*. To bestow all *Ecclesiastical Benefices*

fices in the Kings gift under 20 *l.* yearly in the Kings Books, and for this and other causes he was ever till of late years a Clergy man.

His *Oath* is to do right to all manner of People poor and rich, after the Laws and Customs of the Realm, and truly Counsel the King; to keep secret the Kings Counsel, nor suffer so far as he may, that the Rights of the Crown be diminisht, *&c.* *Oath.*

From the time of *Henry* 2. the Chancellours of *England* have been ordinarily made of *Bishops*, or other *Clergy-men*, learned in the Civil Laws, till *Henry* 8. made Chancellour, first Sir *Thomas More*, and after him *Thomas Audley*. After whom also was made Lord Chancellour Sir *Richard Rich* Knight, Lord *Rich* (a Common Lawyer) who had been first the said Kings Sollicitor, and afterwards Chancellour of his Court of Augementation, from whom is descended the present Earl of *Warwick*, and the Earl of *Holland*; since which time there have been some Bishops, but most Common Lawyers.

This High Office is in *France durante vita*, but here, is *durante bene placito Regis.*

The Salary from the King is 848 *l. per Annum*, and when the Star-Chamber was up, 200 *l. per Annum* more for his Attendance there. *Salary.*

The Lord Chancellour or Lord Keeper *Creation*

 (who

(who differ only in Name) is created *per traditionem magni Sigilli sibi per dominum Regem*, and by taking his *Oath*.

The Great Seal being lately taken from *Edward Earl of Clarendon* Lord Chancellour, was by His Majesties great favour bestowed upon Sir *Orlando Bridgman*, with the Title of Lord Keeper of the Great Seal of *England*.

Lord Treasurer. The Third Great *Officer* of the Crown is the Lord *High Treasurer* of *England*, who receives this high Office by delivery of a *White Staffe* to him by the King, and holds it *durante bene placito Regis*.

Anciently he received this Dignity by the delivery of the *Golden Keys* of the *Treasury*.

Oath. His *Oath* is little different from that of the Lord Chancellour.

Office. He is *Præfectus Ærarii*, a Lord by his *Office*, under whose Charge and Government is all the Kings *Revenue* kept in the *Exchequer*. He hath also the *check* of all the *Officers* any way employed in collecting *Imposts*, *Customs*, *Tributes*, or other Revenues belonging to the *Crown*. He hath the gift of all *Customers*, *Controlers*, and *Searchers* in all the *Ports* of *England*.

He hath the nomination of the *Escheators* in every County, and in some Cases by Statute is to appoint a *Measurer* for the length and breadth of Clothes.

He, with others joyned in Commission with

with him, or without, letteth Leases of all the Lands belonging to the Crown. He giveth *Warrants* to certain Persons of Quality to have their *Wine* Custom free.

The Annual *Salary* of the Lord High Treasurer is in all 383 *l.* 7 *s.* 8 *d. per Annum.* Since the decease of *Thomas Wriothesly* last Earl of *Southampton*, and last Lord High Treasurer of *England*, this Office hath been executed by a Commission granted to three eminent Persons, *viz.* the Lord *Ashley*, Sir *Thomas Clifford*, and Sir *John Duncomb.*

Lord President.

The Fourth *Great Officer* named in the Statute 31 *Hen.* 8. is the Lord *President* of the Kings Privy Council, an Officer as antient as King *John*'s time, was usually called *Consiliarius Capitalis.* His Office is to attend upon the King, to propose business at Council-Table, and then to report to the King the several Transactions there. It hath been alwayes granted by Letters Patents under the Kings Great Seal *durante bene placito.* This Office of later times is grown obsolete, the last that had this honour, was the late Earl of *Manchester.* Now the Lord *Keeper* usually supplies his place.

Lord Privy Seal.

The Fifth, the Lord *Privy Seal*, who is a Lord by his Office, under whose hands pass all Charters and *Grants* of the King, and *Pardons* signed by the King, before they come to the *Great Seal of England* also divers other matters of less concernment

cernment, as for payments of Money, &c. which do not pass the Great Seal.

He is by his Place of the Kings *Privy-Council*, and Chief Judge of the *Court of Requests*, when it shall be re-continued; and besides his Oath of Privy Counsellour, takes a particular Oath as Lord *Privy Seal.*

His Salary is 1500 *l. per Annum.*

His Place according to Statute is next to the *Lord President* of of the *Kings Council.*

Dignity. It is an Office of great Trust and Skill, that he put not this Seal to any Grant without good Warrant under the Kings *Privy Signet*; nor with Warrant, if it be against Law or Custom, until that the King be first acquainted.

This great Officer is mentioned in the Statutes of 2 *Rich.* 2. and then ranked amongst the Chief Persons of the Realm.

And is at present enjoyed by *John Lord Roberts*, *Baron Roberts* of *Truro*, late Lord Lieutenant of *Ireland*, and executed by Commissioners under him, who are Sir *Edward Deering*, Sir *Thomas Strickland*, and *Robert Milward* Esquire.

Chamberlain. The Sixth *Great Officer* of the Crown is the Lord *Great Chamberlain* of *England*, an officer of great Antiquity, to whom belongs *Livery* and *Lodging* in the Kings Court, and certain Fees due from each *Archbishop* and *Bishop* when they do their *Homage* or *Fealty* to the King, and from all

all *Peers* of the Realm at their *Creation*, or doing the *Homage* or *Fealty*, and at the *Coronation* of any King to have 40 Ells of *Crimson Velvet* for his own Robes, and on the *Coronation* day before the King riseth, to bring his *Shirt*, *Coyfe*, *Wearing Clothes*, and after the King is by him apparelled and gone forth, to have his *Bed* and all *Furniture* of his *Bed-Chamber* for his Fees, all the Kings *Night Apparel*, and to carry at the Coronation the *Coife*, *Gloves*, and *Linnen* to be us'd by the King upon that occasion; also the *Sword* and *Scabbard*, and the *Gold* to be offered by the King, and the *Robe-Royal* and *Crown*, and to *undress* and *attire* the King with his Robes-Royal, and to serve the King that day before and after *Dinner* with *water* to wash his hands, and to have the *Basin* and *Towels* for his Fees, &c.

This Honour was long enjoyed by the Earls of *Oxford*, from the time of *Hen.* I. by an *Estate Tayle* or *Inheritance*, but in the two last Coronations by the Earls of *Lindsey*, and that by an Estate of Inheritance from a Daughter or Heir General claimed and controverted.

The Seventh *Great Officer* is the Lord *High Constable* of *England*, so called some think from the Saxon *Cuning*, by contraction King and Stable, *quasi Regis columen*, for it was antiently written *Cuninstible*, but rather from *Comes Stabuli*, whose Power and Jurisdiction was anciently

Constable

ciently so great, that after the death of *Edward Bagot* or *Stafford*, Duke of *Buckingham* 1521, the last *High-Constable* of *England*, it was thought too great for any Subject.

But since, upon occasion of Coronations (as at that of King *Charles* the Second, was made the late Earl of *Northumberland*) and at Solemn Trials by Combat (as at that which was intended between *Rey* and *Ramsey*, 1631, was made *Robert* Earl of *Lindsey*) there is created *pro illa vice* a Lord *High Constable*. His Power and Jurisdiction is the same with the *Earl Marshal*, with whom he sits *Judge* in the *Marshals Court*, and takes place of the *Earl Marshal*.

Earl Marshal.

Norfolk

The Eighth *Great Officer* of the Crown is the *Earl Marshal* of *England*, so called from *Mare* in the old Saxon (*i. e.*) Horses; and *Schal*, *Præfectus*. He is an Earl, some say, by his *Office*, whereby he taketh as the Constable doth, Cognisance of all matters of *War* and *Arms*, determineth *Contracts* touching Deeds of Arms *out of the Realm* upon Land, and matters concerning *Wars* within the Realm, which cannot be determined by *Common Law*.

This Office is of great antiquity in *England*, and antiently of great Power.

The last Earl Marshal was *Henry Howard* Earl of *Arundel*, who died in 1652, his Father *Thomas* Earle of *Arundel*, and he enjoying that Office onely for the term of their lives by the Kings Letters Patents.

At

At the Coronation of His Majesty now Raigning, the present Earl of *Suffolk* for that Solemnity onely was made *Earl Marshal*.

At present that great Office is executed in part by a Commission granted by His Majesty to *John* Lord *Roberts*, Lord *Privy Seal*, to *Henry Pierpoint* Marquis of *Dorchester*, to *Edward Montague* Earl of *Manchester* and Lord Chamberlain, and to *Charles Howard* Earl of *Carlisle*, &c.

The Ninth and last Great Officer of the Crown is the Lord *High Admiral of England*, whose Trust and Honour is so great, that this Office hath usually been given either to some of the Kings younger Sons, near Kinsmen, or to some one of the highest and chiefest of all the Nobility. *Admiral*

He is called *Admiral* from *Amir* in *Arabick*, and ἅλιος in the *Greek*, that is *Præfectus Marinus*, a word borrowed from the Eastern Empire, where such kind of Compounds were much in request, and introduced into *England* after the Wars in the *Holy Land* by King *Richard*, or King *Edward* the First.

The Patent of the Lord *Admiral* did anciently run this, *Angliæ*, *Hiberniæ*, & *Aquitaniæ*, *Magnus Admiralus*; but at present thus, *Angliæ & Hiberniæ ac Dominiorum & Insularum earundem*, *Villæ Calesiæ & Marchiarum ejusdem*, *Normandiæ*, *Gasconiæ*, & *Aquitaniæ*, *Magnus Admi-*

rallus & Præfectus Generalis Classis & Marium dictorum Regnorum.

To the Lord High Admiral of *England* is by the King intrusted the management of all *Maritime Affairs*, as well in respect of *Jurisdiction* as *Protection*. He is that High Officer or Magistrate to whom is committed the Government of the Kings *Navy*, with Power of decision in all Causes *Maritime*, as well *Civil* as *Criminal*; of all things done upon or beyond the Sea in any part of the World, all things done upon the Sea *Coasts* in all *Ports* and *Havens*, and upon all Rivers below the *first bridg* next toward the Sea.

The Lord Admiral hath the power to commissionate a *Vice-Admiral*, a *Reer-Admiral*, and all Sea-Captains, also *Deputies* for particular Coasts, *Coroners* to view dead bodies found on the Sea Coasts, or at Sea, Commissioners or Judges for exercising Justice in the Court of Admiralty, to imprison, release, &c.

He hath sometimes a Commission to bestow Knighthood to such as shall deserve it at Sea.

To the Lord Admiral belongs by Law and Custom all *penalties* and *amercements* of all Transgressors at *Sea*, on the *Sea Shore*, in *Ports*, and from the first Bridge on Rivers toward the Sea; also the goods of *Pyrates*, *Felons*, or *Capital Faulters*, condemned, outlawed, or *horned*. Moreover all *Waifs*, *Stray Goods*, *Wrecks* of *Sea*, *Deodands*, a share of all lawful *Prizes*, *Lagon*, *Fetson*, and *Flotson*, as our

Law-

Lawyers term it; that is, Goods lying in the Sea on Ground, Goods floting on the Sea, and goods cast by the Sea on the Shore, not granted to Lords of Mannors adjoyning to the Sea: All great Fishes, as *Sea-Hogs*, and other Fishes of extraordinary bigness, called *Royal Fishes*, except only *Whales* and *Sturgeons*.

This *High Dignity* is at present enjoyed by the Kings only Brother the Illustrious Prince *James* Duke of *York*.

CHAP. XII.

Of the Kings Court, *the Ecclesiastical, Civil, and Military Government thereof, with a Catalogue of the Kings Privy Counsellors, of the Kings Judges, Sergeants,* &c.

THe Court of the King of *England* is a *Monarchy* within a *Monarchy*, consisting of *Ecclesiastical*, *Civil*, and *Military* Persons and Government.

Ecclesiastical Government.

For the Ecclesiastical Government of the Kings Court, there is first a *Dean* of the Kings Chappel, who is usually some grave Learned Prelate, chosen by the King, and who as Dean acknowledgeth no *Superiour* but the King; for as the Kings Palace is exempt from all inferiour Temporal Jurisdiction, so is his Chappel from all

Spiritual

Spiritual; it is called *Capella Dominica*, the *Demean* Chappel, is not within the Jurisdiction or Diocess of any Bishop, but as a *Regal Peculiar* exempt and reserved to the Visitation and Immediate Government of the King, who is *Supreme Ordinary*, and as it were Prime Bishop over all the Churches and Bishops of *England*.

By the Dean are chosen all other Officers of the Chappel, *viz.* a *Subdean* or *Præceutor Capellæ*; 32 Gentlemen of the Chappel; whereof 12 are *Priests*, and one of them is *Confessor* to the Kings Houshold; whose Office is to read Prayers every Morning to the Family, to visit the sick, to examine and prepare Communicants, to inform such as desire advice in any Case of Conscience or Point of Religion, &c.

The other 20 Gentlemen, commonly called *Clerks* of the Chappel, are with the aforesaid Priests to perform in the Chappel the Office of Divine Service in *Praying, Singing, &c.* One of these being well skilled in *Musick* is chosen *Master of the Children*, whereof there are 12 in Ordinary, to instruct them in the Rules and Art of Musick for the service of the Chappel. Three other of the said Clerks are chosen to be *Organists*, to whom are joyned upon *Sundays Collar-days*, and other *Holydays*; the *Saickbuts* and *Cornets* belonging to the Kings Private Musick, to make the Chappel Musick more full and compleat.

There

There are moreover 4 Officers called *Vergers*, from the Silver Rods carried in their hands, also a *Sergeant*, 2 *Yeomen*, and a *Groom* of the Chappel.

In the Kings Chappel *thrice* every day Prayers are read, and Gods Service and Worſhip performed with great *Decency*, *Order*, and *Devotion*, and ſhould be a *Pattern* to all other Churches and Chappels of *England*.

The King hath alſo his private Oratory where ſome of His Chaplains read Divine Service to the King on working dayes every Morning and every Evening.

Twelve days in the year, being high and Principal Feſtivals, His Majeſty after Divine Service, attended with His Principal Nobility, adorned with their *Collars of the Garter*, in a grave ſolemn manner at the *Altar Offers* a ſum of *Gold* to God, *in ſignum ſpecialis Dominii*, that by His Grace he is King, and holdeth all of him.

All Offerings made at the Holy Altar by the King and Queen, did antiently belong to the diſpoſal of the Archbiſhop of *Canterbury*, if his Grace were preſent, whereſoever the Court was, but now to the Dean of the Chappel, to be diſtributed amongſt the poor.

Thoſe 12 days are, firſt *Chriſtmas*, *Eaſter*, *Whitſunday*, and *All Saints*, called *Houſhold-days*; upon which the *Beſant* or *Gold* to be offered, is delivered to the King by the Lord *Steward*, or ſome other of the principal Officers; then *New-years-day*, *Twelf-*

day.

day, upon the later of which *Gold*, *Frankincense* and *Myrrhe*, in several purses are offered by the King: Lastly, *Candelmas*, *Annunciation*, *Ascension*, *Trinity Sunday*, St. *John Baptist*, and *Michaelmass-day*, when onely *Gold* is offered. Upon *Christmass*, *Easter*, and *Whitsunday*, His Majesty usually receives the Holy *Sacrament*, none but two or three of the principal Bishops communicating with Him.

The King hath also (besides many *Extraordinary*) 48 *Chaplains* in *Ordinary*, who are usually eminent Doctors in Divinity; whereof four every Moneth wait at Court to preach in the Chappel on Sundays and other Festivals before the King, and in the Morning early on Sundays before the Houshold, to read Divine Service before the King, out of Chappel daily as afore mentioned, twice in the Kings private Oratory, to give Thanks at Table in the Clerk of the Closets absence.

In time of *Lent*, according to Antient Laudable Custom, the Divine Service and Preaching is performed in a more Solemn manner:

Antiently at Court there were Sermons in *Lent* onely, and that in the Afternoon, in the open Aire, and then only by Bishops, Deans, and Principal Prebendaries: Our Ancestors judging that time enough, and those persons only fit to teach such an Auditory their duty to God and Man. Antiently also the Lent Preachers were all appointed by the Archbishop of *Canterbury*. Now on the first

Wednesday

Wednesday called *Ashwednesday*, in the Morning, begins the Dean of the Chappel to preach, on each *Wednesday* after one of His Majesties more eloquent *Chaplains*, every Friday the Dean of some Cathedral or Collegiate Church: on the last *Friday* called *Good-Friday*, is always to preach the Dean of *Westminster*; on every *Sunday* in *Lent* some *Right Reverend Bishop* preacheth, and on the last *Sunday* of *Lent*, called *Palm-Sunday*, is to preach an *Archbishop*, and upon *Easter-day* the Lord *High Almoner*, who is usually some principal Bishop, that disposeth of the Kings *Almes*, and for that use receiveth (besides other moneys allowed by the King) all *Deodands & Bona Felonum de se*, to be that way disposed.

In *France* the *Grand Aumosnier* is principal of all the *Ecclesiastiques* of the Court, and all Officers of the Kings Chappel; he receiveth their Oaths of Allegiance, and himself swears only to the King for that Office; he hath the disposition of all *Hospitals*, the Charge for delivering Prisoners pardoned by the King at his coming to the Crown, or at his Coronation or first entrance into any of his Cities.

Under the Lord High Almoner there is a *Subalmoner*, two *Yeomen*, and two *Grooms* of the *Almonry*.

Besides all these, the King hath a *Clerk* of the Closet or *Confessor* to His Majesty, who is commonly some Reverend discreet Divine extraordinarily esteemed by His Majesty;

Majesty, whose *Office* is to *attend* at the Kings Right hand during Divine Service, to resolve all *doubts* concerning spiritual matters, *&c.*

The present Dean of the Chappel is Doctor *Blanford* Bishop of *Oxford*, whose Fee is 200 *l.* yearly and a Table, his Sub-dean is Doctor *Jones*, whose Fee is 100 *l.* yearly.

The Fee of each Priest and Clerk of the Chappel is 70 *l.* yearly.

The *Clerk of the Closet* is Doctor *Crew* Dean of *Chichester*, a younger Son to the Lord *Crew* of *Stene* in *Com. Northampton*, receives 20 Nobles Fee *per anuum.*

The Lord *High Almoner*, is Doctor *Henchman*, Bishop of *London*, hath no Fee; his *Sub-Almoner* is Doctor *Perinchef*, whose Fee is 6 *l.* 6 *s.* 10 *d.*

Civil Government.

Steward Ormond

Treasury Newport

For the *Civil Government* of the *Kings Court*, the cheif Officer is the Lord *Steward*, called also in the time of *Henry* the Eighth, *The Great Master of the Kings Houshold*, after the French Mode, but *Primo Mariæ*, and ever since called *The Lord Steward of the Kings Houshold.*

The State of the *Kings House* is committed to him, to be ruled and guided by his discretion; and all his commands in Court to be obeyed and served. And as his Power is great, so is his Dignity, State, and Honor. The *Steward* and *Treasurer* within the *Kings House*, saith, *an old Manuscript*, *represent the State of an Earl.*

He hath Authority over all Officers and Servants of the *Kings House*, except those of *His Majesties* Chappel, Chamber, and Stable, &c.

He by his Office, without any Commission, judgeth of all disorders, as *Treasons*, *Murders*, *Felonies*, *Bloodsheds*, committed in the Court, or within the *Verge*, which is every way within Twelve miles of the cheif Tunnel of the Court (onely *London* by Charter is exempted,) for the Law having an high esteem of the dignity of the *Kings* setled *Mansion-House*, laid out such a Plot of Ground about his House (as a *Haut Pas* or *Foot-Carpet* spred about the *Kings Chair* of Estate, that ought to be more cleared and void, then other places) to be subject to a special exempted Jurisdiction depending on the *Kings Person* and Great Officers, that so, where the *King* comes, there should come with him, Peace, and Order, and an Awfulness and Reverence in Mens hearts: Besides, it would have been a kinde of eclipsing of the *Kings Honor*, that where the *King* was, any Justice should be sought, but immediately from the *Kings* own Officers; and therefore from very ancient times, the Jurisdiction of the *Verge*, hath been executed by the *Lord Steward*, with great ceremony, in the nature of a *Peculiar Kings Bench*, and that not onely within, but without the *Kings Dominions*: For so it is recorded, that one *Engleam* of *Nogent* in *France*, for stealing Silver Dishes out of the House of *Edward* the First, King of *England*,

England, then at *Paris* (after the matter had been debated in the Council of the King of *France*, touching the Jurisdiction, and ordered, That the King of *England* should enjoy this Kingly Prerogative of His Houshold) was condemned by Sir *Robert Fitz-John*, then *Steward* to the King of *England*, and hanged in Saint *Germains* Fields.

The *Lord Steward* is a *White-staff Officer*; for he in the *Kings Presence*, carrieth a White-staff, and at other times going abroad, it is carried by a Foot-man bare-headed. This White-staff is taken for a Commission; at the death of the King, over the Herse made for the Kings Body, he breaketh this Staff, and thereby dischargeth all the Officers, whom the succeeding King, out of His meer Grace, doth re-establish each one in his former Office.

This eminent employment is now enjoyed by *James* Duke of *Ormond*, whose Fee is 100*l.* yearly, and Sixteen dishes daily each Meal, with Wine, Beer, *&c.*

The next Officer is the *Lord Chamberlain*, who hath the oversight of all Officers belonging to the *Kings Chamber*, except the Precincts of the *Kings Bed-Chamber*, which is wholly under the *Groom of the Stole*; and all above Stairs; who are all sworn by him (or his Warrant to the *Gentlemen Ushers*) to the King. He hath also the oversight of the Officers of the *Wardrobes*, at all *His Majesties* Houses; and

and of the removing *Wardrobes*; or of *Beds*, of the *Tents*, *Revels*, *Musick*. *Comedians*, *Hunting*, and of the *Messengers*, of the *Trumpetters*, *Drummers*, of all *Handicrafts*, and *Artisans*, retained in the *Kings Services*.

Morever, He hath the oversight of the *Heralds* and *Pursivants*, and *Sergeants at Arms*; of all *Physicians*, *Apothecaries*, *Surgeons*, *Barbers*, &c. To him also belongeth the oversight of the *Chaplains*, though himself be a *Layman*; contrary in this particular to the ancient Custom of *England*, and Modern Custom of all other Kingdoms, where Ecclesiasticks are never under the ordering of Laymen.

Also of the Charges of Coronations; Marriages, Entries, Cavalcades, Funerals, &c.

The Fee of the *Lord Chamberlain* of the *Kings House*, is 100 *l.* yearly, and Sixteen dishes each Meal, with all the Appurtenances.

This Office is now in the hands of *Edward Montague*, Lord *Kimbolton*, Viscount *Mandevile*, and Earl of *Manchester*; as also Knight of the most Noble Order of the Garter.

Most of the above-named Offices and Places, are in the gift and disposal of the *Lord Chamberlain*.

The Third Great Officer of the *Kings Court*, is the *Master of the Horse*, anciently called *Comes Stabuli*, or *Constable*, to whom

whom a higher employment and power was then given, and this taken from him.

This Great Officer hath now the ordering and disposal of all the *Kings Stables*, and *Races*, or *Breed of Horses*; and had heretofore of all the *Posts* of *England*. He hath also the power over *Escuiries*, and *Pages*, over the *Footmen*, *Grooms*, *Riders* of the *Great Horses*, *Farriers*, *Smiths*, *Coachmen*, *Sadlers*, and all other *Trades* working to the *Kings Stables*; to all whom he (or by his Warrant the *Avener*) giveth an Oath to be true and faithful.

He hath the Charge of all *Lands* and *Revenues*, appointed for the *Kings* breed of Horses, and for Charges of the *Stable*, and for *Litters*, *Coaches*, *Sumpter-Horses*, *&c.*

He onely hath the Priviledge to make use of any *Horses*, *Pages*, *Footmen*, belonging to the *Kings Stable*.

At any *Solemn Cavalcade* he rides next behinde the *King*, and leads a *Lear Horse of State*.

This Great Honor is now enjoyed by *George* Duke of *Buckingham*. His yearly Fee is *666 l. 16 s. 4 d.* and a Table of Sixteen dishes each Meal.

The account of the *Stables* for *Horse-Meat*, *Livery Wages*, and *Board Wages*, are brought by the *Avener*, being cheif Clerk of the *Avery*, to be passed and allowed by the Board of the *Green-Cloth*.

Under these Three Principal Officers of

His

His Majesties Houshold, are almost all the other Officers and Servants.

First, under the *Lord Steward* in the *Compting-house*, is the

Treasurer of the Houshold.
Comptroller.
Cofferer.
Master of the Houshold.
Two Clerks of the Green-Cloth.
Two Clerks Comptrollers.
One Sergeant.
Two Yeomen.
The Cofferers Clerks, or Clerks of the Assignment.
The Groom.
Two Messengers.

It is called *The Compting-house*, because the Accompts for all expences of the *Kings Houshold*, are there taken daily by the *Lord Steward*, the *Treasurer*, the *Cromptroller*, the *Cofferer*, the *Master of the Houshold*, the *Two Clerks of the Green-Cloth*, and the *Two Clerks Comptrollers*, who also there make Provisions for the Houshold, according to the Law of the Land, and make Payments and Orders for the well-governing of the Servants of the Houshold.

In the *Compting-house* is the *Green-Cloth*, which is a Court of Justice continually sitting in the *Kings House*, composed of the Persons last mentioned; whereof the Three first are usually of the *Kings Privy Council*. To this Court, being the first and most ancient Court of *England*, is committed the charge and oversight

oversight of the *Kings Court Royal* for Matters of Justice and Government, with Authority for maintaining the *Peace* within Twelve miles distance, wheresoever the Court shall be; and within the *Kings House* the power of correcting all the Servants therein that shall any way offend.

It is called *The Green-Cloth*, of a *Green-Cloth* whereat they sit, over whom are the Arms of the *Compting-house*, bearing *Vert a Key, and a Rod Or, a Staff Argent Saultier*, signifying their Power to reward and correct, as Persons for their great wisdom and experience thought fit by *His Majesty* to exercise both these *Functions* in *His Royal House*.

The *Treasurer* of the *Kings House* is always of the *Privy Council*, and in absence of the *Lord Steward* hath power with the *Comptroller*, and *Steward* of the *Marshalsea*, to hear and determine *Treasons*, *Felonies*, and other Inferior Crimes committed within the *Kings Palace*, and that by Verdict of the *Kings Houshold*.

Houshold Servants within the *Check Roll*, if any be found guilty of Felony, no benefit of Clergy is to be allowed him. Anciently this Court might have held *Pleas* of *Freehold* also.

His yearly Fee 124 *l.* 14 *s.* 8 *d.* and a Table of Sixteen dishes each Meal. He bears a White Staff, and is at present Sir *Thomas Clifford*.

The

The *Comptrollers Office* is to controul the Accompts and Reckonings of the *Green-Cloth*.

His yearly Fee is 107 *l.* 12 *s.* 4 *d.* a Table of Sixteen dishes each Meal. He bears a White-Staff, and is at present *Francis* Lord *Newport*.

The *Cofferer* is also a Principal Officer, hath a special charge and oversight of other Officers of the House; for their good demeanor and carriage in their Offices, and is to pay the Wages to the *Kings Servants* below Stairs; and for Provisions, by the direction and allowance of the *Green-Cloth*.

His yearly Fee is 100 *l*, a Table of Seven dishes daily, and is now Colonel *William Ashburnham*.

The next is the *Master of the Houshold*, whose Office is to survey the Accompts of the House.

His Fee One hundred Marks, and Seven dishes daily, enjoyed by Sir *Herbert Price*.

All *Bills of Controulment*, *Parcels*, and *Brievments*, are tolted and allowed by the *Clerks Comptrollers*, and summed up by the Clerks of the *Green-Cloth*.

The Two Clerks of the *Green-Cloth*, are, Sir *Henry Wood*, and Sir *Stephen Fox*, and the *Two Clerks Comptrollers*, Sir *William Boreman*, and Sir *Winston Churchill*.

The

The yearly Fee to each of these Four, is 48 *l.* 13 *s.* 4 *d.* And between them, Two Tables of Seven dishes to each Table.

The rest of the *Compting-House* being less considerable, shall for brevity be past over; and for other Officers below Stairs, onely their names and number shall be noted, their Fees being not considerable, except the Sergeants Fee of each Office; onely the *Reader* may here take notice, that although the King pays still the ancient Fees, which at first were of above Ten times the value they are now; yet the Perquisits in many Offices, make sometimes a place of 10 *l.* Fee, to be worth near 500 *l.* *per annum.*

In the *Acatery* or the *Caterers Office*, A Sergeant, *Robert Angel*; a Clerk, Purveyors for Flesh and Fish, Yeomen; in all, Twelve persons.

In the *Poulty*, A Sergeant, *Simon Ager*, a Clerk, Yeomen, Grooms, Purveyors; in all, Ten persons.

In the *Bake-house*, A Sergeant, *Nicholas Johnson*; a Clerk, divers Yeomen; a Garnitor, divers Purveyors, Grooms, and Conducts; in all, Seventeen persons.

In the *Wood-yard*, A Sergeant, Mr. *Bland*; a Clerk, Yeomen, Groom, and Pages; in all, Eight persons.

In the *Scullery*, A Sergeant, *William Dike*; a Clerk, Yeomen, Grooms, and Pages; in all, Twelve persons.

In the *Larder*, A Sergeant, a Clerk, Three Yeomen, Three Grooms, Two Pages.

In

In the *Pastry*, A Sergeant, *William Astley*; a Clerk, Yeomen, Grooms, and Children; in all, Eleven persons.

Note, That from the *Pastry*, to the *Acatery*, as the Clerk of one Office dies, the Clerk of the next under Office succeeds; and from the *Acatery*, as any of the Clerks of the *Avenary*, *Spicery*, or *Kitchin* die, the Clerk of the *Acatery* succeeds; and from thence, to be one of the *Clerks Controuler*, then Clerk of the *Compting-house*, then *Master of the Houshold*, lastly, *Cofferer of the Houshold*: Higher then which, this Succession goes not.

Note also, That in each Office there is a Succession from one to another; as one of the Children may come to be Groom, then Yeoman, then Gentleman, then Sergeant, as he happens to out live them above him.

In the *Pantry*, A Sergeant, *Francis Cob*, Yeomen, Grooms, Pages, &c. In all, Eleven.

In the *Cellar*, A Sergeant, *Richard Dalton*; a Gentleman, Yeomen, Grooms, Purveyors, Pages; in all, Twelve.

In the *Buttery*, A Gentleman, *Robert Ermley*, Yeoman, Grooms, Pages, Purveyors; in all, Eleven.

In the *Pitcher-house*, A Yeoman, Grooms, Page, and Clerk; in all, Five persons.

In the *Spicery*, Three Clerks and a Grocer.

In the *Chandlery*, A Sergeant, Sir *Thomas Monings* Baronet; Two Yeomen, Two Grooms, and a Page; in all, Six persons.

In the *Wafery*, A Yeoman, and a Groom.

In the *Confectionary*, A Sergeant, Two Yeomen, a Groom, and a Page.

In the *Ewry*, A Sergeant, *Ed. Wynn*; a Gentleman, Two Yeoman, a Groom, and Two Pages.

In the *Laundry*, A Yeoman, a Groom, Three Pages, and a Draper.

In the *Kitchin*, Five Clerks, Three to the King,

viz. { *Henry Firebrase*, *John Clements*, *Ralph Jackson*, } Esquires.

And Two Clerks to the Queen,

viz. { *John Manly*, *Thomas Vivian*, } Esquires.

The cheif of these Five Clerks hath a Fee and Diet equal to an Officer of the *Green-Cloth*: A Master Cook to the King, *John Sayer*; a Master Cook to the Queen, *Abraham Harcourt*; a Master Cook to the Houshold, *William Austin*: Each of these Three, a Table of Five Dishes, Six Yeomen, Seven Grooms, Five Children; in all Twenty six persons.

In the *Boyling-House*, A Yeoman, Two Grooms.

In the *Scalding-House*, Yeomen, Grooms, and Pages; in all Six.

Harbingers, Two Gentlemen, *Peter Watson*, first Gentleman, Six Yeomen.

In

In the *Almonry*, Sub-Almoner, Two Yeomen, two Grooms.

Porters at Gate, A Sergeant, Sir *Edward Brett*, Two Yeomen, Four Grooms.

Cart-takers, Six in number.

Surveyors of the Dresser, Two persons.

Marshals of the Hall, Four.

Sewers of the Hall, Five.

Waiters of the Hall, Twelve.

Messenger of the Compting-House, One.

Bell-Ringer, One.

Long Cart-takers, Four.

Wine-Porters, Eight.

Wood-Bearer, One.

The Cock of the Court, One.

Supernumerary Servants to the last King, viz. *In the Poultry* Two. *In the Almonry* One. *And in the Pastry*, One.

Besides the forenamed Officers below Stairs, there are also under the said *Lord Steward*, all the Officers belonging to the *Queens Kitchin, Cellar, Pantry, &c.* And to the *Kings Privy Kitchin*, and to the *Lords Kitchin*, together with *Children, Scowrers, Turn-broaches, &c.* In all, Sixty eight.

A List of His Majesties Servants in Ordinary above Stairs.

GEntlemen of the Bed-Chamber, whereof the first is called *Groom of the Stole*, that is according to the signification of the word in *Greek*, from whence first the *Latines*, and thence the *Italian* and *French* derive it *Groom* or *Servant* of the *Robe* or *Vestment*: He having the Office and Honor to present and put on His Majesties first Garment or Shirt every morning, and to order the things of the Bed-Chamber.

The Gentlemen of the Bed-Chamber, consist usually of the prime Nobility of *England*. Their Office in general, is each one in his turn to wait a week in every quarter in the Kings Bed Chamber, there to lie by the King on a Pallet-Bed all night; and in the absence of the Groom of the Stole to supply his place. Moreover, they wait on the King when He eats in private, for then the Cup bearers, Carvers, and Sewers do not wait.

The yearly Fee to each, is a 1000 *l.*

Their Names fellow according to their Order,

John Earl of *Bath*, Groom of the Stole, and first Gentleman of the Bed-Chamber.

George Duke of *Buckingham*.

Charles

Charles Duke of *Richmond.*
Christopher Duke of *Albemarle.*
William Duke of *Newcastle.*

Earl of { *Ogle.* *Ossory.* *Suffolk.* *Rochester.* }

Lord { *Gerrard.* *Crofts.* *Lauderdale.* *Mandevil.* *Buckhurst.* }

The Vice-Chamberlain is Sir *George Carteret.*

Keeper of His Majesties Privy-Purse, is Mr. *May.*

Treasurer of the Chamber is Sir *Edward Griffin.* He pays Riding and Lodging wages as the *Lord Chamberlain* shall direct.

Doctor *Wren*, Surveyor General of His Majesties works.

Master of the Robes, belonging to His Majesties Person, is at present *Laurence Hide*, Second Son to the Earl of *Clarendon.* His Office is to have the ordering of all His Majesties Robes; as those of *Coronation*, of St. *Georges* Feast, and of *Parliament*; also, of all His Majesties Wearing Apparel, of His Collar of Esses, Georges, and Garters beset with Diamonds and Pearls.

Grooms of the Bed-Chamber.

Henry Seymour,	Esquires.
John Ashburnham,	
Thomas Elliot,	
David Walter,	
William Legg,	
Sylvius Titus,	
Thomas Killegrew,	
Robert Phillips,	
Edward Progers,	
Richard Lane,	
James Hammilton,	
Henry Coventry.	

These are to be under the degree of Knights.

Their Office is to attend in the Kings Bed-Chamber, to dress and undress the King in private, &c. The yearly Fee to each, is 500 *l.*

Pages of the Bed-Chamber are Six.

Francis Rogers.
Hugh Griffith.
Mauniae de la Dale.
Theodosius Randu.
William Chiffins.
Arundel Bull.

The Fifth of these, is also Keeper of the Kings Cabinet Closet.

Gentle-

Gentlemen Ushers of the Privy-Chamber.

Marmaduke Darcy Esquire.
Sir *Paul Neal*.
John Milton Esquire.
Sir *Thomas Not*.

These wait, one at a time, in the Privy-Lodgings, &c.

Gentlemen of the Privy-Chamber in Ordinary.

Midsummer Quarter.

Sir *Edward Griffin*.
Sir *Francis Cobb*.
Bullen Reymes.
Colonel *Carlos*.
Sir *Robert Benlos*.
Sir *Thomas Sands*.
Edward Vernon.
William Neal.
Sir *Richard Onseley*.
Sir *John Cotton*.
Ambrose Pudsey.
Francis Berkley.

Michaelmass Quarter.

John Hall.
Sir *Edward Sutton*.
Sir *Robert Hilliard*.

Sir William Heyward.
Sir Samuel Moreland.
William Walter.
Sir John Locket.
Sir Robert Killegrew.
Sir William Sanderson.
Sir Charles Wheeler.
Francis Berkley.
John Dawes.

Christmass Quarter.

Edward Grey.
Sir Joseph Seymore.
Sir Peter Killegrew.
Sir Edward Savage.
Sir Thomas Nevil.
Henry Markham.
Sir John Morton.
Sir John Elws.
Sir Jonathan Trelawny.
John Scot.
Sir John Dawet.
John Beaumont.

Lady-day Quarter.

Peregrine Bertue.
Sir Thomas Daniel.
Sir Jacob Ashley.
Sir Francis Lawley.
Robert Thomas.
Sir Gilbert Gerrard.
Sir Francis Clark.

Sir *John Mince.*
Sir *William Swan.*
Colonel *Charles Progers.*
John Crook.
Sir *Philip Carteret.*

In number Forty eight; all Knights or Esquires of note.

Their Office is Twelve every Quarter, to wait on the Kings Person within doors and without, so long as His Majesty is on Foot; and when the King eats in the Privy Chamber, they wait at the Table, and bring in His Meat. They wait also at the Reception of Ambassadors; and every Night, two of them lye in the Kings Privy-Chamber.

A Gentleman of the Privy-Chamber, by the Kings Commandment onely, without any written Commission, is sufficient to Arrest any Peer of *England*; as Cardinal *Woolsey* acknowledged.

Grooms of the Privy-Chamber in Ordinary, in number Six; all Gentlemen of quality.

Viz.
Maurice Wynn.
James Progers.
Adrian May.
Robert Thompson.
James Elliot.
Thomas Rosse.

These (as all Grooms) wait without Sword, Cloak, or Hat: Whereas the Gentlemen of the Privy-Chamber wear always Cloak and Sword.

In the Presence Chamber, Gentlemen-Ushers daily Waiters in Ordinary, are Four, whereof the first hath that considerable office of *Black Rod*, and in time of Parliament is to attend every day the Lords House; and is also Usher of the most Honorable Order of the Garter: But at present, the first Gentleman Usher hath resigned these last-named Offices to the second Gentleman-Usher, daily waiter. They are these that follow,

Sir *John Ayton*.
Sir *Edward Carteret*.
Richard Marsh Esquire.
Thomas Duppa Esquire.

Their Office is to wait in the Presence-Chamber, and to attend next the Kings Person; and after the Lord Chamberlain, and the Vice-Chamberlain, to order all Affairs; and to obey these, are all under Officers above Stairs.

Gentlemen-Ushers, *Quarter-Waiters in Ordinary*, in number Eight.

Viz.
Francis Bowman,
Paul French,
Richard Bagnal,
Edward Bowman,
Peter Watson,
Nicholas Levet,
Ralph Whistler,
Nicholas Slaney,
Esquires.

These wait also in the Presence-Chamber, and are to give Directions in the absence of of the Gentlemen-Ushers; Daily Waiters to the Grooms and Pages, and other under Officers; who are to attend in all Offices next below the Gentlemen-Ushers, Quarter Waiters.

The Grooms of the Great Chamber, are Fourteen; the Pages of the Presence Chamber Four.

Six Gentlemen Waiters.

Cup-Bearers in Ordinary.

James Halsal Esq;
Charles Littleton Esq;
Sir *William Fleetwood* Knight.
Sir *Philip Palmer* Knight.
Mr. *Ayrskin* Esq;

Carvers in Ordinary.

John Trelawny
John Cooper
Christopher Amias
William Champneys
} Esquires.

Sewers to the Person in Ordinary.

Richard Irwyn Esquire.
Thomas Man Esquire.
Sir *John Covert.*
Bevil Skelton Esquire.

Esquires of the Body in Ordinary.

Ferdinando Massum.
Richard March.
Sir *John Hanmore.*
Henry Norwood.
Andrew Newport.
Thomas Cheek.

Their

Their Office to guard the Kings Person by night, to set the Watch, and give the Word, and keep good order in the whole House by night, as the *Lord Chamberlain*, and his other Officers are to do by day.

The Sewers of the Chamber, are Eight.

Groom Porter, Thomas Offley Esquire.
His Office to see the Kings Lodgings furnished with Tables, Chairs, Stools, Firing; to furnish Cards, Dice, *&c.* to decide Disputes arising at Cards, Dice, Bowlings, *&c.*

There are *Sixteen Sergeant at Arms*, all Gentlemen or Knights attending upon His Majesty: There are also Four other *Sergeants at Arms*, whereof one attends the Lord President of *Wales*, another attends the Speaker of the House of Commons, and another the Lord Lieutenant of *Ireland*.

CHAPLAINS in Ordinary, Four for every Moneth, as followeth.

January.	February.
Dr. *Brideock.*	Dr. *Pierce.*
Dr. *Jos. Beaumont.*	Dr. *Shute.*
Dr. *Colebrand.*	Dr. *Dupert.*
Dr. *Mense.*	Dr. *Cradock.*

March.

March.

Dr. *Reeves.*
Dr. *Brough.*
Dr. *Sancroft.*
Dr. *Barnes.*

April.

Dr. *Maine.*
Dr. *Compton.*
Dr. *Stillingfleet.*
Dr. *Tillotſon.*

May.

Dr. *Fell.*
Dr. *Sudbury.*
Dr. *Bathurſt.*
Dr. *Only.*

June.

Dr. *Wood.*
Dr. *Carlton.*
Dr. *Baſire.*
Dr. *Neale.*

July.

Dr. *Cartwright.*
Dr. *Caſtillian.*
Dr. *Smith.*
Dr. *Maggot.*

Auguſt.

Dr. *Fleetwood.*
Dr. *Iſaac Barrow.*
Dr. *Thorne.*
Dr. *Offley.*

September.

Dr. *Pearſon.*
Dr. *Stradling.*
Dr. *Perinchief.*
Dr. *Creighton.*

October.

Dr. *Outtram.*
Dr. *Bell.*
Dr. *Thomas Tilley.*
Dr. *Smalwood.*

November.

Dr. *Alleſtree.*
Dr. *Benſon.*
Dr. *John Lloyd.*
Dr. *William Lloyd.*

December.

Dr. *Hodges.*
Dr. *Hardy.*
Dr. *Ball.*
Dr. *Lamplugh.*

Theſe Forty eight Chaplains in Ordinary, areuſually Doctors in Divinity, and for

for the most part Deans or Prebendaries, and all Principal Predicators.

Physitians in Ordinary to His Majesties Person, are,

Sir *Alexander Fraser*,

Sir *John Baber*,

Doctor *Clark*,

Doctor *Hinton*, assigned to attend upon the Queen.

Physitians in Ordinary to the Houshold.

Doctor *Waldron*.

Doctor *Scarborough* for the *Tower* of *London*. Moreover, there are above a dozen more able Physitians, who are the Kings sworn Servants, but wait not.

Jewel House, Sir *Gilbert Talbot*, Master and Treasurer, and three under Officers, called *Yeomen* and *Grooms*.

Whose Office is to take charge of all Vessels of Gold or Silver gilt for the King and Queens Table, of all Plate in the *Tower*, of Chains and loose Jewels, not fixed to any Garment.

The Master of *Ceremonies*, is Sir *Charles Cotterel*, Fee 200 *l*. One Assistant *Clement Cotterel* Esquire, Fee 120 *l*. and one Marshal.

Amongst His Majesties Servants in Ordinary, are to be reckoned the Three *Kings of Arms*, Six *Heralds*, or *Dukes of Arms*, as they have been heretofore stiled, and Four *Pursuivants at Arms*. The now Kings of of Arms being these: First, Sir *Edward Walker* Knight, whose Title is *Garter*, and unto whose Office, it cheifly belongeth to attend and direct at those Ceremonies and Solemnities, as concern the most Noble Order of the *Garter*; and to Marshal the Solemn Funerals of the Knights of that Order; as also of the Peers of this Realm; and to direct in all things else relating to Arms, which do appertain to the Peerage.

Secondly, Sir *Edward Bish* Knight, whose Title is *Clarenceux*, and his Office cheifly to regulate, and direct the Proceedings at such Solemn Funerals of all degrees, under the Peerage of this Realm, as shall be celebrated in his Province, which is the Counties on the South of *Trent*, and whatsoever else there relateth to Arms.

Thirdly, *William Dugdale* Esquire, whose Title is *Norroy*, and whose Office is chiefly to regulate and direct as aforesaid throughout his Province on the North of *Trent*.

The *Six Heralds, or Dukes at Arms*, are these.

Elias Ashmole, *Windsor Herald*, Esq;
Henry St. George, *Richmond*, Esq;
Thomas Lee, *Chester*, Esq;
Sir *Thomas St. George* Knight, *Somerset*.
John Wingfield, *York*, Esq; And
Robert Chaloner, *Lancaster*, Esq;

The Four *Pursuivants*, are these, *viz.*
Henry Dethick, Rouge-Croix.
Francis Sandford, Rouge-Dragon.

Thomas

Thomas Holford, Portcullice. And
Thomas Segar, Blewmantle.

The Offices of which *Heralds* and *Pursuivants*, besides their Services (*viz.* all or some of them) at great Solemnities, as aforesaid, is, together with the said Kings of Arms, to attend at all Publick Solemnities; and they, or some of them to Proclaim War and Peace, carry Defiances, Summon Fortified Places, or Rebels in Arms, Proclaim Traitors; and to do their best service in whatsoever relateth to the Nobility and Gentry of this Realm, in point of Honor and Arms.

Also amongst *His Majesties Servants in Ordinary*, are reckoned.

One
- *Geographer*, Major *John Scot.*
- *Historiographer.*
- *Hydrographer.*
- *Library Keeper.*
- *Poet Laureat.*
- *Publick Notary.*

Of *Wardrobes*, the King hath (besides the *Great Wardrobe*, whereof a particular account shall be given elswhere) divers standing *Wardrobes* at *Whitehal*, *Windsor*, *Hampton-Court*, the *Tower of London*, *Greenwich*, *&c.* whereof there are divers Officers. Lastly, *Removing Wardrobes*, whereof there is *One Yeoman*, *Two Grooms*, and *Three Pages*.

In the Office of the Tents, Toyls, Hays, and Pavillions. Two Masters, Four Yeomen, One

One Groom, One Clerk Comptroler, One Clerk of the Tents.

A Master of the Revels Office to order all things concerning Comedies, &c. There is One Yeoman, One Groom.

Engraver, Sculptor, One in each Office.

In the Office of the Robes, besides the Master aforementioned, there is One Yeoman, Three Grooms, One Page, Two Purveyors, One Brusher, One Trailor, One Dyer, One Girdler, One Clerk, One Laceman, One Cutter and Racer, Two Embroiderers, Two Silkmen, One Shoomaker, One Perfumer, One Feather-Maker, One Milliner, One Mercer, One Hosier, One Draper, One Surveyor of the Dresser and Chamber, *&c.*

Falconers, Sir *Allen Apsley,* Master of the Hawks, and other Officers under him, about *London,* and other places belonging to the King; in all, Thirty three.

Huntsmen for the Buck-hounds in Ordinary, John Carey Esquire, Master of the *Buck-hounds,* and under him a Sergeant, and Thirty four other persons.

Otter-hounds, Simon Smith Esquire, Master of the *Otter-hounds.*

Huntsmen for the Harriers, Master of the Harriers, Mr. *Elliot,* and five under him.

Armory at the Tower, Master of the Ordnance, now in several Commissioners, *William Legg* Lieutenant of the Ordnance, and Master Armorer, and Seventeen under Officers.

Messengers of the Chamber in Ordinary, First two Clerks of the Check, then Forty more; in all, Forty two.

Musitians

Musitians in Ordinary, Sixty two.

Trumpetters in Ordinary, *and Kettle-Drummers*; are in all, Fifteen.

Drummers and Fifes, Seven.

Apothecaries Two. One for the Kings Person, and one for the Houshold.

Chirurgeons Five.

Barbers Two.

Printers Two. Another for the Oriental Tongue.

Book-binder One.

Taylors Two.

Stationers Two.

Post-Masters for all the Post-Towns in *England*, All sworn to, and paid by the King.

A Master of the Game of *Cock-fighting*.

Two Sergeant Skinners, Two Embroiderers.

Two Keepers of the Privy Lodgings.

Two Gentlemen, and one Yeoman of the Bows.

One Cross-bow-Maker, one Fletcher.

One Cormorant Keeper.

One Hand-Gun-Maker.

One Master and Marker of Tennis.

One Mistress-Sempstress, and one Laundress.

One {
Perspective-Maker.
Master Fencer.
Haberdasher of Hats.
Comb-Maker.
Coffee-Maker.
Sergeant Painter.
Painter.
Limner.
}

One

One { Picture Keeper. Silver-Smith. Goldsmith. Jeweller. Perruque-Maker.

One Keeper of Phesants and Turkies.

Joyner, Copier of Pictures, Watch-Maker, Cabinet-Maker, Lock-Smith, of each one.

Game of the Bears and Bulls, One Master, one Sergeant one Yeoman.

Operators for the Teeth, Two.

Coffer-Bearers to the Back-Stairs, Two.

One Yeoman of the *Leash*.

Watermen, Fifty five.

Upholster, Letter-Carrier, Foreign Post, of each one.

Officers belonging to Gardens, Bowling-Greens, Tennis-Courts, Pall-Mall, Ten persons.

Keeper of the Theater in *Whitehal*.

Cutler, Spurrier, Girdler, Corn-Cutter, Button-Maker, one of each.

Embosser, Enameler, of each one.

Writer, Flourisher, and Embellisher, Scenographer, or Designer of Prospects, Letter-Founder, Geographer, of each one.

Comedians, Seventeen Men, and Eight Women Actors.

Gunner, Gilder, Cleanser of Pictures, Scene-keeper, Coffer-maker, Wax-Chandler, one of each.

Keeper of Birds and Fowl in S. *James's Park*, One.

Keeper of the Volery, Goffe-Club-Maker, Serjeant Painter, one for each.

With

With divers other Officers and Servants under the Lord Chamberlain; to serve His Majesty upon Extraordinary occasions and services.

Note that many of these Offices and Places are of good Credit, great Profit, and enjoyed by Persons of quality, although not here named for want of good information.

A List of His Majesties Officers and Servants under the Master of the Horse.

FIrst are 12 *Querries*, so called from the French word *Escuyer*, derived from *Escurie* a *Stable*. Their Office is to attend the King on Hunting on Progress, or on any occasion of riding abroad, to help His Majesty up and down from his Horse, &c.

Of these there are 4 called *Querries* of the *Crown Stable*, viz.

Sir *William Armorer*.
Captain *John Mazine* Esquire.
James Porter Esquire.
John Mazine Jun. Esquire.

The other 8 are called *Querries* of the *Hunting Stable*, viz.

Andrew Cole Esquire.
Sir *Charles Alderlee* Knight.

Thomas

Thomas Windham Esquire.
Sir *Nicholas Armorer* Knight.
Henry Progers Esquire.
Sir *Robert Pye*, Knight.
Wakelife Esquire.
Walter Strickland Esquire.

The Fee to each of these is onely 20 *l.* yearly, according to the antient Custom, but they have allowance for Diet to each 100 *l* yearly, besides Lodgings and two Horse Liveries.

Next is the *Chief Avener*, from *Avena Oates*; whose yearly Fee is 40 *l.* and this place with all the following, are in the Gift of the *Master of the Horse.* This Office at present hath *Richard Mason* Esquire.

There is moreover one Clerk of the *Stable*, *William Morgan* Esquire, 4 Yeomen Riders, 4 Child Riders, Yeomen of the Stirrup, Sergeant Marshal and Yeomen Farriers, 4 Groom Farriers, Sergeant of the Carriage, 3 Surveyors, a Squire and Yeoman Sadlers, 4 Yeomen Granators, 4 Yeomen Purveyors, a Yeoman Peckman, a Yeoman Bit-maker, 4 Coachmen, 8 Littermen, a Yeoman of the Close Waggon, 64 Grooms of the Stable, whereof 30 are called Grooms of the *Crown Stable*, and 34 of the *Hunting* and *Pad Stable*, 26 Footmen in their Liveries to run by the Kings Horse.

There is (besides some other Officers not here

here named) an Ancient Officer in the Kings Houshold, called *Clerk of the Mercat*, who within the Verge of the Kings Houshold is to keep a Standard of all Weights and Measures, and to burn all false Weights and Measures; and from the Pattern of this Standard are to be taken all the Weights and Measures of the Kingdom.

There are divers other Offices belonging to the King of great importance, which are not subordinate to any of the 3 fore-mentioned Great-Officers, as *Master of the Great Wardrobe*, *Postmaster*, *Master of the Ordnance*, *Warden of the Mint*; whereof in the Second part of the *Present State*.

In the Court of King *James* there were many more Offices, and to many Offices there belonged many more persons, which King *Charles the First* much lessened, and the present King now Raigning hath yet lessened much more.

Upon the King are also attending in his Court the Lords of His Privy Council, the Reverend Judges, the Learned Colledge of Civilians, the Kings Council at Law, the Kings Sergeants at Law, the Masters of Requests, Secretaries of State, Clerks of the Signet, Clerks of the Council, Keeper of the Paper Office or Papers of State.

The

The Names of the Lords of His Majesties Most Honourable Privy Council.

His Royal Highness the Duke of *York*.
His Highness *Prince Rupert*.
Gilbert Lord Archbishop of *Canterbury*.
Sir *Orlando Bridgman*, Lord Keeper of the Great Seal.
John Lord *Roberts* Lord Privy Seal.
George Duke of *Buckingham*, Master of the Horse to His Majesty.
James Duke of *Ormond*, Lord Great Steward of His Majesties Houshold.
William Cavendish, Duke of *Newcastle*.
Henry Lord Marquis of *Dorchester*.
Awbrey Earl of *Oxford*.
James Earl of *Ossory*.
Robert Earl of *Lindsey* Lord Great Chamberlain of *England*.
Edward Earl of *Manchester*, Lord Chamberlain to His Majesty.
John Earl of *Bridgewater*.
Robert Earl of *Leicester*.
Henry Earl of St. *Albans*.
Edward Earl of *Sandwich*.
John Earl of *Bath*, Groom of the Stole to His Majesty.
Arthur Earl of *Anglesey*.
Charles Earl of *Carlisle*.

William

William Earl of *Craven*.

Jo. Earl of *Rothes*, His Majesties Commissioner in *Scotland*.

Jo. Earl of *Lotherdaile*, Secretarie of State in *Scotland*.

Jo. Earl of *Middleton*.

John Earl of *Tweedale*.

Richard Earl of *Carbery*, Lord President of *Wales*.

Roger Earl of *Orrery*.

Humphrey Lord Bishop of *London*.

Henry Lord *Arlington*, one of His Majesties Principal Secretaries of State.

Francis Lord *Newport*, Comptroler of His Majesties Houshold.

Densel Lord *Holles*,

John Lord *Berkeley*.

Anthony Lord *Ashley*, Chancellour of the Exchequer.

Sir *Thomas Clifford* Knight, Treasurer of His Majesties Houshold.

Sir *George Carteret* Knight, Vice-Chamberlain to His Majesty.

Sir *John Trevor* Knight, one of His Majesties Principal Secretaries of State.

Sir *Thomas Ingram* Knight, Chancellour of the *Dutchy*.

Sir *William Morice* Knight.

Sir *John Duncom* Knight.

Sir *Thomas Chichly*.

The Names of all the Kings Judges, the Kings Councel at Law, and the Kings Sergeants at Law, &c.

IN the High Court of *Chancery.*

The Right Honourable Sir *Orlando Bridgeman* Knight and Baronet; Lord-Keeper of the Great Seal, with whom sits as Assistants,

Sir *Harbottle Grimston* Baronet, Master of the Rolls.

Sir *William Child* Knight, Doctor of Laws.

Sir *Justinian Lewin* Knight, Doctor of Laws.

Sir *Thomas Estcourt* Knight.

Sir *Mundiford Brampstone* Knight, Doctor of Laws.

Sir *Nathaniel Hobart* Knight.

Sir *William Glascock* Knight.

Sir *John Coel* Knight.

Sir *Robert Steward* Knight.

Sir *Timothy Baldwin* Knight, Doctor of Laws.

Sir *Andrew Hacket* Knight.

Sir *William Beversham* Knight.

These twelve are called Masters of *Chancery.*

In the Court of the Kings Bench.

Sir *John Keeling* Lord Chief Justice of the Kings Bench.

Sir *Thomas Twisden* Knight and Baronet.

Sir *William Morton* Knight.
Sir *Richard Rainsford* Knight.

In the Court of the Common Pleas.

Sir *John Vaughan* Knight, Lord Chief Justice of the *Common Pleas*.
Sir *Thomas Tirrel* Knight.
Sir *John Archer* Knight.
Sir *William Wilde* Knight and Baronet.

In the Court of the Exchequer.

Sir *Matthew Hale* Knight, Lord Chief Baron of the Exchequer.
Sir *Christopher Turner* Knight.
Sir *Timothy Littleton* Knight.
Clement Spelman Esq;

These are all the Principal Judges in *England*, who to the Kings High Honour and His Kingdoms great happiness are persons for Knowledge, Courage, Uncorruptness, &c. equal if not superiour to any other in former Kings Raigns.

The Kings Sergeants and Learned Council at Law.

Sir *John Maynard* Knight, the Kings Sergeant at Law.
Sir *Heneage Finch* Knight and Baronet; the Kings Attorney General.
Sir *Edward Turner* Knight and Baronet, the Kings sollicitor General.
Sir *Job Charleton* Knight, Chief Justice of *Chester*, His Majesties Sergeant at Law.

Sir

Sir *William Scroggs* Knight, His Majesties Sergeant at Law.

Sir *Edward Thurland* Knight, His Majesties Councel, learned in the Law.

Mr. *North*, Son to the Lord *North*, His Majesties Councel, learned in the Law.

Robert Milward Esquire, His Majesties Justice at *Chester*, and Councel learned in the Law.

The Queen Consorts Councel at Law.

Mr. *Montague* the Queens Attorney General.

Sir *Robert Atkins* Knight of the *Bath*, the Queens Sollicitor General.

Sir *Frederick Hyde* Knight, Her Majesties Sergeant at Law.

The Queen Mothers Councel was

Sir *Peter Ball* Knight, Attorney.

Henry Win Sollicitor.

The Duke of York's *Councel.*

Sir *Edward Thurland* Attorney.

Sir *Francis Goodrick* Sollicitor.

Sergeants, at Law.

Sergeant.
- *Nudigate.*
- *Windham.*
- *Fountain.*
- *Seys.*
- *Waller.*
- *Brome.*
- *Tournour.*
- *Ellys.*
- *Hardres.*
- *Wilmott.*
- *Goddard.*
- Sir *Rich. Hopkins* Kt.
- *Flynt.*
- *Turner.*
- *Barton.*
- Sir *John Howel* Knight.
- Recorder of *London.*
- *Bramstone*
- Sir *Henry Peckham* Kt.
- *Goodfellow.*
- *Baldwin.*
- *Powys.*
- *Jones.*

The Chief Judges and Doctors of the Civil Law.

Sir *Giles Sweit* Judge of the Arches, Knight Doctor of Laws.

Sir *Lionel Jenkins* Knight Doctor of Laws, Judge both of the Prerogative Court and of the Admiralty.

[illegible] *Robert Wiseman* the Kings *Advocate*; Knight, Doctor of Laws. Sir

Sir *Richard Chaworth* Knight, Doctor of Laws, Advocate to the Lord High Admiral.

Sir *Walter Walker* Knight, Doctor of Laws.

John Milles Doctor of Laws.

Sir *Timothy Baldwin* Knight, Doctor of Laws.

Thomas Exton Doctor of Laws, Chancellour to the Lord Bishop of *London.*

John Clark Doctor of Laws, His Majesties Professor of Law in *Cambridge.*

The present Secretaries of State are,

Henry Lord *Arlington*, whom for his eminent services at home and abroad, both in War and Peace, His Majesty was pleased to advance into the place of Sir *Edward Nicolas.*

And Sir *John Trevor*, who for his great abilities and succesful Negotiations had that honour and trust conferred upon him, when Sir *William Morice*, late Secretarie of State, was by His Majesties gracious consent permitted to retire from business.

The King hath four Masters of Requests, *who are at present,*

Colonel *Gervase Holles.*
Sir *Thomas Beverley.*
Sir *John Berkenhead.*
Sir *Charles Cotterel.*

Clerks of the Council are,

Sir *Richard Brown.*
Sir *Edward Walker.*
Sir *John Nicolas.*
Sir *Robert Southwell.*

Clerks of the Signet are,

Sir *Philip Warwick.*
Sir *John Nicholas.*
Sidney Beare Esquire.
Trumbal Esquire.

The Keeper of the *Paper Office*, or Papers of State at *Whitehal*, is that most ingenious and worthy person *Joseph Williamson* Doctor of Laws.

Of the Military Government *in the* Kings Court.

AS in a Kingdom, because Civil Governours proposing Temporal, and Ecclesiastical Governours Eternal Rewards and Punishments, are not sufficient to secure Peace; therefore a Military force is always in readiness: So in the Kings Court besides Civil and Ecclesiastical Officers, it is thought necessary alwayes to have in readiness Military Officers and Soldiers, to preserve the Kings Person; whereupon depends the Peace and Safety of all his Subjects. Be-

Belonging peculiarly to the Kings Court (besides above 4000 Foot, and above 500 Horse, who are always in Pay and readiness to assist upon any occasion) there are Guards of Horse and Foot.

The *Horse-Guard*, which the French call *Garde du Corps*, the Germains *Lieb Guardy*, we corruptly *Life Guard*, that is, *the Guard of the Kings Body*, hath consisted of 500 Horsemen, all or most Gentlemen and old Officers, commanded by the Captain of the Guard, now *James* Duke of *Monmouth*, whose Pay is 30 *s.* a day, and each Horseman 4 *s.* a day. The e Horse have been divided into Three parts, whereof 200 under the immediate Command of the Captain of the Guard, 150 under Monsieur *le Marquis de Blanford*, and 150 under Sir *Philip Howard*, whose Pay to each is 20 *s.* a day.

Under the Captain of the Guard are now onely two Liestenants, Sir *Thomas Sandis*, and Major General *Egerton*; the Coronet is Mr. *Villars* Son to the Lord *Grandison*, also a Quartermaster and four Brigadeers.

The Office of the Captain of the Life Guard is at all times of War or Peace to wait upon the Kings Person (as oft as he rides abroad) with a considerable number of Horsemen well armed and prepared against all dangers whatsoever?

At home within the Kings House it is thought fit that the Kings Person should have a Guard both above and below Stairs,

In the *Presence Chamber* therefore wait the Honourable Band of *Gentlemen Pensioners*, first instituted by King *Henry* 7. and chosen usually in all times since out of the best and most antient Families of *England*, not only for a faithful Guard to the Kings Person, but to be as a Nursery to breed up hopeful Gentlemen, and fit them for employments both Civil and Military, as well abroad as at home, as Deputies of *Ireland*, Ambassadours in Foreign Parts, Counsellors of Estate, Captains of the Guard, Governours of Places, and Commanders in the Wars both by Land and Sea; of all which there have been examples, as *George* Lord *Hunson* Captain of the Pensioners at the death of Queen *Elizabeth*, intimated in a Letter to King *James* before he came into *England*.

Their Office is to attend the Kings Person to and from his Chappel, only as far as the Privy Chamber; also in all other Solemnities, as *Coronations*, *Publick Audience of Ambassadours*; &c. They are 50 in number, over whom there is a Captain, usually some Peer of the Realm; a Lieutenant, a Standard-Bearer, and a Clerk of the *Checque*, who are at present as followeth:

The Band of Gentlemen Pensioners.

John Lord *Belasys* Captain 360 *l.*
Sir *John Bennet* Knight of the *Bath*, Lieutenant 260 *l.* yearly.

Sir

Sir John Walpoole Knight, *Standard*-Bearer 200 *l.* yearly.

Tho. Wynne Esquire, Clerk of the *Check* 119 *l.* 1 *s.* 3 *d.* yearly.

John Dingley Esquire.
Edward Harbert Esquire.
Thomas Hayles Esquire.
William Sheldon Esquire.
Sir *Thomas Rowe* Knight.
Edward Brooks Esquire.
Sir *Reginald Foster* Baronet.
Richard Harrison Esquire
John Rootes Esquire.
Sir *George Courthop* Knight.
Sir *Philip Honywood* Knight.
Sir *Richard Hatton* Knight.
Sir *Edward Alston* Knight.
Charles Skrimsher Esquire.
William Cowper Esquire.
Seafoule Gibson Esquire.
Sir *George Tash* Knight.
Charles Crompton Esquire.
John Raymond Esquire.
Sir *Edmund Barker* Knight.
Harbert Palmer Esquire.
Roger Coleman Esquire.
Anthony Gawdy Esquire.
Edward Coleman Esquire.
Fleetwood Dormer Esquire.
Brett Norton Esquire.
Sir *John Rea* Knight.
William Dikenson Esquire.
Allington Paineter Esquire.
John Freeman Esquire.
Hugh Tente Esquire.

John Kirke Esquire.
Brooke Estwicke Esquire.
Edward Alston Esquire.
Richard Fifield Esquire.
George Farrington Esquire.
Sir Thomas Gery Knight.
Walter Rea Esquire.
William Forde Esquire.
Thomas Eyre Esquire.
Edward Games Esquire.
John Kirke Junior Esquire.
Richard Wigmore Esquire.
Robert Dacres Esquire.
Charles Radley Esquire.
Thomas Shotterden Esquire.
Roger Conysby Esquire.
Edward Cowper Esquire.
William Fairfaix Esquire.

The Fee to each of these is 100 *l.* yearly.

Richard Child Gentleman Harbinger to provide Lodgings for them, his Fee 70 *l.* 11 *s.*

Ordinarily wait only one half of this Band, and by Quarter.

Upon extraordinary occasions all of them are summoned.

Their ordinary Arms are Gilt Pole-axes.

Their Arms on Horsback in time of War, are Curassiers Arms with Sword and Pistol.

The Band of Pensioners is not under the Lord Chamberlain, but only under their own Officers, and are usually sworn by

the

the Clerk of the *Cheque*; whose Office is to take notice of those that are absent when they should be upon their duty.

Their Standard born in time of War is, *A Cross Gules in a Field Argent*, also 4 *Bends*.

Again, In the first Room above Stairs, called the *Guard Chamber*, attend the Yeomen of the Guard of His Majesties Body; whereof there were wont to be 250 men of the best quality under Gentry, and of larger stature than ordinary (for every one of them was to be 6 foot high.) There are at present 100 Yeomen in daily waiting, and 70 more not in waiting, and as any of the 100 shall die, his place to be filled up out of the 70. These wear Scarlet Coats down to the Knee, and Scarlet Breeches, both richly guarded with Black Velvet and rich Badges upon their Coats before and behind. Moreover Black Velvet round broad-crownd Caps (according to the mode used in the Reign of *Henry* 8.) with Ribbons of the Kings colour. One half of them of late bear in their hands Harquebuzes and the other half Partisans, with large swords by their sides. They have Wages and Diet allowed them. Their Office is to wait upon the King in his standing Houses, 40 by day, and 20 to watch by night; and about the City to wait on the *Kings* person abroad by Water or Land.

The Captain of this Guard is at present *George* Lord Vicount *Grandison*, whose Fee is 1000 *l.* yearly. Lieu-

Lieutenant is Coll. *Thomas Howard*; Fee 500 *l.*

Ensigne *Edward Sackvile* Esquire, Fee 300 *l.*

Clerk of the Cheque *Richard Smith*; Fee 150 *l.*

Four Corporals, Fee to each 150.

The Kings Palace Royal (*ratione Regia Dignitatis*) is exempted from all Jurisdiction of any Court Civil or Ecclesiastical, but onely to the Lord Steward, and in his absence to the Treasurer and Comptroler of the Kings Houshold, with the Steward of the *Marshalsey*, who may by vertue of their Office, without Commission hear and determine all Treasons, Felonies, Breaches of the Peace, committed within the Kings Court or Palace. The most excellent Orders and Rules for the demeanour and carriage of all Officers and Servants in the Kings Court are to be seen in several Tables hung up in several Rooms at the Court, and signed with the Kings own hand, and worthy to be read of all Strangers.

The Kings Court or House where the King resideth, is accounted a place so sacred, that if any man presume to strike another within the Palace where the Kings Royal Person resideth, and by such stroke only draw blood, his right hand shall be stricken off, and he committed to perpetual prison and fined. By the Antient Laws of *England* only striking in the Kings Court was punisht with death and loss of goods.

To

To make the deeper impreſſion and terrour into mens minds for ſtriking in the Kings Court, it hath been ordered that the puniſhment for ſtriking ſhould be executed with great Solemnity and Ceremony, in brief thus:

The Sergeant of the Kings Wood-yard brings to the place of execution a ſquare Block, a Beetle, Staple, and Cords to faſten the hand thereto, the Yeoman of the Scullery provides a great fire of Coals by the Block, wherein the Searing Irons brought by the Chief Farrier, are to be ready for the Chief Surgeon to uſe. Vinegar and Cold Water brought by the Groom of the Saucery; the Chief Officers alſo of the Cellar and Pantry are to be ready, one with a Cup of Red Wine, and the other with a Manchet, to offer the Criminal after the Hand cut off and the ſtump ſeared; the Sergeant of the Ewry is to bring Linnen to wind about and wrap the Arm. The Yeoman of the Poultry a Cock to lay to it, the Yeoman of the Chandry ſeared Clothes, the Maſter Cook a ſharp Dreſſer Knife, which at the place of execution is to be held upright by the Sergeant of the Larder, till Execution be performed by an Officer appointed thereto, *&c.* After all he ſhall be impriſoned during life, and Fine and Ranſome at the Kings Will.

In the Kings Court not only ſtriking is forbidden, but alſo all occaſions of ſtriking, and therefore the Law ſaith, *Nullas*

Citationes

Citationes aut summonitiones licet facere infra Palatium Regis apud Westm. vel alibi ubi Rex residet.

The Court of the King of *England* for Magnificence, for Order, for Number and Quality of Officers, for rich Furniture, for Entertainment and Civility to strangers, for plentiful Tables; might compare with the best Court of *Christendom*, and far excel the most Courts abroad; of one whereof see the Description made by an ingenious Person beyond Sea, writing to a Friend of his at Court there, *Annon in inferno es Amice, qui es in Aulâ ubi Dæmonum habitatio est, qui illic suis artibus, (humana licet effigie) regnant, atque ubi Scelerum Schola est, & Animarum jactura ingens, ac quicquid uspiam est perfidiæ ac doli, quicquid crudelitatis ac inclementiæ, quicquid effrænatæ superbiæ & rapacis avaritiæ, quicquid obscenæ libidinis ac fœdissimæ impudicitiæ, quicquid nefandæ impietatis & morum pessimorum, totum illic acervatur cumulatissime, ubi stupra, raptus, incestus, adulteria; ubi inebriari, jurare, pejerare, Atheismum profiteri palam principum & nobilium ludi sunt, ubi fastus & tumor, ira, Livor, fœdaque cupido cum sociis suis imperare videtur, ubi criminum omnium procella, virtutumque omnium inenarrabile naufragium,* &c.

But the Court of *England* on the contrary hath been (and is hoped ever will be) accounted (as King *James* adviseth in his *Basilicon Doron*) a *Pattern of Godli-*

nes*s*

ness and all *Honesty* and *Vertue*; and the properest School of *Prowess* and *Heroick Deameanour*, and the fittest Place of *Education* for the *Nobility and Gentry*.

The Court of *England* hath for a long time been a *Pattern* of *Hospitallity* to the *Nobility* and *Gentry* of *England*. All Noblemen or Gentlemen, Subjects or Strangers that came accidentally to Court, were freely entertained at the plentiful Tables of His Majesties Officers. Divers Services or Messes of Meat were every day provided Extraordinary for the Kings Honour. Two hundred and forty Gallons of Beer a day were at the Buttry Barr allowed for the Poor, besides all the broken Meat, Bread, *&c.* gathered into Baskets and given to the Poor at the Court Gates by two Grooms and two Yeomen of the Almonry, who have Salaries of His Majesty for that Service.

The Magnificent and abundant plenty of the Kings Tables hath caused amazement in Forreigners, when they have been informed that in the last Kings Reign before the troubles, there were daily in his Court 86 Tables well furnisht each Meal, whereof the Kings Table had 28 Dishes, the Queens 24; Four other Tables 16 Dishes each; Three other 10 Dishes each; Twelve other had 7 Dishes each; Seventeen other Tables had each of them 5 Dishes; Three other had 4 each; Thirty two other Tables had each 3 Dishes, and Thirteen other had each 2 Dishes: In all about Five hundred

Dishes

Dishes each Meal, with Bread, Beer, Wine, and all other things necessary. All which was provided most by the several Purveyors, who by Commissions legally and regularly authorised, did receive those Provisions at a moderate price, such as had been formerly agreed upon in the several Counties of *England*, which price (by reason of the value of Money, much altered) was become low, yet a very inconsiderable burthen to the Kingdom in General, but thereby was greatly supported the Dignity Royal in the eyes of Strangers as well as Subjects. The English Nobility and Gentry, according to the Kings Example were incited to keep a proportionable Hospitality in their several Country Mansions, the Husbandman encouraged to breed Cattel, all Tradesmen to a cheerful industry, and there was then a free Circulation of Moneys through the whole body of the Kingdome. There was spent yearly in the Kings house of gross Meat 1500 Oxen, 7000 Sheep, 1200 Veals, 300 Porkers, 400 Sturks or young Beefs, 6800 Lambs, 300 Flitches of Bacon, and 26 Boars: Also 140 dozen of Geese, 250 dozen of Capons, 470 dozen of Hens, 750 dozen of Pullets, 1470 dozen of Chicken. For Bread 36400 Bushels of Wheat, and for Drink 600 Tun of Wine, and 1700 Tun of Beer. Moreover of Butter 46640 pounds, together with Fish and Fowl, Venison, Fruit, Spice, proportionable. This prodigious plenty in the Kings Court, caused Forreigners

reigners to put a higher value upon the King, and caused the Natives who were there freely welcome (for by order of the Kings house, some of his Officers went daily to *Westminster-Hall* in Term time, between Eleven and Twelve a Clock, to invite Gentlemen to eat of the Kings *Acates*, and in Parliament time to invite the Parliament men) to increase their affection to the King, it being found as necessary for the King of *England* this way to endear the English, who ever delighted in Feasting; as for the Italian Princes by sights and shews to endear their Subjects who as much delight therein.

Moreover the Court is an eminent *Pattern* of *Charity* and *Humility* to all that shall see the performance of that antient Custom by the King and the Queen, on the Thursday before *Easter*, called *Maunday Thursday*, wherein the King in a solemn manner doth wash the Feet, cloath and feed as many poor old men as His Majesty is years old, bestowing on every one Cloth for a Gown, Linnen for a Shirt, Shooes and Stockings, a Joul of Salmon, a Poll of Ling, 30 Red and 30 White Herrings, all in clean Wooden Dishes, 4 Six penny Loaves of Bread, and a Purse with a 20*s*. piece of Gold.

The Queen also doth the like to divers poor women.

CHAP.

CHAP. XIV.

Of the Queen Consorts *Court.*

THe Queens Court, sutable to the *Consort* of so great a King, is Splendid and Magnificent.

Her Majesty hath all Officers and a Houshold apart from the King; for the maintenance whereof there is setled 40000 *l. per annum.*

For the Ecclesiastique Government of her Court, there is first the *Grand Almoner*, Lord *Philip Howard*, Brother to the Duke of *Norfolk*.

He hath the superintendency over all the Ecclesiastiques belonging to the Queen.

Father *Antonio Fernandez* is Her Majesties Confessor.

Bishop *Russel* Almoner.

Father *Patrick* Almoner.

Father *Paul de Almeida* Almon.

Father *Manoel Pereira* Alm.

Doctor *Thomas Godden* Treasurers of the Chappel.

2 Other Preachers Portuguez, Father Master *Christopher del Rosario* a Dominican; and Father *Antonio* a Franciscan.

5 Clerks of the Chappel.

6 English Fathers Benedictins, Chaplains.

11 Franciscan Friers, Chaplains.

Divers Persons belonging to the Musick of the Chappel; to serve at the Altars, two Porters, *&c.*

For

For the Civil Government of her Majesties Court, there is a Council consisting of Persons of great worth and dignity.

Lord Keeper.
Earl of *Manchester.*
Earl of *Chesterfield.*
Earl of *Sandwich.*
Lord *Holles* Steward of the Revenue.
Lord Vicount *Brounker* Chancellor and Keeper of her Majesties Great Seal.
Lord Vicount *Cornbury* Chamberlain.
Lord *Arlington.*
Lord *Ashley.*
Lord *Baltamore.*
Sir *Thomas Clifford.*
Sir *John Trevor.*
Sir *Thomas Ingram.*
Sir *John Duncomb.*
Ralph Montague Esquire, Master of the Horse.
George Montague Esquire.
Sir *William Killegrew* Knight, Vicechamberlain.
Sir *Heneage Finch.*
Sir *Richard Bellings* Principal Secretary and Master of Requests.
John Harvey Esquire, Treasurer and Receiver General.
William Montague Esquier, Attorney General.
Sir *Robert Long* Knight and Baronet.
Sir *Charles Harbert.*

Sir

Sir Henry Wood.
Sir Robert Atkins Knight of the *Bath*, Sollicitor General.
Sir John Arundel Knight.
John Hall Esquire, Surveyour General.
Francis Slingsby Esquire.
Henry Slingsby Esquire.

Gentlemen Ushers of the Privy-Chamber.

Sir Hugh Chomley Baronet.
George Porter Esquire.
Alexander Stanhope Esquire.
Francis Roper, Esquire.
John Hall, Esquire.

Cup-bearers.

Sir Nicholas Slaning Knight of the *Bath*.
Henry Guy Esquire.

Carvers.

Sir Gabriel de Sylviis Knight.
Sir John Elwes Knight.

Sewers.

Sir Charles Windham, Knight.
John Griffith Esquire.

Five Gentlemen Ushers daily waiters.

Ten Grooms of the Privy-Chamber.

Seven Gentlemen Ushers, Quarter-waiters.

Apothe-

Apothecary, Chirurgeon.

Six pages of the Bed-Chamber attending at the Back-Stairs.

Four Pages of the Presence.

Officers belonging to the Robes.

A Surveyor, Proveditor, Clerk, Yeoman, Groom, Page, Taylor, and Brusher.

Twelve Grooms of the Great Chamber.

One Porter of the Back-Stairs.

A Master of the Queens Barge, and 24 Watermen.

Groom of the *Stole*, Lady of the Robes and of the Privy-Purse, is the Countess of *Suffolk*.

Seven other Ladies of the Bed-Chamber, *viz*. Dutchess of *Buckingham*, Dutchess Dowager of *Richmond*, Countess of *Bath*, Countess of *Castlemain*, Countess of *Falmouth*, Lady *Marshal* and Lady *Gerard*.

Mrs *Charlotte Killegrew* Keeper of the Sweet Coffers.

Six Maids of Honour.

These are to be all Gentlewomen unmarried, over whom is placed a Governess called the Mother of the Maids; who is the Lady *Sanderson*.

There are also 6 Chambriers or Dressers.

Lady

Lady *Scroop*, who is also Madam Nurse; Lady *Killegrew*, Lady *Frascr*, Lady *de Sylviis*, Mrs *Thornhil*, and Lady *Clinton*.

A Laundress, a Semstress, a Starcher, a Necessary Woman.

These are all paid by Her Majesty, out of Her own Revenue.

There are besides divers Officers below Stairs and belonging to Her Majesties Table and Stable paid by the King, for which there is allowed Twenty thousand pounds more.

CHAP. XV.

Of the Queen Mothers *Court*.

THe Highest Office in Her Majesties Court was that of Lord Chamberlain and Steward of her Majesties Revenue, lately enjoyed by *Henry* Lord *Germain* Earl of St. *Albans*, whose Salary was and a Table of Dishes.

Monsieur *Vantelet* Vice-Chamberlain, whose salary was 200 *l. per annum*.

The third place was her Majesties Chancellour, enjoyed by Sir *J. Winter*, Sir *Henry Wood*, and Sir *Robert Long*; whose salary was and a Table of Dishes.

The

The next was the Lord *Arundel* of *Warder*, and the Count of the Empire, Master of the Horse, whose salary was

Then her Majesties Secretary *Sir John Winter*.

The Treasurer, Receiver General of Her Majesties Revenues, *Sir Henry Wood*.

Sir *Thomas Bond* Comptroler of the Houshold, whose salary was

Sir Thomas Ork and divers other Officer of the Robes.

Four Gentlemen Ushers of the Privy Chambers, to each of which was 130 *l.* salary *per annum*. and Diet.

Two Cup bearers, two Carvers, two Sewers, two Gentlemen Ushers of the Presence Chamber, Salary to each 120 *l.* and diet all these at a table together.

Four Grooms of the Privy Chamber; salary 60 *l.* and diet.

Four Gentlemen Ushers Quarter Waiters, salary 60 *l.* and diet.

Four Pages of the Presence.

Eight Grooms of the Great Chamber.

For Guarding Her Majesties Person, she had first a Captain of her Guard, the Earl of *St. Albans*.

A Lieutenant, Monsieur *de la Chapelle*.

An Exempt of the Guards, Monsieur *Fremon*.

24 Gentlemen Soldiers in Black Velvet Cassocks and Golden embroidered Badges, marching or waiting about the Person of Her Majesty (when in Sedan, or at Chap-

pel

pel or Table, or Coach with two Horses) on foot with Halberts; and when in Coach and 6 Horses, on Horseback with Carabins; in all places within doors as without, covered.

For to take care of Her Majesties Health, There was one Physitian and one Apothecary.

For to wait on Her Majesty in her Bed-Chamber, There were first the Ladies of the Bed Chamber; the chief whereof was,

The Dutchess Dowager of *Richmond*, Sister to the present Duke of *Buckingham*, who was Groom of the Stole.

And the Countess of *Newport* Lady of the Chamber.

Of the Privy Chamber there were 4 Ladies all English, Fee 150 *l.* each one; they lately were the Lady *Price*, the Lady *Bond*, &c.

Women of the Bed-Chamber 8 or 9, partly French, and partly English.

In the Laundry, The Lady *Sanderson* was the Chief Laundress.

1 Seamstress.

1 Starcher.

In the Stable, the Chief *Query* or *Escuyer* was Sir *Edward Wingfield*.

The many Officers in the Buttry, Cellar, Pantry,

Pantry, Ewry, *&c.* shall be for brevity passed over.

Her Majesty had also four Coaches with 6 Horses each, also 12 Footmen, a Barge with 12 men in Liveries: Moreover Pages of the Back Stairs 4, *&c.*

In the Chappel.

There was first the Lord Almoner Abbot *Montague*, 800 *l.* *per annum.*

Father *Lambart* Confessor to her Majesty, a Frenchman, 300 *l. per annum.*

Father *Gough* Priest of the Oratory; Clerk of Her Majesties private Chappel, and Assistant to the Confessor an Englishman, 200 *l. per annum.*

A Lay Brother of the Oratory, 40. *l.*

Besides these, there was adjoyning to the Chappel a Convent of Capuchins, wherein was a Father Guardian, 7 other Priests and two Lay Brothers all French; whose Office was to perform the Office of the Chappel daily, also to Preach on Sundayes and Holy-dayes, and in *Lent* three dayes every week; for the maintenance of these Her Majesty allowed 500 *l. per annum.*

Her Majesties Revenue was for her Joynture 30000 *l.* yearly, and of His Majesty a Pension of 30000 *l.* more out of the *Exchequer.*

Divers other Offices belonging to Her Majesties Court, as Master of Buck-Hounds, and Bows and Musick.

Master of the Queens Games.

CHAP. XVI.

Of the Duke *of* York's *Court.*

GEntleman of the Bed-Chamber and Groom of the *Stole* the Earl of *Peterborough.*

Gentleman of the Bed-Chamber, the Lord *Hawley.*

Treasurer of the Houshold, Sir *Alan Apsly*, his Fee 400 Marks, or *266 l.* 13 *s.* 4 *d.*

Comptroller, Sir *Jonathan Trelany* 266*l.* 13 *s.* 4 *d.*

Secretary, *Matthew Wren* Esquire, 200 *l.*

Keeper of the Privy Purse, Marquis *de Blanquefort*, 100 *l.*

Master of the Robes and Groom of the Bed-Chamber, *Edward Villiers* Esquire, 266 *l.* 13 *s.* 4 *d.*

Six other Grooms of the Bed-Chamber.

Richard Nicols, *Robert Worden,* *Richard Talbott,* *Henry Savile,* *Roger Vaughan,* *Henry Howard,* *Thomas Thynn*, late Envoye Extraordinary in *Swethland.*	each 200 *l.*

Belonging to His Royal Highness Chappel.

Almoner Doctor *Henry Killigrew*; 100 *l.*

Five Chaplains.

Dr. *William Clark.*
Dr. *William Thomas,*
Dr. *Richard Watson,*
Dr. *Turner,*
Mr. *Doughty*, 50 *l.*

Chaplain to his Royal Highness as Lord High Admiral *Mr Woodroof.*

Sacristan, 40 *l.*

Keeper of the Closet, 40 *l.*

Gentleman-Usher, 80 *l.*

Four Gentlemen-Waiters, each 40 *l.*

Yeoman of the Robes, Mr. *Lawrence du Puy*, 60 *l.*

Brusher, 40 *l.*

Yeoman of the Wardrobe, *Philip Kin-nersly*, 80 *l.*

Two Barbers, each 80 *l.*

Four Pages of the Back-Stairs; each 80 *l.*

One Groom of the Privy-Chamber,

One Groom of the Presence,

A Fire-maker in the Presence,

One Physitian, Sir *Charles Starborough*, 200 *l.*

One Chirurgeon.

One Apothecarie.

A Secretarie of the Languages, 100 *l.*

A Gentleman-Harbinger, 50 *l.* besides Riding-Charges, 8 *s.* 4 *d. per diem.*

Semstress and Laundress to the Body, Mrs *du Puy*, 150 *l.*

Laundress to the Table, Mrs *Katherine Atkinson*, 150 *l.*

Yeoman of the Wine Cellar, Mr *Jeuks* 50 *l.*

Yeomen of the Beer Cellar, Mr *Pierce*, 40 *l.*

Yeoman of the Poultry and Larder, 30 *l.*

Yeoman of the Woodyard and Scullery, 30 *l.*

Of the Pantry and Ewry 30 *l.*

Po[illegible] 5[illegible] *l.*

Keeper of the Arm[illegible], 50*l*

Trumpeter. 30 *l.*

Necessary Woman, 40 *l.*

Chamber-Keeper to the Maids, 10 *l.*

Buttleman.

One

One Clerk to the Commissioners, 50 *l.*
Messenger to the Commissioners, 71 *l.* 18 *s.* 4 *d.*
Door-Keeper to the Commissioners.

Clerk of the Kitchin, 50 *l.*
Master Cook, 40 *l.*
Second Cook, 30 *l.*
Three Turn-broaches, each 18 *l.* 5 *s.*
One Scourer, 18 *l.* 5 *s.*
Pan keeper,
Porter of the Kitchin,
Cole-Carrier,
Porter at *Whitehall*,
Gardiner.

Officers of His Highnesses Revenue.

Treasurer of the Revenue, Sir *Alan Apsley.*
Attorney General, Sir *Edward Turner* 40 *l.*
Sollicitor General, Sir *Edward Thurland*, 40 *l.*
Sollicitor, *Charles Porter* Esquire, 40 *l.*
Auditor General, *Thomas Holder* Esquire, 180 *l.*
Assistant to the Auditor *M. Broad.*
Messenger to the Revenue, Mr *Dutton*, 71 *l.* 18 *s.* 4 *d.*

Officers of the Admiralty.

Sir *William Turner.*
Mr *David Bud.*

Master of the Buckhounds, Mr. *Walsingham*, 500 *l.*

Three Huntsmen of the Buckhounds.

Four Huntsmen of the Fox hounds.

Teacher of the Setting Dogs.

Master of the Barges, 50 *l.*

Twenty four Watermen.

Pensioners.

Officers and Servants in his Highnesses Stable.

Henry Jermin Esquire, Master of the Horse, 266 *l.* 13 *s.* 4 *d.*

Two Escuyries, each 100 *l.*

Clerk of the Stables, 60 *l.*

Surveyour of the Stable, 40 *l.*

Yeoman Rider, 80 *l.*

Two Pages of Honour, each 100 *l.*

Fourteen Foot-men, each 39 *l.*

Fifteen Grooms, each 32 *l.* 10 *s.*

Three Coachmen, each 78 *l.* for themselves, 3 Postilions, and three Helpers, together with Linnen, Stockings, and Liveries twice a year.

Two Sumpter-men, each 26 *l.*

Three Muleteers, each 26 *l.*

Porter of the Stables, 32 *l.* 10 *s.*

Officers and Servants belonging to Her Royal Highness the Dutchess.

GRoom of the Stole, Countess of *Rochester*, 400 *l.*

Lady of the Bed-Chamber, Countess of *Peterborough*, 200 *l.*

Four Maids of Honour.

Mrs *Arabel Churchil*, 20 *l.*
Mrs *Dorothy Howard*, 20 *l.*
Mrs *Anne Ogle*, 20 *l.*
Mrs *Mary Blague*, 20 *l.*
Mother of the Maids; Mrs *Lucy Wise*.

Four Bed-Chamber-Women.

Mrs *Katherine Elliot*, 200 *l.*
Mrs *Margeret Dawson*, 150 *l.*
Mrs *Lelis Cranmer* 150 *l.*
Lady *Apsley*, 150 *l.*

Starcher, Mrs *Mary Roche*, 50 *l.*
Semstress Mrs *Ellen Green*, 50 *l.*
Laundress, Mrs *Mary Cowdre*, 250 *l.*
Lace Mender.

Secretary to her Highness, Sir *Philip Froud*, 100 *l.*
Two Gentlemen Ushers, each 80 *l.*
Four Gentlemen waiters,

Four Pages of the Back-ſtairs, each 40 *l.*
Maſter Cook, 40 *l.*
Neceſſary Woman, 40 *l.*
Eighteen Watermen, each 2 *l.*

Maſter of the Horſe to the Dutcheſs; is Sir *Richard Powle*, 266 *l.* 13 *s.* 4 *d.*
Two Eſcuyries, each 100 *l.*
Eight Footmen, each 39 *l.*
Four Coachmen, each 78 *l.* for themſelves, Poſtillions, and Helpers.
Five Grooms, each 32 *l.* 10 *s.*
Two Chairmen, each 39 *l.*

Officers and Servants to the Duke of Cambridge.

GOverneſs, Lady *Francis Villiers*, 400 *l.*
Under-Governeſs, Mrs *Mary Kilbert*, 150 *l.*
Wet-Nurſe, 80 *l.*
Dry Nurſe, 80 *l.*
Tutor of the French Tongue, Monſieur *Leſne*, 100 *l.*
Three Rockers, each 70 *l.*
Laundreſs to the Body, 60 *l.*
Semiſtreſs,
Laundreſs to the Table,
Page of the Back-ſtairs, 60, *l.*
Neceſſary Woman, 40 *l.*
Cook 38 *l.* 5 *s.*
Muſitian 31 *l.* 4 *s.*
Four Footmen,

One

One Groom,
One Coachman, Postillion, and Helper.

Officers and Servants belonging to the Lady Mary.

TWo Dressers,
Mrs *Anne Walsingham*, 80 *l.*
Mrs *Mary Langford* 80 *l.*

Rocker, Mrs *Jane Leigh* 70 *l.*
Semstress,
Laundress, Mrs *Elizabeth Brooks* 90 *l.*

Page of the Back-stairs, 60 *l.*
Dancing-Master, 200 *l.*
Singing-Master, 100 *l.*

Servants to the Lady Anne.

DResser,
Three Rockers,
Semstress,
Page of the Back-stairs,
Necessary Woman.

His Royal Highness upon all occasions when he goes aboad without the King, hath for his particular Guard a gallant Troop of Horse, commanded by Monsieur *de Blancfort*.

CHAP. XVII.

Of the Three States *of* England, *and first of the* Clergy, *and therein of their Dignity, Name, Degrees,* &c.

Clergy their Dignity.

ALL the Subjects of *England* are divided into *Clegy* and *Laity*;, The Laity sub-divided into *Nobility* and *Commonalty*. These are called *Ordines Regni*, or the *Three States*, and first of the Clergy.

As *Heaven* is more honourable than *Earth*, the *Soul* than the *Body*; so is the *Spiritual Function* more excellent than the *Civil*, and the *Saccrdotal* Dignity higher then the *Secular*: and therefore in *England* the *Clergy*, *cæteris paribus*, hath ever had (according to the practice of all other Civilized Nations since the World began) the preference and precedence of the *Laity*, and hath in all times been reputed the first of the Three States.

Names.

The Clergy so called, because they are Gods Κλῆ[illegible] or *Portion*; for although all Christians may be stiled Gods Portion as well as God's Servants, yet amongst Christians those Persons whom God hath set apart, and seperated from common use to to his Service, to be as it were his Domestick servants; are more peculiarly the the Lords Portion; and therefore from the first Age of Christianity, the Persons so set apart, have been called *Clerici*, Clerks.

As in the *State*, so in the *Church*, the Laws and Constitutions of *England*, would not that there should be a *parity* and *equality* of all persons. *Quippe in Ecclesia nihil magis inæquale quam æqualitas.* And therefore in conformity to the first Times and Places of Establisht *Christianity*, so soon as the *Christian Faith* was by Authority received in *England*, one of the Clergy was in every City ordained a *Bishop*; who hath (to avoid Confusion, which usually springs from equality) a preeminence over the rest of the Clergy within certain Precincts. *Degrees.* *Bishop.*

Afterwards the Bishops being necessitated to meet about Publick Affairs of the Church, as *Consecrations*, *Consultations* for remedy of general disorders, for *Audiences Judicial*, when the actions of any Bishop should be called in question; or *Appeals* from Bishops, *&c.* It seemed requisite to our Ancestors (according to other Christian Churches (ever since the first *Nicene Council*) to have amongst a certain number of Bishops one to be chiefest in Authority over the rest; from thence named *Archiepiscopus*, Arch or Chief Bishop. *Archbishop.*

For

Suffragan Bishops.

For easing the Bishop of some part of his burthen, as the number of Christians waxed great, or the Diocess was large, there were ordained in the Primitive Times *Chorepiscopi*, *Suffragan*, or *Subsidiary* Bishops. Accordingly in the English Church of a long time there have been such ordained by the name of Bishops *Suffragans* or *Titular* Bishops; who have the Name, Title, Stile, and Dignity of Bishops, and (as other Bishops) are consecrated by the Arch-bishop of the Province; each one to execute such Power, Jurisdiction, and Authority, and receive such Profits as is limited in his Commission by the Bishop or Diocesan, whose Suffragan he is.

Suffragan Bishops by an Act of Parliament of *H.* 8. still in force, are to be only of these Towns following.

The *Suffragan Bishop* for the Diocess of *Canterbury* must be at *Dover* only, for *York* at *Nottingham* and *Hull*, for *London* at *Colchester*, for *Durham* at *Berwick*, for *Winchester* at *Guilford*, *Southampton*, and the Isle of *Wight*; for *Lincoln* at *Bedford*, *Leicester*, *Grantham*, and *Huntingdon*; for *Norwich*, at *Thetford* and *Ipswich*; for *Salisbury* at *Shaftsbury*, *Melton*, and *Marlborough*; for *Bath* and *Wells* at *Taunton*; for *Hereford*, *Bridgenorth*; for *Coventry* and *Lichfield*, *Shrewsbury*; for *Ely* at *Cambridge*; for *Exeter* at *St Germains*; for *Carlisle* at *Perith*. These only to be the Sees of Bishops Suffragans, and no more Suffragans allowed, then so

many

many to each Diocese, as above mentioned: In Publick Assemblies they were to take place next after the Temporal Peers of the Realm. In the absence of the Bishops, employed oft upon Embassies abroad, or residing at Court to advise the King, these did usually supply their places. A Suffragan Bishop is made, in case the Archbishop or some other Bishop, for the better Government of his Diocess, desire the same; and in such case the Bishop is to present two able men for any one place aforenamed, whereof His Majesty chooseth one.

For a supply of able and fit persons to assist Bishops, or to be made Bishops, it seemed good to Reverend Antiquity; that in every Diocess a certain number of the more prudent and pious Pastors should be placed in a *Collegiate* manner, at every *Cathedral* or *Episcopal See*; where they might not only be ready to assist the Bishop in certain weighty Cases; but also fit themselves (by gaining experience and loosing by little and little their former familiartiy with the inferiour Countrey Clergy) for Government and Authority in the Church.

Accordingly in every *Cathedral* Church in *England*, there are a certain number of *Prebendaries* or *Canons*, and over them a *Dean*, in Latine *Decanus*, from [illegible]; because antiently set over ten Canons at the least: who is sometimes stiled *Alter Episcopi Oculus*, the other being the *Archdeacon*, who (though a *Presbyter* himself) is so named for his Charge over the *Deacons*;

Dean.

Archdeacon.

cons; who are to be guided and directed by him under the Bishop.

Next is the *Rural Dean*, so called because he had usually charge over Ten Country Parsons. He was antiently called *Archipresbyter*, because he had the guidance and direction of other *Presbyters*.

In the last place are the Pastors of every Parish, who are called *Rectors*, unless the *Predial* Tythes be *impropriated*, and then they are called *Vicars, quasi vice fungentes Rectorum*.

In *England* are 2 *Archbishops* 24 *Bishops*, no *Suffragan Bishops* at present, 26 *Deans* of Cathedrals aud Collegiate Churches, 60 *Archdeacons*, 544 Prebendaries, many *Rural Deans*, and about 9700 *Rectors* and *Vicars*, besides *Curates*, who for certain Stipends assist such Rectors and Vicars that have the care of more Churches than one.

These (if it be considered of what great Learning and Abilities they are; what great Authority and Sway they usually bear over the Laity, to incline, lead, and draw them; what great Priviledges and Immunities they do or ought to enjoy, and how much means they possess) may well be reputed the first Member of the Three Estates of *England*.

Priviledges of the Clergy.

It hath been provided, not without singular wisdom, that as the ordinary course of common affairs is disposed of by general Laws; so likewise mens rarer incident Necessities and Utilities should be with

special

ſpecial equity conſidered. Hence is it that ſo many *Priviledges*, *Immunities*, *Exemptions*, and *Diſpenſations*, have been to the Clergy of *England* granted in all times: Our Anceſtors thinking it very reaſonable that as *Soldiers* were wont by the *Roman Emperours* to be endowed with certain *Priviledges* for their warding and fighting to preſerve the State from *external* Enemies, ſo the Clergy ought to have certain Immunities and Priviledges for their *watching* and *ſpiritual* warfare to preſerve the State from *internal* Enemies; the *World*, the *Fleſh*, and the *Devil*; *Ut ſerventur immunes Clerici, quo Caſtris ſuis ſedulo commorantes, & vigiles excubias ducentes ſummo cæli Imperatori illæſos populos repræſentent, Legibus effectum eſt, ut quam plurima iis Privilegia conceſſa ſint, tum ad eorum perſonas, tum bona ac res ſpectantia.*

Of *Priviledges*, ſome belong to *Archbiſhops*, ſome to *Biſhops*, as they are ſo; and ſome belong to them and to the inferiour Clergy, as they are *Eccleſiaſtiques* or *Churchmen*.

Archbiſhops. Before the coming of the *Saxons* into *England*, the *Chriſtian Britains* had 3 Archbiſhops, *viz.* of *London*, *York* and *Caerleon* an antient great City of *South-Wales* upon the River *Uske* (as aforementioned.) Afterward the *Archiepiſcopal See* of *London* was by the *Saxons* placed at *Canterbury*, for the ſake of St *Auſtin* the Monk

Monk, who first preached the Gospel there to the *Heathen Saxons*, and was there buried. The other of *Caerleon* was translated to St *Davids in Pembrook-shire*, and afterward subjected wholly to the See of *Canterbury*, since which all *England* and *Wales* reckon but two *Archbishops*, *Canterbury* and *York*.

Canterbury. The Archbishop of *Canterbury* antiently had *Primacy* as well over all *Ireland* as *England*, and the Irish Bishops received their *Consecrations* from him; for *Ireland* had no other Archbishop until the year 1152, and therefore in the time of the Two first *Norman* Kings, it was declared, that *Canterbury* was the *Metropolitan* Church of *England*, *Scotland* and *Ireland*, and the Isles adjacent. He was therefore sometimes stiled a *Patriarch* (and *Patriarcha* was a Chief Bishop over several Kingdoms or Provinces (as an Archbishop is of several Dioceses) and had several Archbishops under him; was sometimes called *Alterius Orbis Papa & Orbis Britannici Pontifex*; and matters done and recorded in Ecclesiastical affairs ran thus, *Anno Pontificatus Nostri primo, secundo, &c.* He was *Legatus Natus*, that is a perpetual *Legantine* Power was annext to that Archbishoprick near 1000 years ago; whereby no other *Legat*, *Nuncio*, or *Ambassadour* from the Bishop of *Rome*, could here exercise any *Legantine* Power without special Licence from the King. He was so highly respected abroad, that in Gene-

ral

ral Councils he was placed before all other Archbishops at the Popes right Foot. He was at home so highly honoured by the King of *England*, (that according to the Practice of Gods own People the Jews, where *Aaron* was next in Dignity to *Moses*, and according to the practice of most other *Christian* States; where the next in Dignity and Authority to the Sovereign, is usually the chiefest Person of the Clergy) he was accounted the second Person in the Kingdom, and named and ranked even before the *Princes of the Bloud*. He enjoyed some special marks of *Royalty*, as to be *Patron* of a *Bishoprick* (as he was of *Rochester*:) to *Coyn Moneys*, to make Knights, and to have the Wardships of all those who held Lands of him *Jure Hominii* (as it is called) although they held in *Capite* other Lands of the King; a *Princely* Prerogative, even against the Kings written Prerogative.

In an antient *Charter* granted by *William* the *Conquerour* to *Lanfranc* Archbishop of *Canterbury*, he is to hold his Lands with the same freedom *in Dominico suo* (as the words are) as the King holdeth his *in Dominico suo* except only in 2 or 3 Cases, and those of no great importance.

It is an Antient Priviledge of the See of *Canterbury*, that wheresoever any Mannors or Advowsions do belong unto that See, that place forthwith becomes exempt from the Ordinary, and is reputed a Peculiar, and of the Diocess of *Canterbury*.

The

The Archbishop of *Canterbury* by the favour of our King, is judged fit to enjoy still divers considerable Pre-eminences. He is *Primat* over all *England* and *Metropolitan*, hath a super-eminency and some Power even over the Archbishop of *York*; hath Power to Summon him to a National Synod, and *Archiepis, Eboracensis venire debet cum Episcopis suis, ad nutum ejus, ut ejus Canonicis dispositionibus obediens existat*

The Archbishop of *Canterbury* is at this day *Primus par Regni*, the first *Peer* of *England*, and next to the Royal Family to precede not only all *Dukes*, but all the *Great Officers* of the Crown.

At the late solemn Coronation of our present Sovereign, it was expresly ordered in doing homage to the King, that according to antient Custom, the Archbishops and *Bishops* should precede even the Duke of *York* and all the Lay Lords.

He is stiled by the King in his Writs directed to him, *Dei Gratia Archiepisc. Cant.* and writes himself *Divina Providentia*, whereas other Bishops write, *Divina Permissione*; and he is said to be *inthroned*, when he is invested in the Archbishoprick.

To crown the King belongs to him, and it hath been resolved, that wheresoever the Court shall happen to be, the King and Queen are *Speciales Domestici Parochiani Domini Ar. Cant.* and had antiently the *Holy Offerings* made at the Altar by the King

King and Queen, wheresoever the Cour should happen to be, if his Grace was there present: also the Power of appointing the *Lent Preachers*, which was thought by our Ancestors much more fit for a Prelate or Spiritual Person to do (as in all other Christian Courts) then for any Lay Lord, as hath been used in *England*, since one *Cromwel* was by *Hen*. 8. made Vicar General, and placed above the Archbishop of *Canterbury*.

The Bishop of *London* is accounted his Provincial *Dean*, the Bishop of *Winchester* his *Chancellour*, and the Bishop of *Rochester* his *Chaplain*.

In writing and speaking to him is given the Title of *Grace* (as is to all Dukes) and *Most Reverend Father in God*.

He hath the Power of all *Probate* of *Testaments*, and granting Letters of Administration, where the party dying had *Bona Notabilia*, that is five pounds worth or above, out of the Diocess wherein he died; or ten pounds worth within the Diocess of *London*; or if the party dying be a Bishop, though he hath no Goods out of the Diocess where he died. Also to make Wills for all such as die intestate within his Province, and to administer their Goods to the Kindred or to Pious uses, according to his discretion; which most transcendent Trust and Power is so anciently in *England* belonging to Bishops, that the best Antiquary cannot find the first Original thereof.

By

By *Stat.* 25 *H.* 8. he hath the *Honour* and *Power* to grant *Licenses* and *Dispensations* in all Cases heretofore sued for in the Court of *Rome*, not repugnant to the Law of God or the Kings Prerogative: As to Allow a Clerk to hold a Benefice in *Commendam* or *Trust*; to allow a Son (contrary to the Canons) to succeed his Father immediately in a Benefice; to allow a Clerk rightly qualified to hold two Benifices with Cure of Souls; to abolish irregularity gotten without a mans own default, as by defect of Body or Birth, or by accidental killing of a Man, *&c.* to abolish the guilt of Simony; to allow a Beneficed Clerk for some certain causes to be *Non-Resident* for some time; to allow a Layman to hold a Prebend, *&c.* whilst by study he is preparing himself for the service of the Church; to grant Dispensations to sick, to old People, to Women with Child, to eat flesh on days whereon it was forbidden; to constitute publick Notaries, whose single Testimony is as good as the Testimonies of any two other Persons. All which forementioned *Licences*, *Dispensations*, &c. the said Archbishop grants by himself, or by his Deputy, called the *Master of Faculties*, in all His Majesties Dominions except *Scotland*; for all the new late acquisitions to this Crown, as *Virginia*, *New-England*, *Barbados*, *Bermudos*, &c. were heretofore added by due Authority to the Province of *Canterbury*, and put under the Diocess of *London*. He hath also the Power to grant *Literas Tuitorias*, whereby

whereby any one that brings his appeal, may prosecute the same without any molestation; to bestow one Dignity or Prebend in any Cathedral Church within his Province upon every Creation there of a new Bishop; who is also to provide a sufficient Benefice for one of the Chaplains of the Archbishop, or to maintain him till it be effected.

By the *Stat. Primo Eliz.* it is provided that the Queen by the advise of the Archbishop might ordain and publish such Rights and Ceremonies as may be for Gods glory, for edifying of the Church, and due Reverence of the Sacraments.

He hath the Prerogative to *Consecrate* a Bishop (though it must be done in the presence and with the assistance of two other Bishops (as every Bishop gives Ordination but with the assistance of Presbyters) to assign *Co-adjutors* to infirm Bishops; to confirm the Election of Bishops within his Province; to call Provincial Synods according to the Kings Writ alwayes directed to him; to be Moderator in the Synods or Covocations; to give his Suffrage there last of all; to visit the whole Province; to appoint a *Guardian* of the *Spiritualities*, during the Vacancy of any Bishoprick within his Province; whereby all the Episcopal Rights of that Diocess belong to him, all Ecclesiastical Jurisdiction, as Visitation, Institutions, &c.

The Archbishop may retain and qualifie 8 Chaplains, which is two more then any Duke by Statute is allowed to do.

under him the Bishopricks of *York*, *Durham*, *Carlisle*, *Chester*, and that of the *Isle of Man*. Only *Durham* hath a peculiar Jurisdiction, and in many things is wholly exempt from the Jurisdiction of the Archbishop.

He had the Rights of a Count *Palatine* over *Hexamshire* in *Northumberland*. May qualifie also 8 Chaplains, and hath within his Province divers other Prerogatives and Priviledges which the Archbishop of *Canterbury* hath within his own Province.

The next in place amongst the Clergy of *England* are the Bishops, so called from the Saxon Word *Bisceop*, and that from the Greek ἐπι κ [illegible] *Speculator*, *Explorator vel Superintendens*, an Officer amongst the Heathen so called, *quia praeerat pani & victui quotidiano: Episcopus enim apud Christianos praeest pani & victui spirituali.*

All the Bishops of *England* are Barons and Peers of the Realm, they are Barons by a threefold manner (which cannot be said of the Lay Lords) they are *Feodal* in regard of their Lands and Baronies annext to their Bishopricks. They are *Barons by Writ*, being summoned by the Kings Writ to Parliament, and they are *created Barons by Patent*, which at their *Consecration* is always exhibited to the Archbishop. They have the Precedence of all Temporal Barons under Vicounts. In the Parliament have place in the *Upper House* in a double capacity, not only as Barons, but as Bishops; for before they were Ba-

rons,

rons, they had in all times place in the Great Council of the Kingdom: and there ever placed on the Kings *right hand*, not only to give their Advice as the Judges do; but *ad tractandum*, *ordinandum*, *statuendum*, *definiendum*, &c. They have the Title of *Lords* and *Right Reverend Fathers*.

All Bishops in *England* have one or two transcendent Priviledges, which seem almost *Regal*; as, In their own Court; to judge and pass Sentence alone by themselves, without any *Colleague* or *Assessor*, which is not done in other of the Kings Courts, for the Bishops Courts (though held by the Kings Authority *Virtute Magistratus sui*) are not accounted to be *properly* the Kings Courts, and therefore the Bishops send forth Writs in their own Names, *Teste* the Bishop, and not in the Kings Name; as all the Kings Courts properly so called do.

Moreover Bishops have this other transcendent Priviledge, to depute their Authority to another (as the King doth) either to their *Bishops Suffragans*, to their *Chancellours*, to their *Commissaries* or other Officers; which none of the Kings Judges may do.

All Bishops have one Priviledge above and beyond all Lay Lords, *viz.* That in whatsoever Christian Princes Dominions they come, their Episcopal Dignity and Degree is acknowledged; and they may, *quatenus Bishops* confer *Orders*, *&c.* whereas no Lay *Baron*, *Vicount*, *Marquis*, nor *Duke*, is in Law acknowledged such; not of of the Dominions of the Prince who conferred those Honours.

The Laws and Customs of *England* are so tender of the Honour, Credit, Reputation and Person of Bishops our Spiritual Fathers, that none might (without special Licence from the King first obtained) be endicted of any Crime before any Temporal Judge.

Upon severe penalty by our Laws no man may raise Reports, whereby *Scandal* may arise to the Person of any Bishop, or Debate and Discord between them and the Commons of *England*.

In Civil Trials, where a Bishop is Plaintiff or Defendant, the Bishop may as well as any Lay Lord, challenge the *Array*, if one *Knight* at least be not returned of the Jury, and it shall be allowed unto him as a Priviledge due to his Peerage.

In Criminal Trials for life, all Bishops by *Magna Charta* and Stat. 25 *Edw*. 3. are to be tried by their Peers, who are Barons, and none under; notwithstanding the late conceit of some Lawyers, that because Bishops may not be on the Criminal Trial of a Peer, therefore are not to be tried by Peers; for so neither may Bishops be tried by a Common Jury, because they may not be on the trial of such men. Moreover, Noble Women may not be on the Trial of Peers, and yet they are to be tried by Peers of the Realm. And there is no *Legal Precedent in England* of a Bishop remaining a Bishop, that ever was tried for his life, but by Peers of the Realm. Antiently indeed Bishops were so exempted, as not at all to be tried by *Temporal* Judges, till after *deprivation* and *degradation*, and then being thereby rendred no Peers, but common Persons, they might be tried by Common Juries.

Since the Reformation, the *English Protestant-Bishops* have been so constantly loyal and true to the Crown (to the envy of *Non-Conformists*) and so free from all Capital Crimes, that there is yet no Precedent in *England* for their manner of Tryal for Life: As for that common Assertion, *That no Lords of Parliament are to be tryed by their Peers, but such as sit there* Ratione Nobilitatis, *and that all Lay-Lords have place in Parliament for that reason.* It is not onely false, but frivolous in the Judgment of very many Judicious Men. And indeed, how absurd and unreasonable must it needs be (let all Men judge) that an Archbishop of *Canterbury*, who is by all acknowledged to be *Primus Par Regni*, should be tried by a Common Jury of Freeholders, when as the meanest Lay Baron, though created but yesterday, may not be tryed by any under Barons?

In *Parliament, Bishops* as *Barons*, may be present and vote at the Tryal and Arraignment of a Peer of the Realm, onely before sentence of Death, or loss of Member be pronounced; that they may have no hand in blood, no hand in destroying, but onely in saving, they have by Canon Law the Priviledge and Injunction to absent themselves, and by Common Law to make Proxies to vote for them.

Primo Eliz. cap. 2. It is expresly declared, That all Lords of Parliament (without any exception of Lords Spiritual) should be tryed in that particular by their Peers.

The Bishops of *England*, enjoy at this day many other Priviledges, as freedom from Arrests, Outlawries; Distress *per Equitaturam* or *in a Journey*; Liberty to hunt in any of the Kings Forests or Parks, to kill one or two Deer, going from or coming to the King upon His Order; to have certain Tuns of Wine free from Impost, *&c.*

The Persons of Bishops may not be seised upon Contempt (as the Persons of Lay-Lords) but their Temporalities onely may be seised.

Every Bishop may by Statute Law qualifie as many Chaplains as a Duke, *viz.* Six.

The Law of *England* attributeth so very much to the Word of a Bishop, That not onely in the Tryal of *Bastardy*, the Bishops Certificate shall suffice, but also in Tryal of *Heresie*, which toucheth a Mans life: Upon the Bishops bare Certificate, that any hath been convicted before him of *Heresie*, the Secular Power puts him to death without any Tryal by his Peers.

The Persons of the Spiritual Governors of the Church of *England*, are of such high and tender respect in the eye of the Law, that it is thought fit to exact the same respect from a Clergyman to his Bishop or Ordinary, as from a Childe to his Father; and

and therefore made the offences of *Parricide* and *Episcopicide* equal, *viz.* Both Petty Treason.

London. Next to the Two Archbishops of *England*, the Bishop of *London* amongst all the Bishops, hath the pre-eminence. *Episcopus Londinensis* (saith an Ancient Record) *speciali quadam Dignitate ceteris anteponendus quia Ecclesiæ Cantuariensis Decanus est Provincialis.* Being Bishop over the *Imperial* and *Capital City* of *England*, it is by a Statute of later times expresly provided, That he should have the preference and precedence of all the Bishops of *England*; whereby he is become (as heretofore the *Lord Prior* of the *Order* of S. *John* of *Jerusalem*) *Primus Baro Regni*, as the Lord *Abergavenny* is *Primus Baronum Laicorum*.

Next amongst those of the *Episcopal Colledge*, is the Bishop of *Durham*, within the Province of *York*, who hath been a *Count Palatine* 6 or 700 years: Wherefore the Common Seal of the Bishoprick hath been of a long time an *Armed Knight*, holding in one hand a *Naked Sword*, and in the other, a *Church*.

He hath also at this day, the Earldom of *Sadberge*, annexed long ago to this Bishoprick by the King.

In the Fifth place, by vertue of the forementioned Statute, is the Bishop of *Winchester*, reputed Anciently Earl of *Southampton*, and so stiled in the Statutes of the

the *Honorable Order* of the *Garter*, by *Henry* the Eighth; though soon after, that Earldom was otherwise disposed of.

After these aforenamed, all the other Bishops take place according to the *Seniority* of their *Consecration*, unless any Bishop happen to be made *Lord Chancellor*, *Treasurer*, *Privy Seal*, or *Secretary of State*; which anciently was very usual, as reputed for their *Piety*, *Learning*, *Single life*, *Diligence*, &c. Far more fit for the advantage and service of the King and Kingdom, than any Laymen: And in such case, a Bishop being *Lord Chancellor*, had place next to the Archbishop of *Canterbury*, and above the Archbishop of *York*; and being *Secretary of State*, had place next to the Bishop of *Winchester*.

All the Bishops of *England* now living, take place as they are ranked in this Catalogue.

Dr. *Gilbert Sheldon*, Lord Archbishop of *Canterbury*, Consecrated Bishop of *London* 1660, and Translated to *Canterbury* 1663.

Dr. *Richard Stern*, Lord Archbishop of *York*, Consecrated Bishop of *Carlisle* 1660, and Translated to *York* 1664.

Dr. *Humphrey Henchman*, Lord Bishop of *London*, Consecrated Bishop of *Salisbury* 1650, and Translated to *London* 1663.

Dr. *John Cosins* Consecrated Bishop of *Durham* 1660.

Dr. *George Morley*, Consecrated Bishop of *Worcester* 1660, and Translated to *Winchester* 1662.

Dr. *William Lucy*, Lord Bishop of St. *Davids*, Consecrated 1660.

Dr. *Benjamin Laney*, Lord Bishop of *Ely*, Consecrated 1660 Bishop of *Peterborough*, thence Translated to *Lincoln* 1663. Lastly, to *Ely* 1667.

Dr. *Gilbert Ironside*, Bishop of *Bristol*, Consecrated 1660.

Dr. *Edward Reynolds*, Consecrated 1660. Bishop of *Norwich*; he is also Abbot of St. *Bennet de Hulmo*, the sole Abbot now remaining in *England*.

Dr. *William Nicolson*, Consecrated Bishop of *Glocester* 1660.

Dr. *Herbert Crofts*, Consecrated Bishop of *Hereford* 1661.

Dr. *Seth Ward*, Consecrated Bishop of *Exeter* 1662. Translated to *Salisbury* 1667.

Dr. *Henshaw*, Consecrated Bishop of *Peterborough* 1663.

Dr. *Rainbow*, Consecrated Bishop of *Carlisle* 1664.

Dr. *Blanford*, Consecrated Bishop of *Oxford* 1665.

Dr. *Dolben*, Bishop of *Rochester*, Consecrated 1666.

Dr. *Davis*, Bishop of *Landaff*, Consecrated 1667.

Dr. *Fuller*,

Dr. *Fuller*, Consecrated Bishop of *Lincoln* 1667.

Dr. *Morgan*, Consecrated Bishop of *Bangor* 1667.

Dr. *Sparrow*, Consecrated Bishop of *Exeter* 1667.

Dr. *Wilkins*, Consecrated Bishop of *Chester* 1668.

Dr. *Gunning*, Consecrated Bishop of *Chichester* 1669.

Dr. *Barrow*, Consecrated Bishop of St. *Asaph* 1670.

Dr. *Robert Creighton*, Consecrated Bishop of *Bath* and *Wells* 1670.

The present Bishops of *England*, for Gravity, Learning, and Piety, equal, if not exceed any of their Predecessors.

These are all Barons and Peers of the Realm; these have place in the *Upper House of Parliament*, and in the *Upper House of Convocation*, and these are the *Lords Spiritual*: Next follow the *Commons Spiritual*, consisting of *Suffragan Bishops*, *Deans*, *Arch-Deacons*, *Prebendaries*, *Rectors*, and *Vicars*; to whom also belong divers considerable Priviledges.

All *Suffragan Bishops*, all *Deans*, *Arch-Deacons*, *Prebendaries*, *Rectors*, and *Vicars*, have Priviledges; some by themselves, others by Proxy, or by Representative, to sit and vote in the *Lower House* of *Convocation*.

No Subsidies or other Tax to the *King*, may legally be laid upon them, without their own consent first had in *Convocation*.

The Clergy (as appears by the words of the *Writ*, as also by *Modus Tenendi Parliam.* And by 21 *Rich.* 2. *cap.* 12.) hath *Per Procuratores Cleri*, Place and Suffrage in the *Lower House* of *Parliament*, as was anciently practised in *England*, and of later years in *Ireland*, (though now not used in either) and as the Bishops still have and use in the *Higher House* of *Parliament*.

No Clergyman may be compelled to undergo any *Personal Functions* or *Services* of the *Commonwealth*, or to serve in *War*. If any Man by reason of his Land, be subject to be elected to any *Servile Office*, if he takes Orders, he is free, and there is a *Writ* purposely to free him.

All Clergymen are free from the *Kings Purveyors*, the *Kings Carriages*, the *Kings Posts*, &c. for which they may demand a *Protection* from the King, *Cum clausula nolumus*.

If a Clergyman acknowledge a *Statute*, his body shall not be taken by vertue of any *Process* thereupon; for the *Writ* runs, *Si Laicus sit*, &c.

Clergymen are not obliged to appear at *Sherives Tourns*, or *Views of Frank Pledge*, there to take their *Oath of Allegeance*, the Ancient Laws presuming, That those, whose Principal Care and Office should be to teach the People *Loyalty* and *Alle-*

Allegeance to their King, could not themselves want *Loyalty*.

By *Magna Charta*, no Clergyman is to be fined or amerced according to his *Spiritual Means*, but according to his *Temporal Estate*, and according to the *Crime* committed.

The *Goods* of Clergymen are discharged by the *Common Law* of *England* from *Tolls* and *Customs* (*Si non exerceant Marchandizas de eisdim*) of *Average*, *Pontage*, *Murage*, *Paviage*; for which they have the *Kings Writ* to discharge them.

The *Glebe Lands* and *Spiritual Revenues* of Clergymen, being held *In pura & perpetua Eleemosyna* (*i. e.*) In *Frankalmoine*, are exempted from Arraying and Mustering of Men or Horses for the War, as appears in a *Statute* still in force, *viz.* 8 H.4. *Num.* 12. in the Unprinted *Rolls* of that *Parliament*.

The Clergy being by their *Function* prohibited to wear a *Sword* or any *Arms* (their *Coat* alone being their defence) cannot serve in Person in War: They serve their *Countrey* otherwise, and for that service have always been thought worthy of their *Spiritual Profits* and *Revenues*, and of the *Kings Protection*.

The Clergy paying to the King *First years Profits* of all *Spiritual Benefices*, called *First Fruits*, and yearly the *Tenth* of all the said *Benefices*; are with great reason thought fit to be exempted from all other *Taxes*; though to give the Laity good example, they often lay *Subsidies*, or other great *Taxes* upon themselves.

It was an Ancient Maxim in *England*, *Nullus pro decimis debet onorari de aliqua reparatione Pontis seu aliquibus oneribus temporalibus.*

These and other Immunities of the Clergy, the Great *Aquinas* thought agreeable to Natural Equity, or the Law of Nature; thence it was, that King *Pharaoh*, *Gen.* 47. when all the Lands of his Subjects were mortgaged to him for Bread, yet spared the Lands of the Priests. So *Ezra* 7. 24. And so in our ancient Laws we finde, *De Danigeldo libera & quieta erat omnis Ecclesia in Anglia & etiam omnis Terra quæ in proprio Dominio Ecclesiæ erat, ubicunque jacebat, nihil prorsus in tali redditione persolvens*; and the reason thereof is added, *Quia magis in Ecclesiæ confidebat Orationibus quam in Armorum defensionibus.*

Many more Priviledges, Immunities, Liberties, and Franchises there, are rightly belonging to the Clergy of *England*; so many, that to set down all, saith Sir *Edward Coke* upon *Magna Charta*, would take up a whole Book.

The Priviledges of the Clergy and Franchises of the Church, were (with the Liberties of the People) granted, confirmed, and setled by the King in full Parliament, *Anno* 1253, in such a solemn manner, as no Story can parallel it: The King stood up with His Hand upon His Brest, all the Lords Spiritual and Temporal stood with burning Tapers in their hands; the Archbishop pronounced as followeth; *By the Authority of God Omnipotent, of the Son, and of the Holy Ghost, &c. We excommunicate, anathematize, and sequester from Our Holy Mother the Church, all those who henceforth knowingly and maliciously deprive and spoil Churches of their Right, and all those that shall by any art or wit rashly violate, diminish, or alter secretly or openly, in Deed, Word, or Councel, those Ecclesiastical Liberties, &c. granted by Our Lord the King to the Archbishops, Bishops, Prelates, &c. For everlasting memory whereof We have hereunto put Our Seal.* After which all throwing down their Tapers extinguisht and smoaking, they all said, *So let all, that shall go against this Curse, be extinct and stink in Hell.*

Since which all Kings of *England* at their Coronations have by Solemn Oaths promised to preserve the same, and they have been confirmed by above 30 Successive Parliaments, commanded to be read once a year in Churches; and if any Act should be made to the contrary, it is to be held for null and void; by the Statute of 4 *Edw.* 3.

Antiently men were very tender and fearful to do any thing that might make them incur the said dreadful censure: but of later times, especially since our Reformation, many men pretending to more Christianity, and to more knowledge, have made

made little conscience of infringing and violating any Rights, Priviledges, or Franchises of the Church or Churchmen; whil'st the Liberties of the People (though very little violated) have been exacted, even to Sedition and Rebellion.

Revenues of the Clergy. To the end that men of the best rank and abilities, should in all times be encouraged to embrace the most painful and severe Profession of a Clergy man, and that the People should the more willingly be guided and conducted by them, Our most Christian Ancestors, according to the Pattern of Gods antient People the Jews, and of all other Christian Common-Wealths, judged it expedient to allot large Revenues, and a most plentiful maintenance to the English Clergy; having observed with *Solomon* that a Wise man for his poverty is too oft contemned and despised, and that there is nothing more contemptible and ridiculous than a poor Clergy-man.

The first Kings of *England* had all the Lands of *England* in Demesne. The second sole Monarch amongst the Saxons Kings *Ethelwolphus*, by the advice of his Nobles, gave for ever to God and the Church both the Tythe of all Goods, and the Tenth part of all the Lands of *England*, free from all Secular Service, Taxations, or Impositions whatsoever; the Charter of Donation is to be seen in *Ingulphus* and other Authors; which Charter thus ends, *Qui augere voluerit nostram donationem* (as many Pious Kings and Nobles since have

have done.) *augeat Omnipotens Deus dies ejus prosperos, si quis vero mutare vel minuere præsumpserit, noscat se ad tribunal Christi rationem redditurum.*

Besides the Tenth of Lands and the Husbandmans profits, Merchants also and Shop-keepers paid to their Spiritual Pastors the Tenth of their Gain, Servants in divers Places the Tenth of their Wages, (as Soldiers in the Kings Armies do now a part of their Pay) and in some places *Ale-sellers* the Tenth Flagon. Also Handicrafts-men and Day-Labourers paid the Tenth of their Wages upon their Oaths, if required.

Per Assisas Forestæ and other Records it doth appear, that Tithes have been paid even of Venison in divers parts of *England*, men making conscience in those days, as amongst the ancient Jews, to pay Tithes of all they possessed.

Besides all those, in some places were paid to the Pastor, Obventions, Oblations, Pensions, Mortuaries, *&c.* so that the English Clergy were the best provided for of any Clergy in the whole World, except only the Nation of the Jews, amongst whom the Tribe of *Levi* being not the 40th part of the 12 Tribes, as appears in the Book of *Numbers*, yet had as Mr. *Selden* confesseth, and that by Gods own appointment, three times the Annual Revenue of the greatest of the 12 Tribes: insomuch that the poorest Priest in the 24 Courses might be reputed a wealthy person.

And

And as amongst the Jews the 24 Chief Priests, for the better maintenance of their Authority and Dignity, had means far exceeding those of the inferiour Clergy, and the High Priest had a maintenance as far exceeding any of the said 24 Priests. So in *England* the Bishops by the great Piety and Bounty of several English Kings, had, in Lands and Revenues Temporal and Spiritual, a maintenance far more ample than those of the Inferiour Clergy, and the Two Archbishops more ample then the Bishops.

William the Couquerour at his coming into *England*, found the Bishopricks then in being so richly endowed with Lands, that he erected them all into Baronies, and every Barony then consisted of 13 Knights Fees at the least.

Besides there belonged to Bishops, several Perquisits and Duties for the Visitations of their Diocesses, for Ordinations, Institutions, *Census Cathedraticus subsidium Charitativum*; which upon reasonable Causes they might require of the Clergy under them, also other Duties, called, *Decimarum quarta, Mortuariorum & Oblationum pensitatio Jus Hospitii, Processio, Litania, Viatici vel Commeatus collatio*; which upon a Journey to *Rome* they might demand. Tenths and First Fruits were antiently paid (as is believed) to the several Diocesans, and was continued to the Bishop of *Norwich* till *Hen*, 8. deprived him thereof, and deprived the Pope of all the rest. Moreover all Cathedral Churches

were

were by divers Kings and Nobles richly furnisht with Lands for the plentiful maintenance of a Dean and a certain number of Prebends; insomuch that together with the Lands given to Monasteries, a third part of the Lands of *England* belonged to the Church and Churchmen; whereby did accrue much benefit to this Nation, great Hospitallity was kept, many Hospitals, Colledges, Churches, Bridges built, and other Publick, Pious, and Charitable Works. All Leases held of them by the Laity, were not only much more easie than other Tenures, but so unquestionable, that there was little work for the Lawyers; so much peaceableness, that 140 sworn Attourneys were thought sufficient to serve the whole Kingdom.

At present the Revenues of the English Clergy are generally very small and insufficent, above a third part of the best Benefices of *England* being antiently by the Popes Grant appropriated to Monasteries towards their maintenance, were upon the dissolution of Monasteries made Lay-Fees; besides what hath been taken by secret and indirect means, thorow corrupt Compositions and Compacts and Customs in many other Parishes; also many large Estates wholly exempt from paying Tithes, as Lands belonging to the Cistertian Monks, to the Knights Templars and Hospitallers. Those Benefices that are free from these things, yet (besides First Fruits and Tenths to the King, and Procurations to the Bishop) are taxed towards the Charges

of

of their respective Parishes, and towards the publick Charges of the Nation above and beyond the proportion of the Laity.

The Bishopricks of *England* have been also since the later end of *H.* 8. to the coming in of King *James*, most miserably robbed and spoiled of the greatest part of their Lands and Revenues; so that at this day a mean Gentleman of 200 *l.* Land yearly, will not change his Worldly estate and condition with divers Bishops: An Attorney, a Shop-keeper, a common Artisan, will hardly change theirs with ordinary Pastors of the Church.

Some few Bishopricks do yet retain a competency, amongst which the Bishoprick of *Durham* is accounted one of the Chief, the yearly Revenues whereof, before the late troubles, were above 6000 *l.* of which by the late Act for abolishing Tenures in *Capite*, was lost obove 2000 *l.* yearly. Out of it an yearly Pension of 880 *l.* hath been paid to the Crown ever since the Reign of Queen *Elizabeth*, who promised in lieu thereof so much in *Impropriations*; which was never performed. Above 340 *l.* yearly paid to several Officers of the County Palatine of *Durham*. The Assises and Sessions duly kept in the Bishops House, at the sole Charges of the Bishop. The several expences for keeping in repair certain Banks of Rivers in *Owdenshire* belonging to that Bishoprick, and of several Houses appertaining to that See. Moreover the yearly Tenths, the First Fruits, and

and Publick Taxes being deducted, there did remain *communibus annis* to the Bishop to keep Hospitallity (which must be Great) and to provide for those of his Family, but about 1500 *l.* yearly. It is true, that for the future, whilst First Fruits and Subsidies cease to be paid, this Bishops Revenue will be raised to 500 *l.* more *per annum*; and then the afore-mentioned 880 *l.* being very lately by His Majesties Gracious Letters Patent under His Great Seal, begun to be released for all times to come, and about 400 *l.* more *per annum* being added to that Revenue in divers Rents lately improved by the present Bishop Dr. *John Cosins* by the abatement of Fines (which otherwise he might have taken to himself) the whole yearly Revenues of this Bishoprick began in the year 1670 to be 3280 *l. per annum.*

Of other Principal Bishopricks the Revenues have been much diminisht, some enjoying not a fourth part of their Antient Rights.

The great diminution of the Revenues of the Clergy, and the little care of augmenting or defending the Patrimony of the Church, is the great reproach and shame of the English Reformation, and will one day prove the ruin of Church and State.

Judicious Mr. *Hooker* (who in the Preface of his Works foretold our late troubles 40 years before they came to pass) observing in his time how the Church was every day robbed of her Dues, and that it it was then an Opinion rife [*That to give to the Church smelt of Judaisme and Popery, and to take from the Church what our Ancestors had given, was Reformation*], declared, that what *Moses* saith in the 90th Psalm, was likely to be verified of *Religion* and *Gods Service* amongst us. The time thereof may be *Threescore years and ten*, if it continue till *Fourscore*, it will be but small joy to those that shall then behold the Condition of the *English Church*; nor the best read Historian can produce one example of a happy *State*, where the *Clergy* hath been exposed to the peoples *Contempt*; which must needs happen where their *Benefices*, their *Maintenance* is *scandalous*, and thereby their *Persons* despicable.

It is the last Trick, saith S. *Gregory*, that the Devil hath in the World, when he cannot bring the *Word* and *Sacraments* in disgrace by *Errors* and *Heresies*, he invented this Project to bring the Clergy into contempt and low esteem, as it is now in *England*; where they are accounted by many as the *dross* and *refuse* of the *Nation*. Men think it a stain to their blood, to place their Sons in that Function, and Women ashamed to marry with any of them; whereas antiently in *England* (as among the Jews, the Tribe of *Levi* was counted noble above all other Tribes, except that of the Royal Tribe of *Judah*) the Function of the Clergy was of so high account and esteem, that not only the best Gentry and Nobility, but divers of the *Sons*

and

and *Brothers* of divers of our English Kings since the Conquest and before, disdained not to enter into *Holy Orders*, and to be Clergymen, as at this day is practised in most other Monarchies of Christendom. *Ethelwolph* Son and Successor to *Egbert* first sole King of *England*, was in Holy Orders, and Bishop of *Winchester* at his Fathers death. *Odo* Bishop of *Bayeux* in *Normandy*, was Brother to *William* the Conquerour. *Henry de Blois* Brother to King *Stephen*, was Bishop of *Winchester*. *Geofry Plantagenet* Son to *Henry* the Second, was Bishop of *Lincoln*. *Henry de Beaufort* Brother to *Henry* the Fourth, was Bishop also of *Winchester*. And of later Times that most prudent *Henry* the Seventh had designed his Second Son to be a Clergyman, to omit many others of Noble Blood. Which Policy is still observed even amongst the few families of the Romish Religion in *England*, wherein are to be found at this day, some Brothers or Sons of *Dukes*, *Marquisses*, *Earls*, and *Barons* in Holy Orders, and all the rest of the Stock of *Baronets*, *Knights*, or *Gentry*: and for this cause find respect not only amongst those of their own opinions; but even of the most sober, moderate, and best civilized Protestants. Whil'st this Policy lasted in *England*, the Clergy were judged the fittest Persons to execute most of the Chief Offices and Places of the Kingdom (according to the Divine Policy amongst Gods peculiar People, where the Priests and Levites were the principal Of-

ficers

ficers and *Judges* in every Court; to whom the People were to be obedient on pain of death) and the Laity did with much Reverence and Respect submit to them. And as then, *Os Sacerdotis, Oraculum erit plebis* (according to that of *Malachi* 2. 7.) So *Os Episcopi Oraculum erat Regis & Regni, & Rex amplectebatur universum Clerum lata fronte & ex eo semper sibi eligebat primos a Consiliis; primos ad officia Regni obeunda. Primi igitur sedebant in omnibus Regni Commitiis & Tribunalibus Episcopi, in Regali quidem Palatio cum Regni Magnatibus; in Comitatu una cum Comite, in Turno cum Vicecomite, & in Hundredo cum Domino Hundredi, sic ut in promovenda Justitia usquequaque gladius gladium adjuvaret & nihil inconsulto Sacerdote vel Episcopo ageretur.* And Because the Weal of the Kingdom and the Service of the King depended so much upon them, and their presence for that end so oft required at *London*, it was judged expedient that every Bishoprick should have a Palace or House belonging to it in or about *London*; and it is known at this day where stood the Houses of every one, except that of St. *Asaph*, which also might probably have had one, but more obscure than some other; that Bishoprick having been, as still, very mean.

Great was the *Authority* of the *Clergy* in those days, and their *Memory* should be precious in these days, if we consider that they were the *Authors* of so great benefits and

and advantages to this Kingdom, that there are few things of any importance for promoting of the welfare of this Church and State, wherein the Bishops and Prelates, under God, have not been the *Principal Instruments*. The Excellent Laws made by King *Ina*, King *Athelstan*, King *Edmund*, and St. *Edward*, from whom we have our *Common Laws*, and our *Priviledges*, mentioned in *Magna Charta*, were all made by the perswasions and advice of *Bishops* and *Archbishops*, named in our *Histories*. The *Union* of the *Two Houses* of *York* and *Lancaster* (whereby a long and Bloody War was ended) was by the most wise Advice and Counsel of Bishop *Morton*, then a Privy Counsellor. The *Union* of *England* and *Scotland*, that inexpressible advantage to both Nations, was brought to pass by the long foresight of Reverend Bishop *Fox* a Privy Counsellor, in advising *Henry* the Seventh to match His Eldest Daughter to *Scotland*, and His Younger to *France*. Most of the *Great Publick Works* now remaining in *England*, acknowledge their ancient and present being, either to the sole Cost and Charges, or to the liberal Contributions, or at least to the *powerful perswasions* of *Bishops*, as most of the best endowed *Colledges* in both our *Universities*, very many *Hospitals*, *Churches*, *Palaces*, *Castles*, have been founded and built by *Bishops*; even that famous chargable and difficult structure of *London-Bridge* stands obliged to the *Liberal Contributions* of an *Archbishop*;

bishop; and it was a Bishop of *London*, at whose earnest request, *William* the Conqueror granted to the City of *London*, so large Priviledges, that in a grateful remembrance thereof, the *Lord Major* and *Aldermen* to this day, upon some solemn days of their resort to S. *Pauls* Church, do go in *Procession* about the *Grave-stone*, where that *Bishop* lies interred.

But above all, The Converting *England* to the *Christian Religion*, the Reforming that *Religion* when corrupted; and since that, the maintenance of the *Doctrine* thereof against all *Romish Writers*, and of the *Discipline* thereof (none of the least good *Offices*) against all the practices and power of the *Puritan* and *Presbyterian Factions*, and all those other *Sectaries* lineally descended from them: All this, and more, is owing (if not solely, yet principally) to *Bishops* and *Prelates*: By the late want of whom to sit at the Stern, how soon was this goodly Vessel split upon the *Rocks* of *Anarchy* and *Confusion*.

Even since the late *Restauration* of *Bishops*, to set down the many considerable Publick Benefits flowing from them, and other Dignified Clergy, would tire the Reader.

What sums of Money have been by them expended in repairing *Cathedral Churches*, *Episcopal Houses*, in founding and building *Hospitals*, in *Charity* to poor Widows of Clergymen utterly ruined by the late *Rebels*, for redeeming of a great number of of poor *Christian Slaves* at *Algier*; what publick and private sums for supplying the *Kings Necessities* at His Restauration, what Expences in Hospitality, *&c.* above and beyond the *Charity* and *Bounty* of others, who have ten times their Wealth and Riches?

To instance in a few, whereof certain information hath been given.

Dr. *William Juxon*, Archbishop of *Canterbury*, deceased, augmented to poor Vicaridges to the value of 11000 *l.* paid for *Redemption* of *Christian Captives*, in *Subsidies*, *Poll-money*, *Benevolences*; *First-Fruits*, *&c.* 10000 *l.* *Repairs* 16000 *l.* Besides, for repairing of S. *Pauls* Church 2000 *l.* To S. *Johns* Colledge in *Oxford* 7000 *l.* In other Charitable Uses 2000 *l.* in all 48000 *l.* Besides all this, he was so kinde to his Tenants, as to abate in their Fines 16000 *l.*

Dr. *Gilbert Sheldon*, late Bishop of *London*, now Archbishop of *Canterbury*, gave for *Redemption* of *Captives*, and other *Charitable Uses*, in *Subsidies*, *Benevolences*, Purchase of *London-House*, Repairs, Building at *Oxford*, First-Fruits, *&c.* 40000 *l.* and abated to his Tenants 17000 *l.* And almost all this whilst he was Bishop of *London*.

Dr. *Brian Duppa*, late Bishop of *Winchester*, gave for Redeeming Captives, Building and endowing *Alms-Houses*, with other *Charitable Deeds*, in *Benevolences*, *Repairs*, *&c.* 16000 *l.* and was so good to his Tenants, as to abate 30000 *l.* in their Fines.

Dr.

Dr. *Frewen*, late Archbishop of *York*, disbursed in publick payments and repairs onely, besides abatements to Tenants, 15000 *l.*

Dr. *Cosins* the forementioned Bishop of *Durham*, having from his first entrance, to the end of Seven years, not received above 19800 *l.* He expended it all, and 5000 *l.* more, either in rebuilding and repairing the Houses and Castles belonging to that *See*, or in rebuilding the Chappel at *Aukland*, and Free-Schools at *Durham*, all which had been ruined by the late Rebels; in founding Two Hospitals and a Publick Library; in founding Eight Scholarships in *Cambridge*: Of which pious and charitable Works, the whole expences came (according to most certain information) to above 22000 *l.* Besides he hath expended in Two Benevolences to the King, in redeeming of Christian Captives at *Algiers*; for his Consecration, *&c.* for the Furniture of the *New Chappel* at *Aukland*, with Plate and other decent Ornaments; for relieving the distressed *Loyal Party*, and other publick and pious uses, above 4400 *l.* All which is here declared more particularly, then the designed brevity of this *Treatise* would handsomely allow, onely thereby to put a stop to the clamor of many persons against this Bishop, and many others; as if they had received vast sums of money, and put it all in their private Purses.

Dr. *Warner*, late Bishop of *Rochester*, though his Fines were but small, yet besides

ſides abatements to Tenants, he gave in Royal Preſents, Benevolences, Subſidies, Redeeming of Captives, *&c.* above 25000 *l.* The Deans and Chapters were proportionably as liberal, to mention in ſome of them.

That of *Canterbury* in Royal Preſents, Charities, Repairs, beſides all Abatements to Tenants, gave 16000 *l.*

That of *Winchester*, in all 45800 *l.*

Durham 15000 *l.*

Ely 14000 *l.*

Exeter near 26000 *l.*

Lincoln 11000 *l.*

Rochester 10000 *l.*

Worcester 9000 *l.*

Windsor in abatements of Fines 9000 *l.* in Royal Preſents 2600 *l.* in Augmentations 6900 *l.* in Repairs 8000 *l.* in Charitable Works above 2000 *l.* In all 28500 *l.*

York 8000 *l.*

Wells 8000 *l.*

The Sum Total of onely theſe abovementioned Biſhops, Deans, and Chapters, amounts to 413800 *l.*

The reſt doubtleſs parted with their money proportionably, and then all Accompts caſt up, the Remainder could not be great. For inſtance in one of the beſt Churches, *Canterbury*, out of their clear Remainder of all the firſt Four years, *viz.* at the end of the year 1664. they had no more then every Prebend 1100 *l.* and the Dean a double ſhare.

As they have then been beneficial to this Kingdom, above and beyond other ranks of Men, so they have had the highest respect, reverence, and esteem.

In all Ages amongst all Nations, amongst *Turks* as well as *Jews*, and *Christians*, it was judged fit, that the Principal *Domestick Servants* of the *King* of *Heaven* and *Earth*, either should be of the chiefest and noblest upon Earth, or at least should be so esteemed.

Such *Reverence* our *Ancestors* bare to that Function, that (as *Selden* observes) to fall down and *kiss the Feet*, was a Ceremony usual towards other *Bishops* and *Principal Prelates*, besides the Bishop of *Rome*. Divers of our *Saxon* and *Norman Kings* and *Nobles*, so respected them, that they constrained them in *Publick Grants* yet to be seen, to sign before the highest of the *Lay Nobles*, and sometimes before the *Kings* own *Sons* and *Brothers*, &c. to take precedence of them, &c.

In the year 1200, Three Kings, *viz.* Of *England*, *Scotland*, and of *South-Wales*, to express their pious and courteous respect to *Hugh*, Bishop of *Lincoln*, disdained not with their own *Royal Shoulders*, to bear his dead Corps to the Grave.

And yet it hath been observed even by *Strangers*, that the *Iniquity* of the present times in *England* is such, That the *English Orthodox Clergy* are not onely hated by the *Romanists* on the one side, and maligned by the *Presbyterian* on the other side (as the *English Liturgy* hath also been for a long

time

time by both of them (a sure evidence of the excellency thereof) and as our *Saviour* was crucified between two Thieves) but also that of all the Christian Clergy of *Europe* (whether *Romish*, *Lutheran*, or *Calvincan*) none are so little respected generally, nor beloved, obeyed, or rewarded, as the present Pious, Learned, Loyal, Orthodox Clergy of *England*, even by some of those who have always professed themselves of that Communion.

O Deus in quæ tempora reservasti nos!

Here followeth a Catalogue of the present Deans in the Provinces both of Canterbury *and* York.

In the Province of *Canterbury*.

Dr. *Turner* Dean of *Canterbury*.
Dr. *Sancroft* Dean of *Pauls*,
Dr. *Dolben* Bishop of *Rochester* and Dean of *Westminster*.
Dr. *Clark* Dean of *Winchester*.
Dr. *Wilford* Dean of *Ely*.
Dr. *Williams* Bishop of *Ossory* and Dean Commendatory of *Banger*.
Dr. *Fell* Dean of *Christ-Church*.
Dr. *Thomas* Dean of *Worcester*.
Dr. *Bredyok* Dean of *Salisbury*.
Dr. *Honywood* Dean of *Lincoln*.

Dr. *Loyd* Dean of *St. Asaph*.
Dr. *Cary* Dean of *Exeter*.
Dr. *Dufort* Dean of *Peterborough*.
Dr. *Crofts* Dean of *Norwich*.
Dr. *Toogood* Dean of *Bristol*.
Dr. *Hodges* Dean of *Hereford*.
Dr. *Brough* Dean of *Glocester*.
Dr. *Wood* Dean of *Litchfield*.
Dr. *Crew* Dean of *Chichester*.
Dr. *Bathurst* Dean of *Bath* and *Wells*.
Dr. *Mew* Dean of *Rochester*.

In the Province of *York*.

Dr. *Hitch* Dean of *York*.
Dr. *Sudbury* Dean of *Durham*.
Dr. *Carlton* Dean of *Carlisle*.
Dr. *Bridgeman* Dean of *Chester*.

Note, That in the Cathedral Churches of St. *Davids* and of *Landaff* there never hath been any Dean, but the Bishop in either is Head of the Chapter, and in the Bishops absence the Chanter at St. *Davids*, and at *Landaff* the Archdeacon.

Note also, That there are some Deans in *England* without any Jurisdiction, only for Honour so stiled; as the Dean of the *Chappel Royal*, and Dean of the Chappel of *St. George* at *Windsor*.

Moreover, some Deans there are without any Chapter, yet enjoying certain jurisdictions, as the Dean of *Croyden*, the Dean of *Battel*, the Dean of *Bocking*, &c.

CHAP.

CHAP. XVIII.

Of the Second State or Nobility of England, *and therein of their Degrees Priviledges, States, Revenues* &c.

Nobiles quasi viri noscibiles, or Notabiles. In all Christian Monarchies, men that have been notable for *Courage*, *Wisdom*, *Wealth*, &c. have been judged fit and worthy to enjoy certain *Priviledges, Titles, Dignities, Honours*, &c. above the Common People, to be placed in an higher Orbe, and to be as a *Skreen* between the King and the inferiour Subjects, to defend the one from Insolencies, and the other from Tyranny; to interpose by their *Counsel, Courage*, and *Grandeur*, where common persons dare not, ought not to be so hardy; to support the King and defend the Kingdom with their lives and fortunes. *Name.* *Use.*

The Nobility of *England* is called the *Peerage of England*, because they are all *Pures Regni*; that is *Nobilitate Pares*, though *gradu impares*.

The *Degrees* of the English Nobility are only five, *viz. Duke, Marquess, Earl, Vicount,* and *Baron*. These are all Peers, but the *Degrees.*

four first are for *State*, *Priviledge*, and *Precedence*, above and before those who are Barons only.

Duke. A Duke in Latine *Dux, a ducendo*, Noblemen being antiently either *Generals* and *Leaders* of Armies in time of War, or Wardens of Marches and Governours of Povinces in time of Peace; afterwards made so for terme of Life, then held by *Lands* and *Fees*, at length made *Hereditary* and *Titular*.

The first *Duke* since the Conquerour was *Edward the Black Prince*, created so by *Edw.* 3. in the 11th year of his Reign. A Duke is at this day created by *Patent*, *Cincture of Sword*, *Mantle of State*, *Imposition of a Cap* and *Coronet of Gold* on his Head, and a *Verge of Gold* put into his hand.

Marquis. *Marchio a Marquis*, was first so called from the Government of *Marches* and Frontier Countries. The first that was so created was *Robert Vere* Earl of *Oxford*, made *Marquis* of *Dublin* in *Octavo* of *Richard* 2.

A Marquiss is created by a *Cincture of a Sword*, *Mantle of State*, *Imposition of a Cap of Honour*, with a *Coronet* and delivery of a *Charter* or *Patent*.

Earl. Earls anciently called *Comites*, because they were wont *Comitari Regem*, to wait upon the King for Counsel and Advice. The *Saxons* called them *Ealdormen*, the *Danes Eorlas* and the *English Earls*. They had

had antiently for the support of their state the third penny out of the Sheriffs Court issuing out of all Pleas of that *Shire* whereof they had their Title, but now it is otherwise.

An Earl is Created by the *Cincture* of a *Sword, Mantle of State put upon him by the King himself, a Cap and a Coronet put* upon his head, and a *Charter* in his hand.

All Earls are stiled by the King *Consanguinei nostri, Our Cousins.* and they antiently did and still may use the style of *Nos.*

All the Earls of *England* are local, or denominated from some Shire, Town or Place, except two, whereof one is personal, as the Earl Marshal of *England*, who is not only honorary as all the rest, but also officiary. The other is nominal, *viz*, Earl *Rivers*, who takes his denomination from an illustrious Family, as the rest do from some noted place.

Vicecomes *quasi Vice Comitis gubernaturus Comitatum.* This Title was first given say some by *Hen. 6.* in the 18th year of his Reign to *John Beaumont*, though it may be found that 5 *H* 5. Sir *Robert Brent* was by the King created a Vicount. *Vicount.*

Vicounts also are stiled by the King *Consanguinei nostri, Our Cousins.*

A Vicount is so made by *Patent.*

In the Laws of the *Longobards* and of the *Normans* this word *Baron* was used for *Vir*, as at this day *Baron* or *Varon* in the *Baron.*

 Spanish

Spanish Tongue is used for the same; so that a Baron is *Vir κατ' ἐξοχὴν Vir Notabilis & Principalis*; so the Chief Burgesses of *London* anciently, and still those of the *Cinque Ports* are called *Barons*.

Anciently those Barons only were accounted Peers of the Realm, that held of the King *per integram Baroniam*, which consisted of 13 Knights Fees, and one third part (each Knights Fee being 20 *l.*) which makes in all 400 Marks, and whoever had so much, was wont to be summoned to Parliament. Now to hold *per Baroniam*, is to hold *per hæriditatem Baronis*, whether greater or less.

Barons in the beginning of the Reign of *H.* 3. were not of so much repute as afterwards, when that King (after that great Rebellion against him was supprest) called by Writ unto Parliament onely such great men as had continued Loyal; which the succeeding Kings observing, they only were accounted Peers of the Realm, that were called by the Kings special Writ, and the others lost their Peerage.

The Earls Palatines and Earls Marches of *England*, had antiently also their Barons under them; as in *Cheshire* there are yet such Barons: but as no Bishops but those that hold immediately of the King, are Peers of the Realm (for the Bishop of *Man*, holding immediately of the Earl of *Derby* is no Peer) so no Barons, but those that hold immediately of the King, are Peers of the Realm.

Caput

Caput Baroniæ is some Castle or Chief Seat of a Nobleman, which is not to be divided amongst Daughters (if there be no Son) but must descend to the Eldest Daughter, *cæteris filiabus aliunde satisfactis.*

Land holden by Barony, doth not make the purchaser that is ignoble to be noble, although the charge of such Tenure doth lie upon him in respect of the Service of the Realm; no more than Land by Villain-Service, doth make the purchaser that is a Freeman a villain, though he shall thereby be bound to his Villain Service due for those Lands.

Barons are sometimes made by *Writ*, being thereby called to sit in the Higher House of Parliament, but most usually by *Patent.*

All the fore-menioned Degrees have the Title of *Lord* from the *Saxon* word *Laford*, *Dominus.*

All the Lords of *England* both *Spiritual* and *Temporal*, are *Feudataries* to the King, and in their Creation, and also in their Succession, do swear an *Oath* of *Fealty*, and do *Homage* to the King their Soveraign, and pay certain Duties, as Signs and Symbols of their Subjection to their *Prince.*

All Honours in *England* are given by the King, who is the sole Fountain of Honour.

The Law of *England* prohibiteth all Subjects of the Realm to receive any Heriditary Title of Honour, or Dignity, of the

Gift of any *Foreign Prince, King* or *Emperour. Est enim jus Majestatis & inter Insignia summæ potestatis.*

None of these *Honours* bestowed by the King on a Family, can be lost, but by want of Issue Male, except where the Patent extends to Issue Female, as sometimes it doth; or else by some heinous Crime; and then that Family cannot be restored to their *Blood* but by *Parliament.*

All Noblemen at their Creation have two Ensigns, to signifie two Duties. Their Heads are adorned *ad consulendum Regem & Patriam tempore pacis*, and they are girt with *a Sword ad defendendum Regem & Patriam tempore belli.*

The several Degrees of the English nobility are differenced and distinguisht one from another by their Titles and Ensigns of Honour.

A *Duke* hath the Title of *Grace*, and being written unto, may be stiled, *Most High, Potent, and Noble Prince. A Marquis, Most Noble and Potent Lord.* An *Earl, Most Noble and Potent Lord.* A *Vicount, Right Noble and Potent Lord.* And, A *Baron, Right Noble Lord.*

Their Coronets are all different. A Baron hath 6 Pearls upon the Circle, given to that honour by the present King. A Vicount hath his Circle of Pearls without number. An Earls Coronet hath the Pearls raised upon Points and Leaves low between. The Marquis a Pearl and a Strawberry Leaf round of equal height. And a Dukes Coronet only Leaves without Pearls.

Note that the Dukes of the Blood Royal bear a Coronet of *Crosses* and *Flower de Luce* which is the same with that of the Prince of *Wales*, and his is the same with the Kings, excepting the *Arches Globe* and *Cross* on the top of the Kings Crown. All the Nobles are more especially distinguisht by their *Robes of Parliament*, by their several *Guards* on their *Mantles* or *Short Cloaks* about their Shoulders. A Baron hath but two *Guards*, a Vicount two and a half; an Earl three, a Marquis three and a half, and a Duke four: Also the Mantle of a Duke, Marquis, and Vicount, is faced with Ermine, that of a Vicount and Baron faced with Plain White Furre.

The Nobility of *England* have in all times enjoyed many considerable Priviledges. *Priviledges.*

All Peers of the Realm being lookt on as the Kings Hereditary constant Councellours, their Persons out of Parliament time are priviledged (as others in Parliament time) from all arrest, unless for Treason, Felony, or breach of Peace, Condemnation in Parliament, or Contempt to the King. No *Supplicavit* can be granted against them; No *Capias* or *Exigent* sued out against them for Actions of *Debt* or *Trespass*. No *Essoin* lies against any Peer of the Realm. In Criminal Causes, Treason, or Felony, they cannot be tried by any other Jury but by a Jury of Peers of the Realm; who are not as other Juries to be put to their Oath, but their Verdict given in upon their Honour sufficeth. In Civil Causes they are not to be empaneled upon any Jury, nor upon any Enquests *de facto*, though in a matter between two Peers. In case any Peer be returned upon any such Jury, there is a special Writ for his discharge. Upon no case to be bound to their good behaviour, nor put to swear they will not break the Peace, but only to promise it upon their Honour; which was ever counted so sacred, as upon no terms to be violated. A Peer of the Realm may not be put to the Rack or Torture to discover the Truth, though accused of High Treason. Every Peer of the Realm called to Parliament, hath the Priviledge in his lawful absence to constitute a Proxy to vote for him, which none of the Commons may do. Also in places of Trust committed to them, they are allowed to make Deputies, by reason of the necessity supposed in the Law of their attendance on the Person of the King, though neither Civil Law nor Common Law allow any others Testimony to be valid, but what is given upon Oath, yet the Testimony of a Peer of *England*, given in upon his Honour, without any Oath, is esteemed valid; and they were wont to be examined upon their Allegeance and the Loyalty of their Chivalry, and to put in their answer to a Bill *super honorem*, without taking an Oath; though of later times that Priviledge, by the neglect of some Lords hath been infringed sometimes.

A

A day of Grace by the favour of the Court is not to be granted to the Plaintiff in any Suit or Action wherein a Peer of the Realm is Defendant; and this by Statute Law, because the Law presumes that a Peer of the Realm must always be ready to attend the Person of the King and the Service of the Common-Wealth, and therefore it is not to be delayed longer than the ordinary use of the Court, but to have expedition of Justice. At the beginning of Parliament when the Oath of Supremacy is exacted of all those of the House of Commons, yet it is not required of any of the Lords, because the King is otherwise assured of their Loyalty and Fidelity, as is presumed. In all Cases wherein the priviledge of Clergy is allowed to other men, and also in divers Cases where that Priviledge is taken away from other men, every Peer of the Realm having Place and Voice in Parliament, shall upon his Request by *Stat.* 1. *Edward* 6. without burning in the hand, loss of Inheritance, or corruption of Blood, be adjudged for the first time as a Clerk convict, though he cannot read. The Title of Lord is due to all that are Barons of *England*, and to none other besides Bishops, and some great Officers of the Kingdom.

Only of Courtesie the Title of *Lord* is given to all the Sons of Dukes and Marquisses, and to the eldest Sons of Earls; and to none under.

All Barons of *England* are exempted from all attendance at *Sheriffe Tourns* or

any

any *Leets*, as others are, to take the Oath of *Allegeance*.

A Peer cannot be outlawed in any Civil Action, because he cannot be arested by any *Capias*, and by the same reason lies no Attachment against him.

By the Custom of *England*, (as is by the Law of the Empire) *Nobiles non torquentur in quibus plebei torquerentur & Nobiles non suspenduntur sed decapitantur*: yet this by the meer favour of the King, and in some cases, especially of Felony, hath been therwise sometimes.

For the suppressing of Riots and Routs, the Sheriff may raise the *Posse Comitatus*, that is, all able men are to assist him; yet may not the Sheriff command the person of any Peer of the Realm to attend that Service.

A Baron of Parliament being sent for by the Kings Writ or Letter, or by his Messenger to come to Court, or to Parliament, or to appear before the Council-Board, or in his Court of *Chancery*, may both coming and returning by the Kings Forest or Park, kill one or two Deer.

In any Civil Trial, where a Peer of the Realm is Plaintiff or Defendant, there must be returned of the Jury at least one Knight, otherwise the Array may be quasht by Challenge.

The Laws of *England* are so tender of the Honour, Credit, Reputation and Persons of Noblemen, that there is a Statute on purpose to prohibit all offence by false reports, whereby any scandal to their

persons

persons may arise, or debate and discord between them and the Commons; and because it is to defend not only Lay Lords but Bishops and all great Officers of the Realm, it is called *Scandalum Magnatum*.

The House of a Peer cannot in some Cases (as in search for prohibited Books, for Conventicles, &c.) be entred by Officers of Justice without a Warrant under the Kings own hand, and the hands of Six of his Privy Council, whereof four to be Peers of the Realm.

No Peer can be assessed towards the standing *Militia*, but by six or more of themselves.

The Law allowing any one of the Commonalty to be arraigned for Felony or Treason *in favorem vitæ* to challenge 35 of his Jury without shewing cause, and others by shewing cause; yet allows not a Peer of the Realm to challenge any of his Jury, or to put any of them to their Oath, the Law presuming that they being all Peers of the Realm, and judging upon their Honour, cannot be guilty of Falshood, Favour, or Malice.

All Peers of the Realm have a Priviledge of qualifying a certain number of Chaplains, who (after a Dispensation from the Archbishop (if to him it seem good) and the same ratified under the Great Seal of *England*) may hold Plurality of Benefices with Cure of Souls: In this manner, every Duke may qualifie Six Chaplains, every Marquis and Earl five

apiece,

apiece; every Vicount four, and every Baron three.

A Peer of the Realm may retain six Aliens born, whereas another may not retain above four.

In case of Amercements of the Peers of the Realm upon Nonsuits, or other Judgments; a Duke is to be amerced onely Ten pounds, and all under onely Five pounds, and this to be done by their Peers, according to *Magna Charta*; although it is oft done now by the Kings Justices, in stead of their Peers.

All Peers of the Realm being constant Hereditary Councellors of the King in His Great Council of Parliament, and being obliged upon the Kings Summons to appear, and attend in all Parliaments upon their own charges, are priviledged from contributing to the expences of any Member of the House of Commons; for which no levy may be made upon any of their Lands, Parcel of their Earldoms or Baronies, any of their ancient Demesns, Copihold, or Villain Tenants.

The Estates of all Peers of the Realm, being judged in the Eye of the Law, sufficient at all times to satisfie all Debts and Damages, satisfaction is to be sought by Execution taken forth upon their Lands and Goods, and not by Attachments, Imprisonments of their Persons, (those are to be always free for the Service of the King and Kingdom) nor by Exigents or *Capias Utlagatum, &c.*

Other

Other Priviledges belong to the Peers of *England*, as Eight Tun of Wine Custom free to every Earl, and to the rest proportionably, *&c.*

Notwithstanding these great Priviledges belonging to the Nobility of *England*, yet the greatest of them (no not the Brother or Son of the King) ever had the Priviledge of the Grandees of *Spain*, to be covered in the Kings Presence, except onely *Henry Ratcliff*, Earl of *Surrey*, as before *Page* 160. Nor had ever that higher Priviledge of the Nobility of *France*, whose Domain Lands, and their Dependants holding them, are exempted from all Contributions and Tallies, whereby they are tied to their King, and so enabled to serve him; that although Rebellions are frequent, yet seldom of long continuance, and never prosperous; whereas the highest born Subject of *England* hath herein no more Priviledge, than the meanest Ploughman, but utterly want that kinde of reward for Ancient Vertue, and encouragement for future Industry.

Precedence. Touching the Places or Precedences amongst the Peers of *England*, it is to be observed, That (after the King and Princes of the Blood, *viz.* the Sons, Grandsons, Brothers, Uncles, or Nephews of the King, and no farther) Dukes amongst the Nobility have the first place, then Marquesses, Dukes eldest Sons, Earls, Marquesses eldest Sons, Dukes younger Sons, Vicounts, Earls

eldest

eldest Sons, Marquesses younger Sons, Barons, Vicounts eldest Sons, Earls younger Sons, Barons eldest Sons, Vicounts younger Sons, Barons younger Sons.

Here note, That it was decreed by King *James*, That the younger Sons of Barons and Vicounts should yield Place and Precedence to all Knights of the Garter, *Quatenus tales*, and to all Privy-Councellors, *Master of the Wards*, Chancellor, and Under-Treasurer of the *Exchequer*, Chancellor of the *Dutchy*, Cheif Justice of the *Kings Bench*, *Master of the Rolls*, Cheif Justice of the *Common Pleas*, Cheif Baron of the *Exchequer*, and all other Judges and Barons of the degree of the Coife of the said Courts, and that by reason of their Honorable Order and Employment; and also to all Bannerets made under the Kings Banner or Standard displayed in an Army Royal in open War, and the King personally present.

Moreover, Observe that all Nobles of the same degree take place according to the Seniority of their Creation.

State. There are certain Marks of State that belong to each degree amongst the Nobility, which they may practise, or not practise at pleasure.

Duke.] A Duke may have in all places out of the Kings presence a Cloth of Estate hanging down within half a yard of the Ground; so may his Dutchess, and her

Train

Train born up by a Baroneſs; and no Earl to waſh with a Duke without the Dukes pleaſure.

A Marqueſs may have a Cloth of Eſtate reaching within a yard of the Ground, and that in all places out of the preſence of the King, or a Duke, and his Marchioneſs to have her Train born by a Knights wife; and no Vicount to waſh with a Marqueſs but at his pleaſure. *Marqueſs.*

An Earl alſo may have a Cloth of Eſtate without Pendants, but onely Fringe, and a Counteſs may have her Train born by a Gentlewoman, out of the preſence of her Superiors, and in their preſence by a Gentleman. *Earl.*

A Vicount may have a Cover of Aſſay holden under his Cup while he drinks, but no Aſſay taken, as Dukes, Marqueſſes, and Earls may have, and may have a Travers in his own houſe. And a Vicounteſs may have her Gown born up by a Woman out of the preſence of her Superiors, and in their preſence by a Man. *Vicount.*

A Baron may alſo have the Cover of his Cup holden underneath whilſt he drinketh, and a Baroneſs may have her Gown born up by a Man in the preſence of a Vicounteſs. *Baron.*

All Dukes eldeſt Sons are born as Marqueſſes, and the younger as Lords, with the

the addition of their Christian Names, as Lord *Thomas*, Lord *John*, &c.

A Marquesses eldest Son is called Lord of a place, and the younger Sons Lord *Thomas*, Lord *John*, &c.

An Earls eldest Son is born as a Vicount, and shall go as a Vicount, and shall have as many Powdrings as a Vicount; so their younger Sons are said to be born as Barons, but shall go after all Barons, and before all Baronets.

An Earls eldest Son is called Lord of a place, and all his Daughters Ladies, but his younger Sons not Lords.

A Vicounts eldest Son is no Lord, nor his Daughters Ladies; and therefore the eldest Son, and the eldest Daughter of the first Vicount of *England*, is said to be the first Gentleman and Gentlewoman without Title in *England*. Yet a Vicounts eldest Son is said to be born as a Baron.

The Princes of the Blood, the Great Officers of the Realm, and the Bishops are to precede, according to an Act of Parliament, 31 *H*. 8.

The Lord Chancellor, Lord Treasurer, Lord President of the Kings Council, Lord Privy Seal, These being Barons or above, shall in Parliament sit above all Dukes, except the Son, Brother, or Nephew of the King.

The Lord High Steward of *England* is not here named, because it was intended that he should not continue beyond the occasion for which he should be made.

Next

Next hath place the Lord Great Chamberlain of *England*, then the Lord High Constable, the Earl Marshal, the Lord High Admiral, Lord Steward of the Kings Houshold, Lord Chamberlain of the Kings Houshold. These shall sit after the Lord Privy Seal, above all of their degree onely. And if the Kings Principal Secretary be a Baron, he takes place of all Barons that are not of the Offices beforementioned; but if he be a Vicount or higher degree, he shall take place onely acaccording to his degree. Also if the Kings Secretary be a Bishop, as anciently was usual, he takes place next to the Bishop of *Winchester*, before all other Bishops that have none of the Offices aforesaid.

All Dukes, Marquesses, Earls, Vicounts, and Barons, not having any of the said Offices, shall take place according to the ancientry of their Creation.

All Dukes eldest Sons have the Title of Earls, and the eldest Son of an Earl, hath the Title of the Earls Barony, and sometimes of the Vicounty, according to the Patent.

A Catalogue of the Peers of England, *according to their Precedence.*

Dukes of the Royal Blood.

JAMES, Duke of *York* and *Albany*, Earl of *Ulster*, Lord High Admiral of *England*, the Kings onely Brother.

Edgar, Duke of *Cambridge*.

Rupert, Duke of *Cumberland*, and Earl of *Holderness*.

The Lord Chancellor, or Lord Keeper of the Great Seal, the Lord Treasurer, and the Lord Privy Seal, take place before all Dukes not of the Blood Royal.

Dukes.

Thomas Howard, Duke of *Norfolk*.
William Seymour, Duke of *Somerset*.
George Villars, Duke of *Buckingham*.
Charles Stuart, Duke of *Richmond*.
Christopher Monk, Duke of *Albemarle*.
James Scot, Duke of *Monmouth*
William Cavendish, Duke of *Newcastle*.

Marquesses.

John Pawlet, Marquess of *Winchester*.
Henry Somerset, Marquess of *Worcester*.

Henry

Henry Pierrepoint, Marquess of *Dorchester*.

Earls.

These three take place in respect of their Offices.

Robert Bertue, Earl of *Lindsey*, Lord High Chamberlain of *England*.

James Butler, Earl of *Brecknock*, Lord Steward of the Kings Houshold.

Edward Montague, Earl of *Manchester*, Lord Chamberlain of the Kings Houshold.

Earls.

Awbrey de Vere, Earl of *Oxford.*
Charles Talbot, Earl of *Shrewsbury.*
Anthony Grey, Earl of *Kent.*
Charles Stanley, Earl of *Derby.*
John Mannours, Earl of *Rutland.*
Theophilus Hastings, Earl of *Huntingdon.*
William Russel, Earl of *Bedford.*
William Herbert, Earl of *Pembroke.*
Edward Clinton, Earl of *Lincoln.*
Charles Howard, Earl of *Nottingham.*
James Howard, Earl of *Suffolk.*
Richard Sackvile, Earl of *Dorset.*
Robert Cecil, Earl of *Salisbury.*
John Cecil, Earl of *Exeter.*
John Edgerton, Earl of *Bridgwater.*
Robert Sidney, Earl of *Leicester.*

James

James Compton, Earl of *Northampton*.
Charles Rich, Earl of *Warwick*.
William Cavendish, Earl of *Devonshire*.
Basil Fielding, Earl of *Denbigh*.
George Digby, Earl of *Bristol*.
Lionel Cranfield, Earl of *Middlesex*.
Robert Rich, Earl of *Holland*.
Gilbert Holles, Earl of *Clare*.
Oliver S. John, Earl of *Bullingbroke*.
Charles Fane, Earl of *Westmerland*.
Edward Montague, Earl of *Manchester*.
Charles Howard, Earl of *Berkshire*.
John Sheffield, Earl of *Mulgrave*.
William Ley, Earl of *Marlborough*.
Thomas Savage, Earl of *Rivers*.
Nicholas Knowles, Earl of *Banbury*.
Henry Mordant, Earl of *Peterborough*.
Henry Grey, Earl of *Stamford*.
Heneage Finch, Earl of *Winchelsey*.
Charles Dormer, Earl of *Caernarvon*.
Blount, Earl of *Newport*.
Philip Stanhop, Earl of *Chesterfield*.
John Tufton, Earl of *Thanet*.
Thomas Weston, Earl of *Portland*.
William Wentworth, Earl of *Strafford*.
Robert Spencer, Earl of *Sunderland*.
James Savil, Earl of *Sussex*.
Nicholas Leak, Earl of *Scarsdale*.
John Wilmot, Earl of *Rochester*.
Henry Jermin, Earl of S. *Albans*.
Edward Montague, Earl of *Sandwich*.
James Butler, Earl of *Brecknock*.
Edward Hyde, Earl of *Clarendon*.
Arthur Capel, Earl of *Essex*.
Robert Brudnel, Earl of *Cardigan*.

Arthur Annesly, Earl of *Anglesey*.
John Greenvile, Earl of *Bath*.
Charles Howard, Earl of *Carlisle*.
William Craven, Earl of *Craven*.
Robert Bruce, Earl of *Alisbury*.
Richard Boyl, Earl of *Burlington*.

Vicounts.

Leicester Devereux, Vicount *Hereford*.
Francis Brown, Vicount *Montague*.
James Fiennes, Vicount *Say* and *Sele*.
Edward Conway, Vicount *Conway*.
Baptist Noel, Vicount *Camden*.
William Howard, Vicount *Stafford*.
Thomas Bellasis, Vicount *Falconbridge*.
John Mordant, Vicount *Mordant*.
George Savil, Vicount *Hallifax*.

Barons.

Nevil, Lord *Abergavenny*.
James Touchet, Lord *Audley*.
Charles West, Lord *de la Ware*.
George Berkley, Lord *Berkley*.
Thomas Parker, Lord *Morley* and *Mont-eagle*.
Francis Lennard, Lord *Dacres*.
Conyers Darcy, Lord *Darcy* and *Menil*.
William Stourton, Lord *Stourton*.
Lord *Sandys de la Vine*.
Thomas Windsor, Lord *Windsor*.
Cromwel, Lord *Cromwel*.
George Ewre, Lord *Ewre*.
Philip Wharton, Lord *Wharton*.

O *William*

William Willoughby, Lord *Willoughby* of *Parham*.
William Paget, Lord *Paget*.
Dudley North, Lord *North*.
William Bruges, Lord *Shandois*.
William Petre, Lord *Petre*.
Charles Gerard, Lord *Gerard*.
Charles Stanhop, Lord *Stanhop*.
Henry Arundel, Lord *Arundel* of *Warder*.
Christopher Rooper, Lord *Tenham*.
Robert Grevil, Lord *Brook*.
Edward Montague, Lord *Montague* of *Boughton*.
William Grey, Lord *Grey* of *Wark*.
John Roberts, Lord *Roberts*.
John Lovelace, Lord *Lovelace*.
John Pawlet, Lord *Pawlet*.
William Mainard, Lord *Mainard*.
George Coventry, Lord *Coventry*.
Edward, Lord *Howard* of *Esrick*.
Charles Mohun, Lord *Mohun*.
William Butler, Lord *Butler*.
William Herbert, Lord *Powis*.
Edward Herbert, Lord *Herbert* of *Cherbury*.
Seymour, Lord *Seymour*.
Francis Newport, Lord *Newport*.
Thomas Leigh, Lord *Leigh* of *Stoneley*.
Christopher Hatton, Lord *Hatton*.
Richard Byron, Lord *Byron*.
Richard Vaughan, Lord *Vaug*.
Francis Carrington, Lord *Carrington*.
William Widdrington, Lord *Widdrington*.
Humble Ward, Lord *Ward*.

Thomas

Thomas, Lord *Culpeper*.
Isaac Astley, Lord *Astley*.
John Lucas, Lord *Lucas*.
John Bellasis, Lord *Bellasis*.
Edward Watson, Lord *Rockingham*.
Charles Gerard, Lord *Gerard* of *Brandon*.
Gilbert Sutton, Lord *Lexinton*.
Charles Kirkhoven, Lord *Wotton*.
Marmaduke Langdale, Lord *Langdale*.
William Crofts, Lord *Crofts*.
John Berkley, Lord *Berkley* of *Stratton*.
Denzil Hollis, Lord *Hollis*.
Charles Cornwallis, Lord *Cornwallis*.
George Booth, Lord *de la Mere*.
Horatio Townsend, Lord *Townsend*.
Anthony Ashley Cooper, Lord *Ashley*.
John Crew, Lord *Crew*, &c.
Henry Bennet, Lord *Arlington*.
John Freschevile, Lord *Freschevile*.
Richard Arundel, Lord *Arundel* of *Trerice*.
Thomas Butler, Lord *Butler* of *More Park*.
Henry Howard, Lord *Howard* of *Castlerising*.

Of Temporal Lords or Peers of *England*, there are at present about One hundred fifty four, whereof there are Ten Dukes, Three Marquesses, Fifty six Earls, Nine Vicounts, and Sixty seven Barons; whereas within Seventy years last past, there was not one Duke, but one Marquess, about Nineteen Earls, Three or four Vicounts, and Forty Lords. *Number.*

Revenue. The Laws and Customs of *England*, always willing that *Decorum* and Conveniency should be every where observed, and considering the Charges and Expences appertaining to the several degrees of Honor, as they belong to Men of Principal Service to the King and Realm, both in time of War and Peace, expected that each of them should have a convenient Estate and Value of Lands of Inheritance, for the support of their Honors and the Kings Service. Therefore anciently when the intrinsick value of a Pound *Sterling* was worth 30 *l.* of our Money now, as appears by the then price of all things, every Knight was to have about Eight hundred Acres, reckoned at 20 *l.* yearly in Land. that is, about 600 *l.* of our Money at this day. A Baron to have Thirteen Knights Fees, and one third part, which amounted to about 267 *l.* Which multiplied by 30, was as much as 8000 *l.* a year at this day. An Earl Twenty Knights Fees, and a Duke Forty. And in case of decay of Nobility, or that they had so far wasted their Revenues, that their Honors could not decently be maintained (as the *Roman Senators* were in such case removed from the Senate) so sometimes some *English Barons* have not been admitted to sit in the *Higher House* of *Parliament*, though they kept the Name and Title of Dignity still.

For the better support of these Degrees of Honor, the King doth usually upon the Creation of a Duke, Marquess, Earl, or

Vicount,

Vicount; grant an Annuity or Yearly Rent, to them and their Heirs, which is so annexed to the Dignity; that by no Grant, Assurance, or any manner of Alienation can be given from the same, but is still incident to, and a support of the same Dignity; contrary to that Principle in Law, *That every Land of Fee-simple may be charged with a Rent in Fee-simple by one way or other.*

To a Duke the King grants 40 *l.* heretofore a considerable Pension, to a Marquess 40 Marks, to an Earl 20 *l.* and to Viconnt 20 Mark. To Barons no such Pensions are ordinarily granted, onely the late King creating *Mountjoy Blount* (the late Earl of *Newport*) Lord *Mountjoy* of *Thurlston,* granted him a Fee of 20 Marks *per annum*, to him and his heirs for ever.

As the King of *England* hath ever had the repute of the richest in Domains of any King in *Europe*; so the Nobility of *England* have been accounted the richest in Lands of any Neighboring Nation; some having above 20000 *l.* yearly, others 15000 *l.* and so many of them above Ten, That if one with another, they have but 8000 *l.* yearly, it will amount to in all amongst the 154 Lords, above Twelve hundred thousand pounds a year, about the Eleventh part of the yearly Revenue of all *England*, which upon computation is found to be about Fourteen Millions yearly.

The English Nobility for Valor, Wisdom, Integrity, and Honor, hath in all former Ages been equal to any in Christendom.

Every Lords House was a kinde of a well-disciplined Court, in so much, that the Gentry, Males, and Females, were wont to be sent thither for vertuous breeding, and returned excellently accomplished.

At home their Table Attendance, Officers, Exercises, Recreations, Garb, was an honor to the Nation.

Abroad they were attended with as brave, numerous, and uniform Train of Servants and Followers, as any in *Europe*; not thinking it consistent with their Honors to be seen walk the Streets almost in *Cuerpo* with one Lacquey, or not that, much less to be found drinking in a Tavern, *&c.*

If some of the English Nobility, by a long continued Peace, excessive Luxury in Diet, want of Action, *&c.* were before the late Wars born more feeble in body then their Ancestors, and by too fine and too full Diet, afterwards were rendred weaker in minde, and then during the late troubles by much licentiousness and want of fit Education, were so debauched, that it was lately difficult to finde (as some are bold to affirm) the Courage, Wisdom, Integrity, Honor, Sobriety, and Courtesie of the Ancient Nobility; yet is it not to be doubted, but that under a Warlike Enterprising Prince all those vertues of their Forefathers may spring afresh.

CHAP. XIX.

Of the Third State or Commons of England, *and therein of Baronets, Knights, Esquires, Gentlemen, Yeomen, Citizens, Handicrafts, &c.*

THe Law of *England*, contrary to the Laws and Customs of other Countreys, calleth none Noble under a Baron; so that not onely all Baronets, all sorts of Knights, all Esquires and Gentlemen, but also the Sons of the Nobility, are by our Law reckoned amongst the *Commons* of *England*; and therefore the eldest Son of a Duke, though by the Courtesie of *England* stiled an Earl, yet shall be Arraigned by the stile of Esquire onely, and may be tried by a Jury of *Common Freeholders*; and in Parliament can sit onely in the *House of Commons*, if elected, till called by the *Kings Writ* to the *Lords House*. Yet doth it seem very absurd, that all Noblemens Sons, with all Knights, Esquires, and Gentlemen, should be esteemed *Plebeians*, but rather as in *Rome*, they were in a middle Rank, *Inter Senatores & Plebem*; or else as in other Christian Kingdoms, they should be considered as the *Minor Nobilitas Regni*: So that as Barons, and all above, may be stiled *Nobiles Majores*; so from a Baron downward to the Yeoman, all may be not unfitly, stiled *Nobiles Minores*.

The Lower Nobility then of *England* consists of Baronets, Knights, Esquires, and Gentlemen.

Baronets. The next Degree to Barons are Baronets, which is the lowest Degree of Honour that is Hereditary. An Honour first instituted by King *James Anno* 1611, given by Patent to a Man and his Heirs Males of his Body lawfully begotten; for which each one is obliged to pay into the *Exchequer* so much money as will for 3 years at 8 *d. per diem*, pay 30 Foot Soldiers to serve in the Province of *Ulster* in *Ireland*, which sum amounts to 1095 *l*, which with Fees doth commonly arise to 1200 *l*.

Baronets have precedence before all Knights except Knights of the Garter, Knights who are Privy Councellors, and Knights Bannerets, made under the Kings Banner or Standard, displayed in an *Army Royal* in open War, and the King personally present, or the Prince of *Wales*: Prince *Henry* by particular mention had liberty to Create Bannerets, See Mr. *Selden*'s Titles of Honour.

Baronets have the Priviledge to bear in a Canton of their Coat of Arms, or in a whole Scutcheon the Arms of *Ulster*, *viz.* In *a Field Argent a Hand Gules*: also in the Kings Armies to have place in the gross near the Kings Standard, with some other particulars for their Funerals.

The

The whole number of Baronets in *England* are not to exceed 200 at one and the same time; after which number compleated, as any for want of heirs come to be extinct, the number shall not be made up by new Creations, but be suffered to diminish; as appears by their Patent.

No Honour is ever to be created between Baronets and Barons.

The first Baronet that was created, was Sir *Nicholas Bacon* of *Suffolk*; whose Successor is therefore stiled *Primus Baronettorum Angliæ*.

Knights.

This Word *Knight* is derived from the German Word *Knecht*, signifying originally a *Lusty Servitor*.

The Germans (as the antient Romans gave their young men *Togam Virilem*) by publick Authority bestowed on their young men able to manage Arms, a Sheild and a Javelin; as fit for Martial Service, and to be a Member of the Commonwealth, accounted before but a part of a Family; and such a young man publickly allowed, they called *Knecht*: whence we had our Institution of Knigthood.

The thing *Knight* is at this day signified in *Latine*, *French*, *Spanish*, *Italian*, and also in the *High* and *Law Dutch* Tongues, by a Word that properly signifies a *Horseman*, because they were wont to serve in War on Horse-back, and were sometimes in *England* called *Radenyhts*, *id est*, *Riding Servitors*; yet our *Common Law* stiles them *Milites*, because they commonly held

Lands in Knights Service, to serve the King in his Wars as Soldiers.

The honour of Knighthood is commonly given for some personal desert, and therefore dies with the person deserving, and descends not to his Son.

Knight of the Garter. In *England* there are several sorts of Knights, whereof the chiefest are those of the Order of St. *George*, commonly called *Knights of the Garter.*

This Order is esteemed the most Honourable and most Antient of any now in use in *Christendom.* It began as appears in the Statutes of this Order, in 1350, and the 23th year of the Warlike and Puissant King *Edward* 3. who was founder there of, and at first made choice of the most Illustrious Persons of *Europe*, to be of that *Royal Society* (no doubt) upon a Martial, and not upon any such Amorous Account as a Garter falling from a Ladies Legge, which ridiculous Story, to the dishonour of the Order, was first fancied by *Polydore Virgil*; and since upon his credit taken up by many late Authors.

It was since commonly called, *The Order of the Garter*, because this only part of the whole Habit of the Order was made choice of at first to be constantly worn, and that to put in mind the Companions of the Order, that as by this Order they were joyned in a firm League of Amity and Concord, so by their Garter, as by a fast tye of affection, they were obliged to love one another. Now least this

strict

strict combination might seem to have any other aime or end, but what was honourable and just, *ad obviandam malam interpretationem* (as the antient Records of *Windsor* speak) the said King commanded that Motto, or Impress to be wrought on the Garter, viz. *Honi soit qui mal y pense*.

The reason why this Motto was put in French, was because then the King of *England* being possest of a great part of *France*, not only our Laws, Pleadings, and Sermons were in French, but that was the ordinary Language in the Court of *England*.

It appears by Antient Writings that this Honorable Company is a Colledge or Corporation, having a great Seal belonging to it, and consisting of a Soveraign Guardian (which is always the King of *England*) and of 25 Companions called *Knights of the Garter*, of 14 Secular Canons, that are Priests; of 13 Vicars who are also Priests; of 26 poor Knights, who have no other Maintenance but the allowance of this Colledge, which is given them in respect of their Prayers, to the Honour of God and of St. *George*, who is the Patron of *England* and of this Order in particular; and none of those Fabulous St *Georges* as some have vainly fancied; but that famous Saint and Soldier of Christ St. *George* of *Cappadocia*, a Saint so universally received in all parts of *Christendom*, so generally attested by the Ecclesiastical Writers of all Ages from the time of his Martyrdom till this day, that no one Saint in

all

all the *Calendar* (except those attested by *Scripture*) is better evidenced.

There be also certain Officers belonging to this Order; as the Prelate of the Garter, which Office is settled on the Bishoprick of *Winchester*. A Chancellor of the Garter; a Register, who of latter times hath been constantly the Dean of *Windsor*, though anciently it was otherwise. The Principal King at Arms called *Garter*, whose cheif Function is to manage and marshal their solemnities at their Installations and Feasts. Lastly, The Usher of the Garter.

There are also certain Orders and Constitutions belonging to this Society touching the Solemnities in making these Knights, their Duties after Creation, and their high Priviledges, too long for this place.

The Colledge is seated in the Castle of *Windsor*, with the Chappel of S. *George*, there erected by King *Edward* the Third, and the Chapter-House.

The Order of the Garter is wont to be bestowed upon the most excellent and renowned Persons for Honor and Vertue; and with it a Blew Garter deckt with Gold, Pearl, and Pretious Stones, and a Buckle of Gold, to be worn daily on the Left Leg; also at High Feasts they are to wear a Surcoat, a Mantle, a high Black Velvet Cap, a Collar of pure Gold, composed of Roses enamelled Red, within a Garter enamelled Blew, with the usual Motto in Letters of Gold, and between each of these Garters a Knot with Taſſels of Gold, together with other Stately and Magnificent Apparel.

They are not to be ſeen abroad without their Garter upon their Left Leg, upon pain of paying Two Crowns to any Officer of the Order who ſhall firſt claim it; onely in taking a Journey a Blew Ribbon under the Boot, doth ſuffice.

Upon the Left-Shoulder, upon Cloak, Coat, or Riding Caſſack, in all places of Aſſembly, when they wear not their Robes, they are to wear an Eſcutcheon of the Arms of St. *George*, that is, A Croſs with a Garter, and this by an Order made *April 1626.* That Ornament and Embelliſhment about the ſaid Eſcutcheon now worn, and called *The Star*, or rather, *The Sun in its Glory*, was at the ſame time enjoyned.

The greateſt *Monarchs of Chriſtendom* have been enrolled, and have taken it for an honor to be of this Order.

There have been of this Order ſince the Inſtitution Eight Emperors, Seven and twenty or Eight and twenty Foreign Kings, beſides many Soveraign Princes, &c.

Note, That none can be of this Moſt Honorable Order, that have been convicted of Hereſie, of Treaſon, or of Cowardiſe.

The Fellows and Companions of the Most Noble Order of St. George, *are at present these that follow, ranked according as they are seated in their several Stalls at* Windsor.

IN the first Stall on the Right hand is the *Soveraign* of the Order King *Charles* the Second, who is Patron and Sole Disposer of the Order.

In the other Stalls on the *Soveraign's* side are thus placed these that follow: 2. *Christian* 5th King of *Denmarke*, 3 The Duke of *York*, 4 Prince *Rupert*, 5 Marquiss of *Brandenbourgh*, 6 Duke of *Buckingham*, 7 Earl of *Bristol*, 8 Count *Marsin*, 9 Earl of *Sandwich*, 10 Duke of *Richmond*, 11 Earl of *Strafford*, the 12th and 13th Stalls are void. On the other side, opposite to these afore-named, are placed in this Order these that follow: 1 *Charles* the 11th of that Name, King of *Sweden*; 2 Prince Elector *Palatine*, 3 Prince of *Orange*, 4 Duke of *Saxony*, 5 Duke of *Ormond*, 6 Duke of *Newcastel*, 7 Prince of *Tarent*, 8 Earl of *Oxford*, 9 Earl of *Manchester*, 10 Duke of *Monmouth*, 11 Duke of *Albemarle*, the 12th and 13th Stalls on this side are void at present.

Note, That antiently Kings and Soveraign Princes were placed according to their

their Creations, but now those only are placed according to their Degrees.

The whole number of Fellows of this Order is not to exceed 26.

In the next place are *Knights, Bannerets, Equites Vexilliferi*, antiently a high Honour, now obsolete, there being at this time none of this Order in *England*. *Knights Bannerets,*

These may bear their Arms with supporters, and none under this Degree.

Knights of the Bath, so called of their *Bathing* used before they are created. The first of this sort were made by *Henry* the Fourth *Anno* 1399. They are now commonly made at the Coronation of a King or Queen, or Creation of a Prince of *Wales*. They wear a Scarlet Ribbon Belt wise. They are still made with much Ceremony, too long here to be described. *Knights of the Bath.*

Other Knights callrd *Equites Aurati*, from the Gilt Spurs usually put upon them, and Knights Batchelors, *quasi Bas Chevaliers*, Knights of low Degree. So Batchelors, in Arts or Divinity, *quasi* Low Knights or Servitors in Arts. These were antiently made by girding with a Sword and Gilt Spurs, and was bestowed onely upon Sword-men for their Military Service, and was reputed an excellent and glorious Degree, and a Noble Reward for couragious Persons; but of late being made more common, and bestowed upon Gown Men; *Knights Batchelors.*

con-

contray to the nature of the thing (as degrees in the University are sometimes bestowed upou Sword-men) it is become of much less reputation. Yet amongst Gownmen it is given only to Lawyers and Physitians, and not to Divines, who may as well become that Dignity, and be Spiritual Knights as well as Spiritual Lords.

These are now made with no other Ceremony but kneeling down, the King with a drawn Sword lightly toucheth them on the Shoulder, after which heretofore the King said in French, *Sois Chevalier au nom de Dieu*, and then *Avances Chevalier*.

When a Knight is to suffer death for any foul Crime, his Military Girdle is first to be ungirt, his Sword taken away, his Spurs cut off with an Hatchet, his Gantlet pluckt off, and his Coat of Arms reversed.

Next among the Lower Nobility are *Esquires*, so called from the French word *Escuyers*, *Scutigeri*, because they were Wont to bear before the Prince in war, or before the better sort of Nobility a Shield, or else perhaps because they bear a Coat of Arms as Ensigns of their descent; and by our Lawyers are called *Armigeri*.

Of this Title are first all Vicounts eldest Sons, and all Vicounts and Barons younger Sons; and by the Common Law of *England* all the Sons of Earls, Marquisses, and Dukes, are Esquires and no more. Next are the Esquires of the Kings Body, mentioned among the Officers of the

Kings

Kings Court; after these are reckoned the eldest Sons of younger Sons of Barons, and of all Noblemen of higher degree then Knights eldest Sons and their eldest Sons for ever; next Esquires created by the King, by putting about their Necks a Collar of Esses, and bestowing on them a pair of Silver Spurs, Lastly, any that are in superiour publick Office for King or State, are reputed Esquires, or equal to Esquires, as Justices of the Peace, Mayors of Towns, so Councellors at Law, Batchelours of Divinity, Law, or Physick, although none of them really are so.

In the last place, among the lower Nobility are accounted the Gentry of *England*, that have no other Title, but are descended of antient Families, that have always born a Coat of Arms.

This kind of Honour is derived from the Germans to the rest of *Christendom*, and was never known in any Country where the German Customs were unknown, as in *Asia*, *Affrica*, and *America*. The Germans antiently warring oft amongst themselves, painted their Scutcheons with the Picture of some Beast, Bird, or other thing for distinction, and put some eminent and visible Mark upon the Crests of their Helmets, and this Ornament both of Arms and Crest descended by inheritance to their Children, to the eldest pure, and to the rest with some note of distinction, such as the Old Master of Ceremonies, in High Dutch *Herealt*, now *Herald* thought fit. Gen-

Gentlemen well descended and well qualified, have always been of such repute in *England*, that none of the higher Nobility, no nor the King himself have thought it unfitting to make them sometimes their Companions.

The Title of Gentleman in *England* (as of Cavalier in *France*, *Italy*, and *Spain*) is not disdained by any Nobleman. All Noblemen are Gentlemen, though all Gentlemen are not Noblemen.

The State of Gentry was antiently such, that it was accounted an abasing of Gentry, to put their Sons to get their Living by Shop-keeping, and our Law did account it a disparagement of a Ward in Chivalry to be married to a Shop-keepers Daughter, or to any meer Citizen; for Tradesmen in all Ages and Nations have been reputed ignoble, in regard of the doubleness of their Tongue, without which they hardly grow rich (for *Nihil proficiunt nisi admodum mentiuntur*, as *Tully* observes, so the Son of *Sirach Eccles*. 26. 29. A Merchant shall hardly keep himself from doing wrong, and an Hukster shall not be freed from Sin:) and therefore amongst the *Thebans* no man was admitted to places of Honour and Trust, unless he had left off Trading ten years before: So by the Imperial Laws a Tradesman is not capable of any Honourable Estate, nor to be a Commander over Soldiers, and therefore the English Nobility and Gentry till within late years, judged it a stain and diminution to the honour and dignity of their Families,

lies; to seek their Childrens support by Shopkeeping, but only (as in all great Monarchies, by Military, Court, State, or Church Employments, much less to subject their Children to an apprentisage, a perfect Servitude; for during that time, whatever they gain by their Masters Trade or their own wit, belongs all to their Master, neither can they lie out of their Masters House, nor to take a Wife, nor Trade of their own, but subject to all Houshold Work, all Commands of their Master, undergo what punishment, and eat and wear what their Master pleaseth; which Marks of Slavery considered, Heralds are of opinion that a Gentleman thereby looses his Gentility for ever, till he can otherwise recover it; and yet, to the shame of our Nation, we have seen of late not only the Sons of Baronets, Knights, and Gentlemen, sitting in Shops, and sometimes of Pedling Trades, far more fit for Women and their Daughters, but also an Earl of this Kingdom subjecting his Son to an Apprentisage and Trade; but the folly of the English in swerving from their Ancestors herein (as in other things) is now apparent, for those young Gentlemen possessing more noble and active spirits, could not brook such dull slavish lives, and being thereby unfitted for other employments, have generally taken ill debauched courses.

The true English Nobility and Gentry have in all times made it their main aim to endow their Sons with such accomplish-

ments

ments especially as might render them capable to defend their Countrey in time of War, and to govern it in times of Peace; for which two things all Gentlemen seem to be born, and therefore their chief Studies have ever been that of the Great Emperour *Justinian*, and should be of all Princes and Nobles, *viz. Domi Leges & foris Arma quam optime callere.*

Priviledges.

The lower Nobility of *England* have fewer and less Priviledges than those in other Monarchies.

Some few Priviledges belong to Knights, *quatenus* Knights. If a Knight be a *Minor*, yet shall he be out of Wardship both for Lands, Body, and Marriage; for though the Law doth judge him not able to do Knights Service till the Age of 21 years, yet the King being Soveraign and Supreme Judge of Chivalry, by dubbing him Knight, doth thereby allow him to be able to do him Knights Service.

Knights are excused from attendance at Court-Leets.

They and their eldest Sons not compellable to find Pledges at the *Visus Franci Plegii.*

Knights by *Magna Charta*, *cap.* 21. are so freed, that no Demesne Cart of theirs may be taken.

The Son and Brother of a Knight, by a Statute Law, are capacitated to hold

more

more than one Benefice with cure of Souls.

By the Stat. *Primo Jacobi* it seems that Knights and their Sons (though they cannot spend 10 *l. per annum*, nor are worth 200 *l.*) may keep Greyhounds, Setting-Dogs, or Nets to take Pheasants or Partridges.

Some Priviledges also belong to Gentlemen. Antiently if an ignoble person did strike a Gentleman in *England*, he was to loose his hand.

A Gentleman by Stat. *Quint. Eliz.* may not be compelled to serve in Husbandry.

The Child of a Gentleman brought up to singing, cannot be taken without the Parents and Friends consent to serve in the *Kings Chappel*, as others may.

The Horse of a Gentleman may not be taken to ride Post.

Note, That as there are some Great Officers of the Crown, who for their Dignity and Worth of their Places, although they are not Noblemen, yet take place amongst the highest of the Higher Nobility; so there are some persons who for their Dignities in the Church degrees, in the University, Offices in the State or Army, although they are neither Knights nor Gentlemen born, yet take place amongst them, so all Deans, Archdeacons, Chancellours, Prebends, Doctors of Divinity, Law, and Physick, Heads of Houses in the University, usually take

place

place next to Knights, and before ordinary Esquires and Gentlemen.

Yet in other Christian Countries where the Civil Law hath its due Credit in such Acts as concern Learning, a Doctor of Law hath precedence of a Knight; as also at Court in Foreign parts, those Doctors that wait on the Prince, precede the Knights who are servants to the Prince; but otherwise Knights usually take place of Doctors.

Likewise all Judges of Courts, Justices of the peace.

All Commissionated Officers in the Army, as Colonels, Master of Aitillery, Quarter-Master General, *&c.*

All higher Officers in the Kings Court or State.

All Sergeants at Law, *&c.* These are wont to precede Esquires.

All Batchelors of Divinity, Law, and Physick, all *Doctors* in the Arts, commonly called Masters of Art, all Barresters in the Innes of Court, all Captains, divers other Officers in the Kings Houshold, *&c.* may equal, if not precede Gentlemen, that have none of those qualifications.

In *England* Gentry (as in *Germany* all Nobility) and Arms are held in *Gavelkind*, descending to all the Sons alike, only the eldest Son beareth Arms without difference, which the younger may not.

Of

Of the lower Nobility in *England* the number is so great, that there are reckoned at present above 500 Baronets more than the first intended number; that is in all above 700, who are possest one with another of about 1200 *l.* a year in Lands. Of Knights above 1400, who one with another may have about 800 *l.* Lands a year. Of Esquires and Gentlemen above 6000, each one possest one with another of about 400 *l.* a year in Lands, besides younger Brothers, whose number may amount to about 16000 in all *England*, who have small Estates in Lands, but are commonly bred up to Divinity, Law, Physick, to Court, and Military Employments, but of late too many of them to Shop-keeping.

The Lands in the possession of the Lower Nobility will amount to about four Millions and sixty thousand pounds yearly.

Next to the Lower Nobility and the first Degree of the Commons or Plebeans, are the Freeholders in *England*, commonly called Yeomen from the High Dutch *Gemen* or *Gemain*, in English *Common*; so in the Kings Court it signifieth an Officer, which is in a middle place between a Sergeant and a Groom, or else from the Low Dutch *Yeaman*, *Some-body*, as the Spaniard calls a Gentlemen *Hidalgo*, *Hijo d'algo*, that is *the Son of Somebody*.

The Yeomanry of *England* having Lands of their own to a good value, and living upon Husbandry, are lookt upon

as

as not apt to commit or omit any thing that may endanger their Estates and Credits, nor apt to be corrupted or suborned, &c. wherefore they are judged fit to bear some Offices, as of Constable, Church-warden, to serve upon Juries, to be Train-Soldiers, to vote in the Election of Knights of the Shire for Parliament, &c.

In Cases and Causes the Law of *England* hath conceived a better opinion of the Yeomanry that occupy Lands, than of Tradesmen, Artificers or Labourers.

Husbandry hath in no Age rendred a Gentleman ignoble nor uncapable of places of Honour.

Amongst the Romans some of the greatest Dictators and Consuls had been once Husbandmen, and some of them taken from Plowing their Ground, to bear those Highest Offices and Dignities; so divers Princes, Kings and Emperours, have exercised Agriculture, and the Grand *Scipio* and the Emperour *Dioclesian* left their Commands to enjoy Husbandry.

By the Statutes of *England* certain Immunities are given to Free-holders and landed men, though they are not Gentlemen: *Vide Stat.* 1 *Jacobi*, *cap.* 27. & *alibi*.

Of the Free holders in *England* there are more in number and richer than in any Countrey of the like extent in *Europe*, 40 or 50 *l.* a year a piece is very ordinary, 100 and 200 *l.* a year in some Counties is not rare, sometimes in Kent 1000 *l.* and 1500.

Besides

Besides these Freeholders (which are so called, because they hold Lands or Tenements inheritable by a perpetual Right to them and their heirs for ever) there are in *England* a very great number of Copiholders, who hold Lands within some Mannors onely by Copy of Court Roll of the said Mannor, *&c.* and have *Jus perpetuum & utile Dominium*, though not *Allodium & directum Dominium*, which Freeholders may improperly be said to have but properly none in *England*, but the King hath.

Amongst the Commons of *England*, in the next place, are reckoned Tradesmen, amongst whom Merchants of Foreign Traffick have for their great benefit to the publick, and for their great endowments and generous living, been of best repute in *England*, and although the Law of *England* look upon Tradesmen and Chapmen that live by buying and selling, as a baser sort of people, and that a Ward within age, may bring his Action of Disparagement against his Guardian for offering any such in Marriage; yet in *England*, as well as *Italy*, to become a Merchant of Foreign Commerce, without serving any Apprentisage, hath been allowed no disparagement to a Gentleman born, especially to a younger brother.

Amongst Tradesmen, in the next place, are Whole-salemen, then Retailers, lastly, Mechanicks or Handicraftsmen. These are all capable of bearing some Sway or Office in Cities and Towns Corporate.

The lowest Member, the Feet of the Body Politick, are the Day-Laborers, who by their large Wages given them, and the Cheapness of all Necessaries, enjoy better Dwellings, Diet, and Apparel in *England*, then the Husbandmen do in many other Countreys.

Liberties and Properties.

As the Clergy and Nobility have certain Priviledges peculiar to themselves, so they have Liberties and Properties common to the Commonalty of *England*.

The Commons of *England* for Hereditary Fundamental Liberties and Properties are blest above and beyond the Subjects of any *Monarch* in the World.

First, No Freeman of *England* ought to be imprisoned or otherwise restrained, without cause shewn for which by Law he ought to be so imprisoned.

Secondly, To him that is imprisoned, may not be denied a Writ of *Habeas Corpus*, if it be desired.

Thirdly, If no cause of Imprisonment be alledged, and the same be returned upon an *Habeas Corpus*, then the Prisoner ought to be set at liberty.

Fourthly, No Soldiers can be quartered in the House of any Freeman, in time of Peace, without his will; though they pay for their quarters.

Fifthly, Every Freeman hath such a full and absolute propriety in his goods, that no

Taxes,

Taxes, Loans, or Benevolences, ordinarily and legally can be imposed upon them, without their own consent by their Representtaives in Parliament. Moreover, They have such an absolute Power, that they can dispose of all they have how they please, even from their own Children, and to them in what inequality they will, without shewing any cause; which other Nations governed by the Civil Law, cannot do.

Sixthly, No Englishman may be prest or compelled (unless bound by his Tenure) to march forth of his County) to serve as a Soldier in the Wars, except in case of a Foreign Enemy invading, or a Rebellion at home. Nor may he be sent out of the Realm against his will, upon any Foreign Employment, by way of an honorable Banishment.

Seventhly, No Freeman can be tryed, but by his Peers, nor condemned but by the Laws of the Land, or by an Act of Parliament.

Eighthly, No Freeman may be fined for any Crime, but according to the Merit of the Offence, always *Salvo sibi contenemento suo,* in such manner, that he may continue and go on in his Calling.

Briefly, If it be considered onely, that ordinarily they are subject to no Laws, but what they make themselves, nor no Taxes but what they impose themselves, and pray the King and Lords to consent unto, their Liberties and Properties must be acknowledged to be transcendent and their worldly condition most happy and blessed; and so far above that of the Subjects of any of our Neighbour Nations, that as all the Women of *Europe* would run into *England* (the Paradise of Women) if there were a Bridge made over the Sea: so all the Men too, if there were but an Act for a general Naturalization of all Aliens.

CHAP. XVI.

Of the Women of England.

TOuching the Women of *England*, there are divers things considerable in the English Laws and Customs; Women in *England*, with all their moveable Goods, so soon as they are Married, are wholly in *potestate viri*, at the will and disposition of the Husband.

If any Goods or Chattels be given to Feme Covert to a Married Woman, they all immediately become her Husbands. She cannot let, set, sell, give away, or alienate any thing without her Husbands consent.

Her very necessary Apparel by the Law is not hers in property. If she hath any Tenure at all, it is *in Capite*, that is, she holds it of and by her Husband, who is *Caput mulieris*; and therefore the Law saith *Uxor fulget radiis mariti*.

All the Chattels personal the Wife had at the Marriage, is so much her Husbands, that after his death they shall not return to to the Wife: but go to the Executor or Administrator of the Husband, as his other Goods and Chattels, except only her *Parapherna*, or *præter dotalia*, which are here Necessary Apparel; which with the consent of her Husband she may devise by Will; not otherwise by our Law; because the property and possession even of the *Parapherna* are in him.

The Wife can make no Contract without her Husbands consent, and in Law matters *sine viro respondere non potest.*

The Law of *England* supposes a Wife to be in so much Subjection and Obedience to her Husband, as to have no will at all of her own: Wherefore if a Man and his Wife commit a Felony together, the Wife by the Law can be neither Principal nor Accessary, the Law supposing that in regard of the Subiection and Obedience she owes to her Husband, she was necessitated thereunto.

The Law of *England* supposes in the Husband a power over his Wife, as over his Child or Servant, to correct her when she offends; and therefore he must answer for his Wives faults, if she wrong another by her Tongue or by Trespass, he must make satisfaction.

So the Law makes it as high a Crime, and allots the same punishment to a Woman that shall kill her Husband, as to a Woman that shall kill her Father or Master, and that is Petty Treason, to be burnt alive.

So that a Wife in *England* is *de jure* but the best of Servants, having nothing her own in a more proper sense than a Child hath, whom his Father suffers to call many things his own yet can dispose of nothing.

The Woman upon Marriage looseth not only the power over her person and her will, and the property of her Goods, but her very Name; for ever after she useth her Husbands Surname, and her own is wholly laid aside; which is not observed in *France* and other Countries, where the Wife subscribes her self by her Paternal Name; as if *Susanna* the Daughter of *R. Clifford* be married to *E. Chamberlayne*, she either writes her self *Susanna Clifford*, or else *Susanna Clifford Chamberlayne*.

Notwithstanding all which, their condition *de facto* is the best in the World; for such is the good nature of Englishmen towards their Wives, such is their tenderness and respect, giving them the uppermost place at Table and elsewhere, the right hand every where, and putting them upon no drudgery and hardship; that if there were a Bridge over into *England* as aforesaid, it is thought all the Women in *Europe* would run thither.

Besides in some things the Laws of *England* are above other Nations so favourable to that Sex, as if the Women had voted at the making of them.

If a Wife bring forth a Child during her husbands long absence, though it be for some years, yet if he lived all the time within

this

this Island, he must Father that Child; and if that Child be her first-born Son, he shall inherit that Husbands Estate if entailed, or left without Will.

If a Wife bring forth a Child begotten by another before Marriage, but born after Marriage with another Man, this later must own the Child, and that Child shall be his Heir at Law.

The Wife after her Husbands death having no joynture setled before Marriage, may challenge the third part of his yearly Rents of Land during her life, and within the City of *London* a third part of all her Husbands moveables for ever.

As the Wife doth participate of her Husbands Name, so likewise of his Condition. If he be a Duke, she is a Dutchess; if he be a Knight, she is a Lady; if he be an Alien made a Denison, she is *ipso facto* so too. If a Freeman marry a Bondwoman, she is also free during the Coverture; whereof also it is said as before, *Uxor fulget radiis Mariti.*

All Women in *England* are comprised under Noble or Ignoble.

Noble Women are so three manner of ways, *viz.* by Creation, by Descent, and by Marriage.

The King, the Fountain of Honour, may, and oft hath created Women to be Baronesses, Countesses, Dutchesses, *&c.*

By Descent such Women are Noble, to whom lands holden by such Dignity do descend as Heir; for Dignities and Titles of Honour for want of Males, do sometimes descend to Females; but to one of them onely, because they are things in their own nature entire, and not to be divided amongst many (as the Lands and Tenements are which descend to all the Daughters equally;) besides by dividing Dignities the Reputation of *Honour* would be lost, and the Strength of the Realm impaired; for the *Honour* and *Chivalry* of the *Realm* doth chiefly consist in the *Nobility* thereof.

By Marriage all Women are Noble, who take to their Husbands any Baron or Peer of the Realm; but if afterwards they marry to Men not Noble, they lose their former dignity, and follow the condition of their later Husband; for *eodem modo dissolvitur earum Nobilitas, quo constituitur*. But Women Noble by Creation, or Descent, or Birth-Right, remain Noble, though they marry Husbands under their degree; for such Nobility is accounted *Character indelebilis*. Here note, that by the *Courtesie* or *England* a Woman Noble onely by Marriage always retaineth her Nobility; and so the Widow of a Knight married to any inferiour person, retaineth by Courtesie the Title and Name gotten by her former Husband; but if the Kings Daughter marry a Duke or an Earl, *illa semper dicitur Regalis*, as well by *Law* as *Courtesie*.

Note also that any Woman who is Noble by Birth if she be married to a Baron takes place according to the Degree of her Husband, though she be a Dukes Daughter;

ter; but if she marry to one under those of the higher Nobility, as to a Knight or a Gentleman, then by courtesie place is given according to her Birth and not her Husband.

Noble-women in the eye of the Law are as Peers of the Realm, and are to be tryed by their Peers, and to enjoy most other Priviledges, Honour, and Respect as their Husbands: Only they cannot by the opinion of some great Lawyers maintain an Action upon the Statute *De Scandalo Magnatum*, the Makers of that Statute meaning only to provide in that Case for the Great Men, and not for the Women, as the words of that Statute seem to import. Likewise if any of the Kings Servants within his Check Roll should conspire the death of any Noblewoman, this were not Felony, as it is, if like Conspiracy be against a Nobleman.

None of the Wives dignities can come by Marriage to their Husbands, although all their Goods and Chattels do; only the Wives dignities with her lands, are to descend to her next Heir: yet is the Courtesie of *England* such, that as the Wife for her Dower hath the third part of her Husbands Lands during her life; so the Husband for the Dignity of his Sex, and for getting his Wife with Child, (which must appear by being born alive) shall have all his Wives Lands (for his Dower, if it may be so called) during his Life.

By the Constitutions of *England* married persons are so fast joyned, that they may not be wholly seperated by any agreement between themselves, but only by sentence of the Judge; and such seperation is either *a Vinculo Matrimonii*, and that is *ob præ-contractum, vel ob contractum per metum effectum, vel ob frigiditatem, vel ob affinitatem, sive Consanguinitatem, vel ob Sævitiam*; or else such seperation is *a Mensa & Thoro*, and that is *ob Adulterium.*

The Wife in *England* is accounted so much one with her Husband, that she cannot be produced as a Witness for or against her Husband.

CHAP. XXI.

Of Children.

THe Condition of Children in *England* is different from those in our Neighbour Countries.

As Husbands have a more absolute Authority over their Wives and their Estates, so Fathers have a more absolute Authority over their Children. Fathers may give all their Estates un-intailed from their own Children; and to any one Child, and none to the rest; the consideration whereof keeps the Children in great awe.

Children by the Common Law of *England* are at certain ages enabled to perform certian Acts.

A Son at the Age of 14 may choose his Guardian, may claim his Land holden in *Socage*; may consent to Marriage, may by Will dispose of Goods and Chattels.

At the Age of 15 he ought to be sworn to his Allegeance to the King.

At 21 he is said to be of full Age, may then make any Contracts, may pass not only Goods but Lands by Will, which in other Countries may not be done till the *Annus consistentiæ*, the Age of 25 when the heat of youth is somewhat abated, and they begin to be staied in mind as well as in growth.

A Daughter at 7 years is to have aid of her Fathers Tenants to marry her, for at those years she may consent unto Marriage though she may afterwards dissent.

At 9 she is Dowable, as if then, or soon after she could *virum sustinere*, and thereby *Dotem promereri*.

At 12 she is enabled to ratifie and confirm her former consent given to Matrimony, and if at that Age she dissent not, she is bound for ever; she may then make a Will of Goods and Chattels.

At 14 she might receive her Lands into her own hands, and was then out of Wardship, if she was 14 at the death of her Ancestor.

At 16 (though at the death of her Ancestor she was under 14) she was to be out of Wardship; because then she might take a Husband who might be able to perform Knights-service.

At

At 21 she is enabled to contract or alienate her Lands by Will or otherwise.

The eldest Son inherits all Lands, and to the Younger Children are disposed Goods and Chattels, and commonly the eldest Son's Wives Portion; and besides they are carefully educated in some Profession or Trade.

If there be no Son, the Lands as well as Goods are equally divided amongst the Daughters.

CHAP.

CHAP. XXII.

Of Servants.

THe Condition of Servants in *England* is much more favourable than it was in our Ancestors dayes, when it was so bad, that *England* was called the Purgatory of Servants, as it was and is still the Paradise of Wives, and the Hell for Horses.

Ordinary Servants are hired commonly for one year, at the end whereof they may be free (giving warning three Moneths before) and may place themselves with other Masters; onely it is accounted discourteous and unfriendly, to take another Mans servant, before leave given by his former Master; and indiscreet to take a Servant without Certificate of his diligence and of his faithfulness in his Service to his former Master.

All Servants are subject to be corrected by their Masters and Mistresses, and resistance in a Servant, is punished with severe penalty; but for a Servant to take away the life of his or her Master or Mistress, is accounted a Crime next to High Treason, and called Petty Treason, and hath a peculiar Punishment Capital.

Foreign Slaves in *England* are none, since Christianity prevailed. A Foreign Slave brought into *England*, is upon landing *ipso facto* free from Slavery, but not from ordinary service.

Some Lands in *England* are holden in *Villanage*, to do some particular Services to the Lord of the Mannor, and such Tenants may be called the Lords Servants.

There is a Twofold Tenure called *Villanage*, one where the Tenure onely is servile, as to Plough the Lords Ground, sow, reap, and bring home his Corn; Dung his Land, *&c.* The other, whereby both Person and Tenure is servile, and bound in all respects at the disposition of the Lord; such Persons are called in Law, *Pure Villains*, and are to do all Villanous Services to improve the Land he holds to the Lords use, themselves to be wholly at the Lords service, and whatever they get is for their Lord: Of such, there are now but few left in *England*. The nearest to this condition, are Apprentices, (that signifies *Learners*) a sort of Servants that carry the Marks of Pure Villains or Bond-slaves (as before in the Chapter of Gentry is intimated) differing however in this, That Apprentices are Slaves onely for a time, and by Covenant; the other are so, at the will of their Masters.

CHAP.

CHAP. XXIII.

Of the ROYAL SOCIETY.

HAving in this small Treatise had occasion to make known to the World by *Name* our Princes, Prelates, Nobles, Great Officers of State, Privy Counsellors, Principal Courtiers, our Judges, Serjeants at Law, Civilians, *&c.* all now living, it will not be altogether impertinent to add hereunto not onely the Names of all those worthy Governors and eminent Professors in our two famous Universities, but also all those who of late have listed themselves for promoting that admirably ingenious design for bettering the condition of humane life, by a vigorous advancement of Real Knowledge, and a speedy Improvement of Arts and Sciences: Of whose beginning, progress, and many very useful Discoveries already made; see that excellent History written by Dr. *Sprat*, since the publishing whereof, divers other profitable and ingenious inventions have also been produced by some of that Society, and will be made publick in due time.

A LIST of the ROYAL SOCIETY in Alphabetical Order.

HIs Sacred Majesty, King *CHARLES* the Second, Founder and Patron.

His Royal Highness *James*, Duke of *York*.

His Highness Prince *Rupert*, Count *Palatine* of the *Rhine*.

His Highness *Ferdinand Albert*, Duke of *Brunswick* and *Lunenbrgh*.

A.

Robert, Earl of *Alisbury*.
Archibald, Earl of *Argile*.
James, Earl of *Anglesey*.
James, Lord *Annesley*.
William Aglonby M. D.
James Alderne M. A.
Thomas Allen M. D.
Elias Ashmole Esquire.
Sir *Robert Atkins* Knight.
Monsieur *Adrian Auzont*.
John Aubrey Esquire.

B.

George, Duke of *Buckingham*.
William, Lord Vicount *Brounker*.

William.

William, Lord *Brereton*.
Sir *John Banks* Knight and Baronet.
Nicholas Bagnal Esquire.
Thomas Bains M. D.
Thomas Ball Esquire.
Peter Ball M. D.
Isaac Barrow B. D.
Ralph Bathurst D. D.
John Beal D. D.
Victor Beaufort.
Vabres de Fresars.
Monsieur *Theodore de Berington*.
Sir *Charles Berkley* Knight of the *Bath*.
Sir *John Berkenhead* Knight.
Robert Boyle Esquire.
John Brook Esquire.
Edward Brown M. D.
David Bruce M. D.
Monsieur *Ismael Bullialdus*.
Mr. *Gilbert Burnet*.
Sir *Edward Byshe* Knight.

C.

Gilbert, Lord Archbishop of *Canterbury*.
Edward, Earl of *Clarendon*.
Charles, Earl of *Carlisle*.
John, Earl of *Crafford* and *Lindsey*.
John, Lord Bishop of *Chester*.
William, Lord *Cavendish*.
Charles, Lord *Clifford*.
Mr. *James Carkesse*.
Dr. *George Castle* D. D.
Sir *Philip Carteret*.
Edward Chamberlayne L. L. D.

Sir

Sir *Winston Churchill* Knight.
Henry Clerk M. D.
Timothy Clerk M. D.
Sir *John Clayton* Knight.
Sir *Clifford Clifton* Knight.
George Cock Esquire.
Colonel *Thomas Collepepyr.*
Mr. *John Collins.*
John Colwal Esquire.
Daniel Colwal Esquire.
Sir *Richard Corbet* Knight.
Edward Cotton D. D. A. D. of *Corn.*
Peter Courtoffe Esquire.
Thomas Cox M. D.
Thomas Cox Esquire.
Daniel Cox Esquire.
John Creed Esquire.
Thomas Crispe Esquire.
William Croon M. D.
Sir *William Curtius* Knight and Baronet.
Sir *John Cutler* Knight and Baronet.

D.

Henry, Marquess of *Dorchester.*
Willi m, Earl of *Devonshire.*
Edward, Earl of *Dorset.*
Monsieur *Vital de Damas.*
John Downs M. D.

E.

Benjamin, Lord Bishop of *Ely.*
Andrew Ellis Esquire.
Sir *George Ent* Knight.
John Evelin Esquire.

F. Mau-

F.

Maurice, Lord Viſcount *Fitz-Harding*.
Sir *Francis Fane* Knight of the *Bath*.
Monſieur *le Febure*.
Sir *John Finch* Knight.
Henry Ford Eſquire.

G.

Sir *Bernard Gaſcon* Knight.
Joſeph Glanvile B. D.
Francis Gliſſon M. D.
Jonathan Goddard M. D.
Sir *William Godolphin* Knight.
Major *John Graunt*.
Mr. *James Gregory*.

H.

Henry, Lord *Howard* of *Norfolk*.
Chriſtopher Lord *Hatton*.
Theodore Haak Eſquire.
William Hammond Eſquire.
William Harrington Eſquire.
Sir *Eraſmus Harby* Baronet.
Sir *Edward Harley* Knight of the *Bath*.
Sir *Robert Harley* Knight.
Shomas Harley Eſquire.
Sir *James Hayes* Knight.
Nathaniel Henſhaw M. D.
Thomas Henſhaw Eſquire.
John Hevelius Conſul of *Dantz*.
Abraham Hill Eſquire.
James Hoar Eſquire.

William.

William Holder D. D.
Robert Hook M. A.
John Hoskins Esquire.
Anthony Horneck M. A.
Charles Hotham Esquire.
Charles Howard of *Norfolk.*
Edward Howard of *Norfolk.*
William le Hunt Esquire.
Monsieur *Christian Huygens de Zulichem.*

I.

Richard Jones Esquire.

K.

Alexander, Earl of *Kincardin.*
Edmund King M. D.

L.

Robert, Earl of *Lindsey*, Lord Great Chamberlain.
Humphrey, Lord Bishop of *London.*
Thomas Lake Esquire.
Sir *Ellis Leighton* Knight.
Monsieur *Leyenberg*, Resident of *Sweden.*
John Lock Esquire.
James Long Esquire.
Richard Lower M. D.
Sir *John Lowther* Knight.
Anthony Lowther Esquire.
Monsieur *Hugues Louis de Lyonne.*

M.

Edward, Earl of *Manchester*; Lord Chamberlain.
Mr. *Nicholas Mercator.*
Christopher Merret M. D.
Sir *Robert Moray* Knight.
Henry More D. D.
Jaques du Molin M. D.

N.

James, Earl of *Northampton.*
Gasper Needham M. D.
Walter Needham M. D.
Sir *Paul Neil* Knight.
Thomas Neil Esquire.
William Neil Esquire.
Edward Nelthrop Esquire.
John Newburgh Esquire.
Sir *Thomas Nott* Knight.

O.

Henry Oldenburg Esquire.
Nicholas Oudart Esquire.

P.

Henry, Earl of *Peterborough.*
Philip Packer Esquire:
Samuel Parker M. A.
Sir *Robert Paston* Knight and Baronet.
John Peirson D. D.
John Pell D. D.

Samuel

Samuel Pepys Esquire.
Sir *William Persal* Knight.
Monsieur *Samuel Petit.*
Sir *William Petty* Knight.
Sir *Peter Pett* Knight.
Peter Pett Esquire.
Walter Pope M. D.
Sir *William Portman* Knight and Baronet, and Knight of the *Bath.*
Francis Potter B. D.
Thomas Povey Esquire.
Henry Power M. D.
Sir *Richard Powle* Knight of the *Bath.*
Henry Powle Esquire.

R.

John, Lord *Roberts*, Lord Privy Seal.
John, Lord Bishop of *Rochester*.
Colonel *Bullen Reymes.*
Thomas Rolt Esquire.
Paul Ricaut Esquire.

S.

Edward, Earl of *Sandwich.*
William, Lord Viscount *Stafford.*
David, Lord Viscount *Stermont.*
Seth, Lord Bishop of *Salisbury.*
William Schroter Esquire.
Sir *James Shaen* Knight and Baronet.
Philip Skippon Esquire.
Sir *Nicholas Slanning* Knight.
Henry Slingsby Esquire.
Francis Smethwick Esquire.
Edward Smith Esquire.

George

George Smith M. D.
William Soam Esquire.
Monsieur *Samuel Sorbiere.*
Sir *Robert Southwel* Knight.
Thomas Sprat M. A.
Alexander Stanhope Esquire.
Sir *Nicholas Stewart* Baronet.

T.

Sir *Gilbert Talbot* Knight.
John, Earl of *Tweedale.*
Christopher Terne M. D.
Thomas Thynne Esquire.
Malachi Trustan M. D.
Sir *Samuel Tuke* Knight.

V.

Count *Charles Ubaldino* of *Mount-Feltre.*
Sir *Theodore de Vaux* Knight.
Cornelius Vermuyden Esquire.
Monsieur *Isaac Vossius.*

W.

George, Lord Bishop of *Winton.*
Edmund Waller Esquire.
John Wallis D. D.
Esau Ward M. A.
Edward Waterhouse Esquire.
Daniel Whistler M. D.
Joseph Williamson Esquire.
Thomas Willis M. D.
Francis Willoughby Esquire.

William Winde
John Winthrop Esquires.
Samuel Woodford

Benjamin Woodrooff M. A.
John Wray M. A.
Matthew Wren Esquire.
Christopher Wren L. L. D.
Thomas Wren M. D.
Sir *Cyril Wyche* Knight.
Sir *Peter Wyche* Knight.
Edmund Wylde Esquire.

Y.

Richard, Lord Archbishop of *York*.
John, Lord *Yester*.

A List of the present COUNCIL *of the* ROYAL SOCIETY *in Alphabetical Order.*

W*Illiam*, Lord Viscount *Brounker*, President.
Robert, Earl of *Alesbury*.
William Ærskin Esquire.
Sir *John Banks* Knight.
Edward Brown M. D.
John, Lord Bishop of *Chester*.
Timothy Clarke M. D.
Daniel Colwal Esquire, Treasurer.
William Croon M. D.
John Evelin Esquire.
Jonathan Goddard M. D.

Henry

Henry, Lord *Howard* of *Norfolk*.
Sir *James Hayes* Knight.
Thomas Henshaw Esquire, Secretary.
Sir *John Lowther* Baronet.
Sir *Robert Moray* Knight.
Sir *Paul Neil* Knight.
Henry Oldenburg Esquire.
Seth, Lord Bishop of *Salisbury*.
Sir *Samuel Tuke* Knight.
Sir *Peter Wyche* Knight.

By the fore-going List, the Reader may perceive how many persons of different Degrees, Religions, Countreys, Professions, Trades, and Fortunes, have united and conspired to lay aside all Names of Distinction, amicably to promote Experimental Knowledge.

At *Arundel* House (by the Bounty of the Right Honorable the Lord *Henry Howard* of *Norfolk*) is at present the Place of their Meeting, the Time is every Thursday at Four of the Clock in the Afternoon.

At *Gresham* Colledge (in the Custody of that most ingenious discoverer and indefatigable Experimenter Mr. *Robert Hook* is their *Repository*, the free and bountiful gift of *Daniel Colwal* Esquire; the present Treasurer of the said Society, wherein are to be seen many Thousands of great Rarities, fetched (some of them) from the farthest corners of the habitable World, as Beasts, Birds, Fishes, Serpents, Flies,

Shells, Feathers, Seeds, Minerals, Earths; some things Petrified, others Ossified, Mummies, Gums, *&c.* Divers of which have been since added by other worthy Members of that Society, and by other ingenious Persons; and in a short time, is like to be (if not already) one of the largest and most curious Collections of the Works of Nature in the World.

Touching their *Library* (the noble gift of the fore-mentioned Lord *Henry Howard*) their *Laboratories*, intended *Colledges*, *&c.* Account shall be given elswhere.

The Names and Titles of the Governors of the several Colledges and Halls in Oxon.

DOctor *Fell*, Dean of *Christ-Church*.

Dr. *Pierce*, President of *Magdalen-Colledge*.

Dr. *Woodward*, Warden of *New-Colledge*.

Dr. *James*, Warden of *All-Souls*.

Sir *Thomas Clayton*, Warden of *Merton*.

Dr. *Newlin*, President of *Corpus Christi*.

Dr. *Barlow*, Provost of *Queens*.

Dr. *Mew*, President of S. *Johns*.

Dr. *Bathurst*, President of *Trinity*.

Dr. *Yates*, Principal of *Brasen Nose*.

Dr. *Say*, Provost of *Oriel*.

Dr. *Ironside*, Warden of *Wadham*.

Dr. *Crew*, Rector of *Lincoln*.

Dr. *Clayton*, Master of *University-Colledge*.

Dr. *Berry*, Rector of *Exeter*.

Dr. *Savage*, Master of *Baliol*.

Dr. *Jenkins*, Principal of *Jesus*.

Dr. *Hall*, Master of *Pembrooke*.

Dr. *Hide*, Principal of *Magdalen-Hall*.

Dr. *Tully*, Principal of *Edmund-Hall*.

Dr. *Lamplugh*, Principal of *Albon-Hall*.

Mr. *Stone*, Principal of *New-Inn*.

Dr. *Eaton*, Principal of *Glocester-Hall*.

Dr. *Crowder*, Principal of S. *Mary-Hall*.
Dr. *Lamphire*, Principal of *Hart-Hall*.

The Names of the Professors and Lecturers in Oxon.

R*Eg. Professor Theologiæ*, Dr. *Allestry*.

Præl. Theologiæ Dominæ Margaritæ, Dr. *Barlow*.

Reg. Professor Medicinæ, Dr. *Hide*.

Reg. Profes. Juris Civilis, Dr. *Swett*.

Pub. Orator. Dr. *South*.

Linguæ Hebraicæ P. Reg. Dr. *Pocock*.

Linguæ Græcæ Prof. Reg. Dr. *Levins*.

Prælector Anatom. Dr. *Paris*, C.C.C.

Prælector Historiæ, Dr. *Lamphire*.

Præl. Natural. Philos. Dr. *Willis*.

Præl. Astron. Dr. *Wren*.

Præl. Geomet. Dr. *Wallis*.

Prælector Moral. Philos. Mr. *Hodges*, *Ch. Ch.*

A

A Catalogue of the Masters of all the Colledges and Halls in the University of Cambridge.

ST. *Peters-Colledge*, Dr. *Beamont*, D.D.

Clare Hall, Dr. *Dillingham*, D. D.

Pembrook-Hall, Dr. *Mapletoft*, D. D.

Corpus Christi-Colledge, *alias Bennet-Colledge*, Dr. *Spencer*, D. D.

Trinity-Hall, Dr. *King*, Doctor in Law.

Gonvile & Caias-Colledge, Dr. *Braddy*, Doctor in Physick.

Kings-Colledge Dr. *Fleetwood*, D. D. and Provost of the said Colledge.

Queens-Colledge, Dr. *Wells*, D. D.

S. *Katherines Hall*, Dr. *Lightfoot*, D.D.

Jesus-Colledge, Dr. *Baldero*, D. D.

Christs-Colledge, Dr. *Cudworth*, D. D.

S. *Johns-Colledge*, Dr. *Turner*, D. D.

Magdalen Colledge, Dr. *Duport*, D. D.

Trinity-Colledge, Dr. *Peirson*, D. D.

Emanuel-Colledge, Dr. *Britton*, D. D.

Sussex and *Sidney-Colledge*, Dr. *Minshal*, D. D.

The Names of the Publick Professors in the University of Cambrdige.

DOctor *Gunning*, the Kings Professor in Divinity.

Dr. *Peirson*, the Lady *Margarets* Professor in Divinity.

Dr. *Clarke*, Professor in the Civil Law.

Dr. *Glisson*, Professor in Physick.

Dr. *Witherington*, Publick Orator.

Mr. *Barrow*, the Mathematick Professor.

Dr. *Cudworth*, the Hebrew Professor.

Mr. *Creiton*, the Greek Professor.

Dr. *Castel*, Arabick Professor.

FINIS.

www.ingramcontent.com/pod-product-compliance
Lightning Source LLC
Chambersburg PA
CBHW021107270326
41929CB00009B/764
* 9 7 8 3 3 3 7 7 9 3 3 6 4 *